CrossRoads

A SOUTHERN CULTURE ANNUAL

2006

Edited by Ted Olson

MERCER UNIVERSITY PRESS | MACON, GEORGIA | 2006

MUP/P355

1400 Coleman Avenue
Macon, Georgia 31207

First Edition.

Book design by Burt & Burt Studio

∞The paper used in this publication meets the minimum requirements of American National Standard for Information Sciences—Permanence of Paper for Printed Library Materials, ANSI Z39.48-1992.

Library of Congress Cataloging-in-Publication Data

CrossRoads / edited by Ted Olson.
p. cm.
ISBN-13: 978-0-88146-037-7 ISBN-10: 0-88146-037-0 (pbk. : alk. paper)
1. American literature—Southern States. 2. Authors, American—Homes and haunts—Southern States. 3. Southern States—Literary collections. 4. Southern States—Biography. 5. Southern States. I. Olson, Ted.

PS551.C76 2004
810.8'0975–dc22

2004009006

Cover photography by William Christenberry
[front] detail, Psalmist Building (winter), Havana Junction, Alabama
[back] detail, Psalmist Building (summer), Havana Junction, Alabama

CONTENTS

INTRODUCTION

This is the third installment of *CrossRoads: A Southern Culture Annual,* a series of yearly anthologies published by Mercer University Press and dedicated to the interdisciplinary study and artistic appreciation of the South (broadly defined) and of Southern culture. It is my hope as editor of *CrossRoads* that readers will find selections that edify their minds and enrich their lives. I also hope that readers will agree that the material contained herein—obtained through general calls-for-papers and through direct invitations—represents a diversity of cultural experiences within the South and chronicles a wide range of intellectual and artistic perspectives about the South. This series affords an opportunity for each volume to elaborate upon themes or topics from previous volumes. Since *CrossRoads* is an ongoing project, it may be hoped that any omissions in coverage between this book and the first and second installments of *CrossRoads: A Southern Culture Annual* may be resolved by the inclusion of complementary material in future volumes of *CrossRoads.* By allowing for—even facilitating—such thematic and topical development, *CrossRoads* can play a role in encouraging the evolution of Southern cultural studies.

The first two volumes of *CrossRoads: A Southern Culture Annual,* published in 2004 and 2005, gathered interesting and often groundbreaking scholarly work that explored such topics as Southern language, literature, visual art, music, and food, and that elucidated Southern perspectives on religion, politics, race, ethnicity, gender, and regional identity. Those two books also contained compelling creative work from a number of leading writers and visual artists hailing from and/or living in the South. People whose works were featured in those two volumes of *CrossRoads: A Southern*

Culture Annual included Margaret D. Bauer, Jeff Biggers, Brooks Blevins, Laura Payne Butler, James E. Cherry, Donald Davidson, G. Wayne Dowdy, Bart Galloway, Kathryn Bright Gurkin, Allean Hale, David Huddle, M. Thomas Inge, Jeff Daniel Marion, Robert Morgan, Mendi Lewis Obadike, James A. Perkins, Ron Rash, R. T. Smith, Suzanne Stryk, Jaclyn Weldon White, and many other scholars and artists.

As a publication project, *CrossRoads: A Southern Culture Annual* continues the editorial approach of *CrossRoads: A Journal of Southern Culture*, a semi-legendary periodical originally published in the early-to-mid-1990s by a dedicated group of graduate students (including myself) affiliated with the University of Mississippi's Center for the Study of Southern Culture. *CrossRoads: A Journal of Southern Culture* featured previously unpublished material by many of the leading scholars and artists committed to interpreting and celebrating the South, including Rob Amberg, A. R. Ammons, Mary Ulmer Chiltosky, James Dickey, Robert Drake, William Ferris, Ann Fisher-Wirth, Wayne Flynt, Ernest Gaines, David Galef, Eugene Genovese, Kathryn Gurkin, Alex Haley, Fred Hobson, Patricia Spears Jones, Jack Temple Kirby, Ed McClanahan, Walter McDonald, Ethelbert Miller, Marilyn Nance, Tom Rankin, John Shelton Reed, Sheryl St. Germain, Jon Michael Spencer, Joel Williamson, and Steve Young.

CrossRoads: A Southern Culture Annual is currently seeking previously unpublished submissions for future volumes. These submissions can include—but are not limited to—analytical academic essays, oral histories, memoirs, profile essays, photo essays, creative writing, and artwork. The main criteria ensuring consideration for *CrossRoads* are that all submitted materials should (to borrow Faulkner's famous phrase) "tell about the South" and that they should do so memorably.

Ted Olson, Editor
CrossRoads: A Southern Culture Annual
ETSU
Box 70400
Johnson City TN 37614

Southerners Anonymous

BY DAVID GOLD

I wasn't always a redneck.

Although I am from the South, indeed from about as far south as it is possible to be born and still get a US passport, growing up I was discomforted by my Southern heritage. For white Southerners of a certain generation, born, say, between *Brown v. Board of Education* and the Carter administration, admitting to your identity is akin to confessing a somewhat tawdry secret. It's not bad enough that as Southerners we're raised to apologize to total strangers just for existing anyway, but worse, we've got actual reason to apologize.

We heard Governor Wallace scream "Segregation!" now, tomorrow, and forever. We watched Bull Connor sic his brownshirts on the Selma marchers. We saw the hoses, the billy clubs, the dogs, the terror turned on people of color and the people of conscience with the courage to support them. We sat in church every Sunday as our preachers denounced Northern agitators, commies, and Jews, and other threats to our peculiar institutions. And maybe we nodded our heads and said, "Amen." Or maybe we knew that Dr. King was right when he said that nothing was more harmful to the cause of justice than good people of conscience remaining silent in the face of evil. But we were too often silent. And even if we were born late enough in the century so that we didn't have to personally take action, so that we could rock along when Neil Young told the Southern Man to listen up on what his Good Book said, our parents and uncles and grandparents weren't so lucky. And in the South, you don't dismiss your ancestors so easily. Even if we joined the cause, we still had their legacy—our legacy—to deal with. And we are still dealing with it. Lyndon Johnson made the decision to support civil rights legislation, knowing it would cost him the South, and it did, as whites left the party in droves. White Southern Democrats, once so numerous they even had their own appellation, Dixiecrats, are today about as easy to find as a homegrown tomato at Wal-Mart. I do love the Southland, but Lord, if we don't got some explaining to do.

If our own sins aren't bad enough, the South has also been poorly served by popular culture, the production of which is largely in the hands not merely of Northern agitators but worse, Californians, for whom we are, literally, the poor Southern cousin. In a day and age when you can't even make fun of some lone, fruitcake, fundamentalist Iraqi terrorist without being denounced by half-a-dozen civil rights organizations, it's still open season on the redneck. In fact, it's always been open season on the redneck. No wonder we have an inferiority complex. We can't help it; it is the way we wuz raised. In comics, TV, the movies, radio, the Southerner has always been portrayed as retrograde and ignorant. Fun-loving sure—Yeeeeeeeehaw! and all that—but green as a pool table, twice as square, and dumb as a box of rocks. Ma and Pa Kettle. Snuffy Smith. Lil' Abner. Foghorn Leghorn. Gomer Pyle. *The Beverly Hillbillies. Hee Haw. The Dukes of Hazzard.*

Lord help us, *The Dukes of Hazzard.*

Nor have we been well served of late by our representatives in the White House. Jimmy, bless his heart, may have been a good Christian and better farmer, but as a president he made a pretty good poet. Bill, God bless him, *was* a great president, but he would have done well to have taken a page from the Jimmy Carter playbook and kept the lust in his heart, instead of letting it leak out all over the Oval Office. And as for George Dubya, well, I'd just like to point out for the record that he was born in Connecticut, went to high school in Massachusetts, and went *back* to Connecticut for college, so we ain't entirely to blame.

All in all, though, is it any wonder we're ashamed?

In my particular case, it was a little easier to hide my Southern roots, as I grew up in Miami, a city which allows one the pretension that one is not really in the South, or even in America. It's kind of like what Mark Twain said about Missouri. If there was ever a Southern author, he was it. Yet he found that though Northerners were happy to look down on him as expected, folks from other parts of the country didn't want to claim him either. Easterners assumed he was a Westerner, Westerners claimed he was an Easterner, and Southerners insisted he was a damn troublemaking Yankee, never mind that Missouri had not only been a slave state but so bat-shit rabid a one that it had damn near caused a constitutional crisis before entering the Union.

Like with the Missouri of Twain's day, folks from certain other parts of the South also view Miami with suspicion. For one thing, it's full of Cubans and New Yorkers, and Southerners can't quite wrap their heads around the idea that someplace with so many foreigners can be Southern. It's also, to be frank, full of Jews. Now as one of the chosen few myself, I'm not about to deny that being circumcised won't get you funny looks sometimes in the locker room. Once when I was five, a kid on the bus told me I was going to burn in Hell because I had killed Jesus. I went home and asked my momma, "Um, who's Jesus? And what's Hell?" And yes, there was that time when a playmate asked if he could feel my horns. But there is a difference between simple ignorance and willful meanness. It's not that Southerners dislike Jews—in fact, many Southern cities have substantial Jewish populations; rather, it's New York Jews they hate. Or, really, just New Yorkers. *Our* Jews is a different matter. "Them Rubensteins down the block? Oh, sure, been here as long as anyone can remember, and good decent Christian folk too."

Another problem with being from Miami is that Miamians don't really have Southern accents. Or at least we like to pretend that we don't. For a brief time, I dated a woman from New York City, a genuine East Village intellectual (Yes, I consorted with the enemy.). One night after dinner she said to me, "Did you know that when you order food you have a Southern accent?"

I'd like to say I shot my beer out my nose in shock all over her black turtleneck, but I honestly had no idea what she was talking about. Southern accent? Are y'all for real? In kindergarten, my friends used to call me Elmer Fudd because I sounded so much like my folks, expatriate New Yorkers both, God bless them for leaving. But as they say back home, denial ain't a river in Egypt. Replaying the dinner conversation in my head—did I just say *ma'am*?—eventually I realized she was right, I *did* sound Southern when I spoke to waitresses. I couldn't help it, it's the way I wuz raised. Even in Miami, the language of politeness is still Southern. Or was. I had to have learned it from somewhere.

And then I started thinking of all the Southern things I had done growing up. Going to the dirt-track stock car races in Hialeah every Saturday night I could beg my momma to take me. Cheering for Dusty Rhodes at the Wednesday-night wrestling matches at the Miami Beach Convention Center; on Thursday morning, all the cool kids in the second grade came to school with voices hoarse from screaming the night before. Fishing off the Haulover pier or a West Miami canal. Strawberry picking in the Redlands. Canoeing in the Glades. All-U-Can-Eat catfish at Stratford's on Hollywood Boulevard, rolled in cornmeal and fried whole on the bone, the way God intended, not filleted the way it's served just about everywhere now. Driving out on the Tamiami Trail for gator wrestling and airboat rides and pulling off the road on the way back to watch the stars, far from the city lights. Stomping through the muck hoping to step on a water moccasin to see if you would really swell up and die a horrible screaming death. Cruising the dangerous parts of town on a Friday night looking not for trouble but for someone smoking ribs outside on a 55-gallon drum. Going mudding in a neighbor's pickup truck and drunkenly catching your wrist on the tailpipe trying to push it out of a bog. Going to the emergency room the next day to be treated for third-degree burns. Heading down to the Keys to drink beer and, well, drink some more beer, which is what one does in the Keys, and try to catch that cool blues musician who always made a batch of gumbo on stage while he played and then passed it out to the audience at the end of his show. Not enough pepper, but man could he play that Stratocaster.

Fact is, Miami is even something of a blues town, and nothing is more Southern than the blues. At Tobacco Road, a 100-year-old shotgun shack of a bar down by the Miami River in the shadows of downtown, I sat no more than five feet from John Lee Hooker as he sat in a rickety folding chair and took us back to Tupelo. I saw Diamond Teeth Mary, who had known Bessie Smith. She had long ago sold off the diamond fillings that had given her her nickname, but she could still moan the blues like the devil was on her trail. I saw Buddy Guy play the blues so funky I could indeed smell it, just as he promised. One evening, I even got to wear Junior Wells' coat. His was blue sharkskin, mine was black, and for one sweet song we traded. Goddamn if he wasn't a 38 short as well.

I used to claim that Miami was so far south you had to go north to get to the South. But Miami is not only in the South, it is surrounded by the South, and not just the South but the *deep* South. The *Deliverance* and *Easy Rider* South. The South of Yankee nightmares. Like a brisket in marinade, it can't help but suck up those good Southern juices. Go 10 miles north, south, or west from the city proper (east is the ocean) and you may as well be floating down the Chattooga with your ass cheeks pinched shut. The Everglades could be the Okefenokee, Homestead, Valdosta. Davie has honest-to-God cowboys. You can still hear twang in Hollywood and Ft. Lauderdale, especially if you go to the right bars. And nothing is more Southern than the Keys. They might not wave the stars and bars down there, and they might drink rum instead of bourbon, but it's not too far a drive down the Lost Highway to Margaritaville, as Jimmy Buffett's cameo on Alan Jackson's "Five O'Clock Somewhere" can attest. Hell, Key West, which calls itself the Conch Republic, has more than once threatened to secede from the US: what could be more Reb than that?

Even if you spend most of your time in Coral Gables or South Beach, you still have to drive through Florida to get anyplace else, and brother let me tell you, there is a whole mess of Florida out there. My Aunt Mickey lived on a few acres about 15 miles outside of Ocala, and driving up to see her half-a-dozen times a year, we got to see a good portion of what Greil Marcus called "the old, weird America." The world-famous, real-live mermaids at Weeki Wachee. The glass-bottomed boats at Silver Springs. Seashells by the Pound. Indian Moccasins and Fireworks. Free Orange Juice Just for Stopping In. Saltwater Taffy Exit Here. Serpent Kingdom. The World's Largest Brahma Bull, which was conveniently just down the road from my Aunt Mickey's place. Aunt Mickey kept chickens, which she taught me how to kill by grabbing them by the heads and snapping their necks, which I must admit I did with delight, though I balked at the gutting and feathering. Aunt Mickey's third husband (in true Southern fashion she had buried the first two and was eyeing a fourth in case this one wore out), Uncle Bill, who wore a thick, silver handlebar mustache and muttonchops beneath his mostly bald head, worked in a slaughterhouse during the week and took in butchering for the neighbors on weekends. He scared the living bejesus out of me. One time when we were out grocery shopping, he taught me how to say "Yes'm" and "No sir" to the store clerk; when I tried it out on my momma that evening, she slapped me for being fresh. When my dad got sick, my folks left me in the care of Aunt Mickey and Uncle Bill for a few months. They promptly enrolled me in the local public school, where, after we recited the pledge to the flag each morning, we sang "Jesus Loves Me, This I Know." I still couldn't quite figure out who this Jesus was or why He loved me—*my* Bible didn't have much to say about it one way or the other—but even then I was Southern enough to know to shut my mouth and learn every single word by heart. Yes'm.

It took me a long time to make my peace with the South. Moving to Texas helped. There I discovered that the blues and folk music I loved so much came from the same place—and often the same players—as the country music I had once so proudly claimed to despise. In Texas, too, I learned to two-step and dance to swing music, picking up some moves I was even able to use when I went salsa dancing back in Miami. Hola y'all. I bought my first pair of cowboy boots in Austin, and dammit if they weren't pretty darn comfortable to walk in. Or dance. I even started playing country music on my guitar, in public, and not one person asked what's this long-haired, dark-skinned, Jewish-Italian, Miami-bastard doing singing "Convoy." What do you know, Lyle was right: Texas does want you anyway.

To this transformation, I owe Willie Nelson. In Austin in the 1970s, during what is now sometimes referred to as the Great Progressive Country Music Scare, Willie brought together the rednecks and the hippies, two great tastes that frankly had never previously gone together before, and created a new class of Southerner, what Texas songwriter Ray Wylie Hubbard once called "hipnecks." Alas, as Hubbard laments, the term never quite took off, but the mixture stuck. Willie made it okay for Southerners to have long hair, smoke pot, and even support progressive political causes—in short, to reclaim their Southern roots.

Yet such reclamation is easier said than done. We reconstructed rednecks still have much prejudice to overcome. For all the talk of the New South, most outsiders are still wary of the Old South, probably not without some cause. In *Redneck Nation*, Michael Graham does a pretty good job of arguing that the South has of late been a particularly bad influence, responsible for dumbing down the rest of the country. (NASCAR figures heavily in his argument.) He may be right. America, it's true, has never been the most intellectual of nations, but only in the South have we raised dumb-ass ignorance to a virtue.

But so what? There's more to us than that. Indeed, much of what is worthwhile in American culture—the cooking, the music, the language, the literature—has Southern roots. Our nation's founding document was written by a farmer from Virginia. And that most American of values, stubborn, stupid, pigheaded independence, was *born* in the South. At the end of the day, there ain't much difference between "So what if we ain't the sharpest axe in the toolshed" and "Don't tread on me." Both are declarations of resistance in the face of colonial hegemony, a rebel yell against tight-ass Yankee prissiness and intolerance. Because (despite regional blending and homogenization in recent years, and despite Hollywood) we are still different. We know it, and *they* know it, and let me tell you, they is scared. And scared people do desperate things, like try to make a real-live version of the

Beverly Hillbillies to keep us in line. Can our little postage stamp of the world survive? Yes, but only if we admit that we belong to it, and it to us. I say let 'em laugh, and when the weather gets hot, graciously invite them over to take a dip in the cement pond. They won't come of course, which'll make it all the sweeter.

In the movie *The Commitments*, a character declares that the Irish are the blacks of Europe. I know exactly what he meant; Southerners, after all, are still the Irish of America.

So say it loud, I'm Southern and proud.

Open Your Mouth and Remove All Doubt

BY ANNA SUNSHINE ISON

Some pertinent jokes: What do you get when you have 32 Kentuckians in one room? *A full set of teeth.* What's a Kentucky property owner? *A guy who's made all the payments on his false teeth.* How do you know the toothbrush was invented in Kentucky? *Because if it had been invented anywhere else, it would be called a TEETHbrush.* How do you know if you're from Kentucky? *You have more guns, dogs, and cars in your yard than teeth in your mouth.*

Many of my family's stories revolve around teeth, or the lack thereof. For the most part, these stories come in two varieties—adventure tales about the moment that owner and pearly whites parted ways (fights and ATV accidents generate the most thrilling details) or humorous anecdotes about life in the aftermath of toothlessness—dentures accidentally attached with Superglue instead of Fixodent, the unfortunate result of eating previously beloved food. My father has always been the grade-A champion storyteller of the family, so it's not surprising that his toothsome tale has held a special spot in the annals of family lore.

At fifteen years of age, my dad was the first of the five children to get dentures. He hadn't lost them in an accident; though he had had plenty of near-brushes and broken legs and burned-off eyebrows, his teeth went naturally. They simply "plumb rotted out of his head." There was some mystique about him, then, when my grandfather took him off to town, and my father came back with a shiny new pair of choppers. As his brothers and sisters gathered around, my father told them that their daddy had driven him down to Northcutt & Sons, the big funeral home out on Old Flemingsburg Road. I'm sure he had their attention then and there—the dark wood and red velvet of Northcutts' has always symbolized unheard-of luxury to my family, and years later at my grandfather's funeral my cousins and I marveled that rich people would let us use their houses to lay out our dead. My father said that Mr. Northcutt led him away from his father into a big long room where rows of teeth lay on trestle tables. My Aunt Lil remembers the shivers that ran down her back—though deep down she knew what a liar my father was—when he talked about how he walked down the aisle, picking up teeth that caught his fancy and sticking them in his mouth until he found a set that fit.

In my generation, my cousin Archie's teeth were the first to go. Initially, no one worried. His baby teeth turned black and rotted away, but baby teeth were just practice teeth after all. We joked that black cats confused him with a Jack O'Lantern when Halloween approached. Eventually, Archie's adult teeth grew in. Not long after, those teeth started rotting, too, or getting knocked out in any variety of boyhood trouble. We would tell him jokes so we could see his funny smile, made up of equal parts of gaps and silver.

Archie wasn't alone. Most of the kids at our rural Elliotville Elementary School had dramatic tooth problems. According to a report by the Center of Excellence in Rural Health, poor oral health has a pernicious effect on educational development in Kentucky. Schoolchildren around our state miss around 20,000 to 30,000 days of class every year because of tooth pain. At the end of 2003, a governmental report showed that Kentuckians had finally beaten out West Virginia to claim the nation's highest rate of toothless adults, and our untreated tooth decay level is four times higher than the national average. Rowan County tried hard to battle this inevitable future. Our teachers handed out free tooth care kits and once a month brought in gallon jugs full of pink bubblegum-flavored fluoride washes that we dutifully swished and spat after lunch. We learned in science class that enamel is the hardest part of our body, tougher even then bone. We went home and looked at our parents, their mouths filled with black holes or caved in where dentures didn't quite fit, and we let this lesson sink in.

I guess it's probably to my mom's credit that my own teeth held out for so long. Her teeth were fine—she was from the Midwest and met my father when he was in Colorado studying archeology through the GI bill. My parents had school loans to pay off and couldn't quite afford a regular dentist, so twice a year she'd take me to get my teeth checked out at the University of Kentucky's dental school. Students there practiced on me, showed me how they made molds of my teeth, and gave me sugar-free lollipops and balloons from the surprise drawer as a reward for good brushing. My mother and I would make a day of it; she'd take me window-shopping afterwards, and we'd go to a restaurant where I'd have soup or a milkshake to comfort my aching teeth before we headed back to the family farm. Years after my first dentist graduated, he regularly sent me lavish tooth-shaped cards on my birthday, illustrated with pictures of dancing molars and inscribed with goofy dental puns.

Eventually, the student dentists started noticing that my teeth, though relatively cavity-free, had entered the crooked adolescent stage. One of the heads of the dental school informed my mother that the slight savings wouldn't make up for the extra gas money and inconvenience, and suggested that we go to the orthodontist in our town. Thus was I delivered into the hands of a Morehead orthodontist who was of the decided opinion that she was entertaining. She gave her patients mugs with her name spelled out in the grotesque mouth of a smiling girl, and she allowed us to choose the colors on the rubber bands she stuck around our braces. This was supposed to make the experience seem worthwhile—to show us that it was okay that our mouths had been transformed into hideous metal constructions at the very stage in our lives when we most cared what our peers thought about us, just so long as we could color-coordinate bands of neon green and purple with our spandex pants, or choose blue and yellow to express our solidarity with Batman.

Soon after that, the Ison family curse caught up with me. Frankly, I know I can't realistically blame it all on genetics or locale. For one thing, my teen angst hit full force, and I decided my appearance was so terrible anyway that there was really no need to spend as much time on a lost cause. I didn't brush quite as well as before. I ate too much candy. And after every visit, when my orthodontist showed me the decline in grades of my *Healthy Tooth Score!* and smarmily admonished me to "brush brush brush harder," a swell of adolescent rebellion surged, and I started caring less and less. Finally, my braces were removed a year early because my still-crooked teeth had become so weak they couldn't withstand the extra weight of the metal. Even those pure pleasures of newly braceless teeth were mitigated. I could eat popcorn, but when I ran my tongue over my teeth I could feel the telltale ridges where the braces had been. I could see them in the mirror, too—darker middles such as where pictures have hung on faded walls or where indelible shadows were burned into white surfaces at Hiroshima.

This couldn't have happened at a worse time. I'll never downplay anyone's journey through adolescence; people who say that those were the best years of life have probably willed themselves into amnesia. But the removal of my braces unfortunately coincided with an entirely new pressure.

The social structure in Rowan County, Kentucky, is strictly divided into those who live within the town limits and those who don't. Morehead is wet; Rowan County is dry. Census figures on racial make-up and education and income levels vary radically between town and country. Kids who went to Morehead Elementary were the children of doctors and realtors and guidance counselors. They could enroll in gifted classes and join soccer teams and put on school plays. But at Elliotville Elementary, where a vast majority of the students received free or reduced lunches, we didn't even have a principal. Our own gym coach taunted us, saying that the name of our school was really Idiotville, but we couldn't spell well enough to notice. Our fifth grade teacher told us that she wasn't racist, but…

Rowan County only has one high school, however, so everyone got thrown together in the end. It's still an oil and water society. Preps hung out in the front hall. Rednecks ruled the back, and they smoked and fought with imperviousness since the members of the administration (made up of town people, mostly) were afraid to set foot in that area. If for some reason there was confusion about who was who, one could tell by their smiles.

By the time my braces were off, we had stopped going to the dental college even for regular checkups. My new doctor was the only dentist in Morehead, and his two children went to high school with me and were town kids. My dad had gone to high school with my dentist, as well as with our high school guidance counselor who silently signed the papers when my cousin Carrie dropped out. The guidance counselor had tried to get me to switch out of my freshman honors English class even though I was doing fine, figuring, I suppose, that any Ison who wanted to take college-bound courses was either drunk or crazy.

And there was the irony. People who lived in town hadn't swooped in from some more idyllic place with better test scores. They had grown up in the same county as we, and though they had gone to college, it was more often than not the local university. They had tried to muffle their accents, but hadn't been able to leave the county for good, had just moved out of the holler to one of the subdivisions within the city limits. Both my parents had master's degrees and good jobs, and were well known in their field. But because our last name was Ison and we lived on the family farm instead of moving up to town, we were to be condescended toward and humored until we learned what was good for us.

I don't mean to impugn my dental care. My dentist was kind and was honestly concerned when none of the techniques we had tried—not extra cleanings, not prescription toothpaste—stopped the declining health of my teeth. But by the time I began to be his patient, I had a full-blown case of orthodontophobia. I didn't mind watching *Little Shop of Horrors* or hearing the sound of drills, but as soon as I got in the car to the dentist's office, I would start to sweat, with fear heavy in my stomach.

On one occasion, this hatred actually worked to my advantage. One winter when I was home from college, I went in for the dreaded root canal. I had tried to prepare myself mentally—after all, according to acquaintances and television sitcoms, root canals involved unmentionable pain. When the session passed with discomfort that was considerable but not unusual, I assumed he had only done prep work and had made an appointment for emergency dental surgery when I got back to my university town. The dentist took an x-ray, looked at the tooth, and discharged me, having completed my root canal.

In the *Iliad,* Homer writes that "fleeting dreams have two gates: one is fashioned of horn and one of ivory." True dreams, dreams that are to be believed, issue out of the gate made of horn. It is from the ivory gate, the gate made of teeth, that the false dreams come. According to dream interpretation books, "If you dream your teeth are loose, there will be failure and gloomy tidings. To dream of spitting out teeth, portends personal sickness, or sickness in your immediate family." It goes downhill from there. In my dreams, my teeth regularly desert me. Sometimes I trip and they fall out of my mouth upon impact. Sometimes I am eating, and they crumble into dust so that they flavor my food. Sometimes I find a path of my teeth and put a hand up to my face to discover an empty mouth.

I wouldn't be surprised to learn that such nightmares are inherited. I don't talk to my father about teeth because that topic puts us both in bad moods. But I can imagine my Aunt Lil, shrunk down into childhood, shivering at the image of someday having to try on dead men's teeth, and I wonder how many bad dreams we've shared.

The last time I went to the dentist back home, my teeth were cleaned by a new person, my dentist's son, newly a graduate of UK's dental school and part of the family practice. He was a junior when I was a freshman, and I had never had a crush on him or been a friend, but I held no antagonism either. He had always been one step removed—friends with my friends, but not of any interest to me—yet now it seemed terribly shameful and unfair that he, someone who had attended Morehead Elementary, could get a good look at my imperfect teeth. If the wait in the lobby hadn't reduced me as usual to a trembling, silent creature, if I had retained any of my usual bravery, I would not even have opened up my mouth, just flashed a close-lipped smile, gotten out of the chair, and left. Instead, I lay there with a spit bib around my neck, listening to him trade jargon with the nurse over my gaping mouth. It didn't matter that I was doing well at an out-of-state college, and was happy, independent, and popular. It didn't matter that he was a consummate professional throughout the whole experience, or that, if I wanted to be really catty, I could gloat to myself that I had *gotten out*, and was just home on vacation before I went to live in Hong Kong, and he was here, back in Morehead, taking up the family business. But none of that quite mattered because he was a town kid, and I was a girl with Kentucky teeth.

A couple of years ago, I accepted a Fulbright grant to research beauty pageant culture in Venezuela. I wanted to study the subject mostly because I didn't understand it. Why did Venezuelans care so much about pageants? Why would a woman submit to multiple cosmetic operations just to be a beauty queen? But while this was my main objective, secretly I also wanted to prove that I could talk to some of the most beautiful women in the world and still feel good about myself, that I was delighted to be who I was and wouldn't change myself even if given the chance. I interviewed past and present beauty queens and their parents, friends, and coaches, and I came away mostly unscathed. There was one man I stayed far away from, though. I could never get up the nerve to open my mouth anywhere near Moises Kaswan, the official dentist of Miss Venezuela, famous for shaping those perfect smiles one sees at Miss Universe.

Sometimes it takes awhile to convince people that I grew up in authentic dirty-kids-in-the-road Appalachia—and that the region even exists anymore after the efforts of Lyndon Johnson and the goodhearted college students who went to Kentucky to save the world. After all, I've been to college, and I don't really have much of an accent. In Venezuela, my roommate used to say, "Just wait until she opens her mouth: then you'll believe her." He meant that my origins are betrayed in some of my expressions—statements like "Well, I'll tell you *what.*" What he didn't mean, but could have meant, was that, though I belie the negative stereotype in every other way, I've got the teeth to prove I'm for real.

Sometimes I try to convince myself that it's the price I pay for taking pride in a questionable origin. And looking at it from the glass-half-full perspective, I should be delighted that I'm nearly twice as old as my dad was when he got his dentures, and I still have a full set of real teeth. Sometimes I dream up scenarios in which my writing, my inherited ability to tell lies, will make me so rich that when the time comes for me to get dentures, I'll obtain a set with a diamond in the center of every other one, or maybe I'll find some decorous fangs.

But mostly, I brush.

Scar Tissue

BY CARLY SACHS

The summer my parents divorced,
I helped my mother jar strawberry preserves.
With my mother, it was all about the filling of jars.
She refused the spoon, grandma's neat precision.
She preferred to scoop up the pulp,
give the jam one more press before sealing it up.
She told me this way she'd recognize which were hers
and which were grandma's from the taste.
I said hers were tart, grandma's were sweet.
I don't remember what happened next.
What I remember is how she refused to wash her hands
for days afterwards, the way red melted to pink,
the way a burn scars so you can never
really say it healed.

The Far and the Near

BY RON RASH

My grandfather was seventy-one years old when he manifested an artistic talent no one in our family, including himself, realized he possessed. That July he had suffered a stroke while stretching barbed wire in his pasture. My Aunt Florence was bringing him lunch and found him draped on the fence like something hung out to dry. The worst thing, my aunt said, had been pulling him free from the wire, for the metal thorns were embedded in his flesh as well as in his flannel shirt.

The doctors told my grandfather's two daughters—my mother and my aunt—that months might pass before he came home, but he recovered more quickly than the doctors anticipated. Within two weeks he was in the hospital's rehabilitation wing walking the black, rubber street of the treadmill. And he was painting.

"He's knows how to *see*," the art therapist told my mother and me when we visited one Saturday. "And it's not just being able to look at something and make a copy. He makes us see the world through his eyes." The therapist shook her head. "It's amazing."

My mother looked across the room where my grandfather sat before an easel, brush and palette in hand.

"All I've ever seen him paint was his house and some farm equipment," my mother said, her voice a mixture of humor and something close to alarm. "Could this be caused by the stroke?"

"No," the therapist said. "It's something he's always had, something he was born with, a gift. He's just finally gotten the chance to show it."

The therapist nodded toward my grandfather. "He's going to need this, because he won't be able to do a lot of the things he's used to doing."

As we drove out of the hospital parking lot my mother looked at me and shook her head. "My goodness, Chad. If your grandmother was alive she'd have a fit seeing him spend a whole afternoon painting. He always looked for a reason not to paint, said he hated doing it worse than anything, even cutting tobacco."

My grandfather left the hospital the first week of July. An orderly placed the suitcase and paintings in the trunk of my mother's car, then an easel and cardboard box filled with art books and supplies beside it.

"That's from Mrs. Watkins, his therapist," the orderly said. "It's a farewell present."

My grandfather had been back home less than an hour when he set up the easel in the front room. While my mother went and cooked supper, my grandfather had me drag an old trunk from the corner to lay his paints and brushes on. He sat down in a ladderback chair and began to work on a painting he'd begun at the hospital. I stood behind him and watched as he completed a river scene. The river was the French Broad, and I knew exactly which section, a shoals above Hot Springs. Nevertheless, my grandfather's hand had created a vividness I'd never seen with my own eyes. A patch of morning sunlight spread over the river's surface like a gold quilt. Willow oak leaves pulsed bright-green like emeralds.

Once home, my grandfather insisted he stay at his own farmhouse instead of living with one of his daughters. My mother and aunt relented only when he agreed that either my first cousin Jarred or I would stay with him those first few weeks. Jarred was sixteen, and I fourteen. I stayed with him during the day and Jarred at night, so I was with him the afternoon my father and uncle loaded up the cattle to sell at the livestock barn in Asheville. We watched from the front porch as the last cow was taken out from the pasture. After my uncle drove the livestock truck through, my father jumped out of the cab and closed the gate.

"No reason for your daddy to close the gate," my grandfather said as we watched the truck disappear up the road. "There's nothing left to keep in."

Each weekday morning, my father let me off at 7:15 on his way to work in Asheville. Jarred would be in the kitchen. He had a construction job that summer, helping to build second homes for wealthy Floridians, but he didn't have to be at work until 8:30. As soon as I got to the farmhouse, Jarred crossed the pasture to bring back the breakfast Aunt Florence had cooked. Jarred ate with us, then cranked up the decade-old Plymouth Fury he'd taken out a loan for the week school let out. The car sputtered and rattled to life, the rotting muffler Jarred couldn't yet afford to replace coughing plumes of black smoke. He would work all day, then come straight back to the farmhouse after he got off at five.

Jarred was the oldest grandchild, and because he had grown up on land adjacent to my grandfather's farm, he'd spent much more time with my grandfather than I had. Jarred had been named after him as well. Although my grandfather tried his best not to show it, his bond with Jarred was, inevitably, deeper. He did not leave the kitchen table until Jarred left for work.

Only then would my grandfather move into the front room and sit before his easel. He would paint all morning, at first Madison County landscapes—barns and fields, streams and mountains. After a month he began to do portraits as well, first one of Jarred standing alone in the pasture, then one of me leaning against the barn. While my grandfather painted, I straightened up the house as best I could, then went outside to mow the grass and hoe the half-acre of corn and beans he'd planted two months before his stroke.

Afternoons we sat on the front porch. My grandfather read the art books or closed his eyes and napped, while I listened to the radio or read musty *Field and Streams* I'd hauled down from the attic. At a few minutes after five, he would start looking down the road for Jarred's Plymouth.

"I've seen milking trails wider than that road down to Mars Hill," my grandfather would say. "I wish some of them state politicians would look at a map and realize there's a lot of North Carolina west of Raleigh. If they did, we might get some decent roads up here."

By the time I went back to school in late August, my grandfather was able to take care of himself. Despite my mother and Aunt Florence's protests, he was again driving his rust-scabbed 57' Ford pick-up to Gus Boyd's store, sometimes going all the way to Hot Springs or Mars Hill. He hoed the corn and beans and cut the grass himself. It was all they could do to keep him from buying some cattle for his pasture.

It was during this time that Reverend Luckadoo approached my grandfather about painting a mural for the baptistry. Reverend Luckadoo had seen several of my grandfather's paintings, including one of the church that now hung in the preacher's living room.

"God has given you a gift, Deacon Hampton" Reverend Luckadoo said, "and this would be a chance to use it to benefit the church."

That my grandfather agreed to do the mural did not surprise me. He'd always been an active member of the church, serving as a deacon for two decades. He frequently offered the morning prayer, and every other Sunday he served as our music director, choosing hymns for the service and then leading the singing.

Reverend Luckadoo looked at my mother and aunt. "But only if we're all in agreement you're healthy enough to do this. It wasn't but two months ago I was visiting you in the hospital."

"I'm not sure this is such a good idea," my mother said.

"What if he had to get on a ladder and fell?" Aunt Florence asked.

"I wouldn't need a ladder," my grandfather said. "Maybe a footstool, but not a ladder."

"Well, a footstool then," Aunt Florence said. "If you fell off a footstool, you could still get hurt."

"Maybe it could be done on weekends," Reverend Luckadoo suggested, then nodded at me. "That way Jarred or Chad could go as well."

"Jarred can't do it," Aunt Florence said. "He works construction all day Saturday. Sundays afternoons he helps at Billy Nelson's gas station as well."

Reverend Luckadoo looked at me.

"It would be a way of contributing to your church, Chad," he said.

"I don't mind doing it," I said, but my lack of enthusiasm was evident.

"It'll just take a weekend," my grandfather said.

"Gus Boyd says he'll donate the paint and brushes," Reverend Luckadoo said. "You just tell him what you need."

The following Saturday morning, my grandfather and I drove toward the church, paint cans and brushes bumping and rattling in the truck bed. We spread old bed sheets over the baptistry. My grandfather handed me a screwdriver.

"Just open the blue paint," he said as he taped a bed sheet to the wall edge, "then bring that piano bench over here. I'm going to start with the sky."

He did not speak loudly, but his voice reverberated from the back pews. I had never been in the church when it was so vacant, and I found the emptiness unsettling. The building felt not so much unoccupied as abandoned. The church seemed somehow darker, as if it were the congregation as much as the hundred-watt bulbs that filled the building with light.

"You'll need to hold the paint can for me," my grandfather said. "This bench will flip over for sure if I'm bending to douse my brush."

I stood beside the piano bench, lifting the blue paint bucket each time the paint thinned on his three-inch brush.

"This isn't going to do," my grandfather said after a few minutes. He handed me the brush, then laid his hand on my shoulder as he stepped from the bench. He took a rag from the back pocket of his coveralls and wiped paint off his thumb and index finger.

"The color isn't thick enough," he said. "I want it to look like the person getting baptized is stepping right into that river."

My grandfather nodded at the cans of paint at our feet. "That paint won't work, but I know some that will." He began to reseal the open cans.

"Let's load this back on the truck, except for the white and brown. Then we'll go trade this for what we need."

"What are going to use instead?" I asked as we drove toward Gus Boyd's store.

"Tractor paint. They only make three colors, but that ought to be enough."

Gus Boyd had five cans of the red tractor paint that Massey-Ferguson made as well as four cans of Ford's blue, but we had to drive to the John Deere dealership in Mars Hill to get our green.

"I reckon I can count this as part of my tithe," my grandfather said as he pulled several worn five dollar bills from his billfold. He adjusted the new John Deere cap the clerk had given him. "Well, at least I got me a new hat."

We were back in the church in forty-five minutes, my grandfather on the bench creating a sky out of Ford tractor paint.

"This is more like it," he said. "See how it makes things look thicker. Now that's a sky you could disappear into."

My grandfather did not want to break for lunch until he finished the upper sky, the part that required he stand on the piano bench, so we worked past noon. I switched the can from hand to hand more often as the hours passed. By the time we finished, the muscles in my wrists and arms ached as though I'd spent the morning lifting dumbbells.

We ate the sandwiches my mother had made and sipped iced tea from mason jars. Then we sat down on the front pew. For a few minutes my grandfather was motionless, his eyes staring intently at the wall.

"I see it now," he finally said, and got up. While I cleaned brushes with kerosene, my grandfather mixed green tractor paint and white house paint. He added more white until the paint lightened to a green, silver-tinged pastel. I'd seen the color before, but I couldn't remember where. My grandfather no longer needed the piano bench, so I carried it back, then sat back down on the front pew and watched.

He worked from the bottom up now, kneeling inside the baptistry pool as his green, silver-tinged river slowly rose inside the glass. He applied the paint in sweeping horizontal swathes, some overlapping, some not, creating the appearance of currents moving behind the glass. He continued to kneel even when he had to raise the brush over his head. From the front pew, my grandfather looked like a man mid-river waving to someone on shore, or perhaps signaling for help.

When the paint on the wall was level with the baptistry glass, he stood up, his left hand pressing the small of his back as he slowly rose to his full height.

"Time to mix some more paints," he said, opening the cardboard box that contained pint canning jars, jars my mother called jelly glasses. I was like an alchemist's assistant as I helped mix red and blue to make a deep purple, white and brown to make a manila color like August wheat, other hues to match the palette he'd already created in his head.

"Don't let him overdo," my mother had warned me before I left the house that morning. "No matter what he thinks, he's still over seventy and recovering from a stroke." As we filled the jelly jars, I checked my grandfather's face for signs of fatigue.

"Shouldn't you rest a few minutes?" I asked.

"No," my grandfather said, "I'm fine."

"You look tired," I said.

My grandfather looked up from the paint he was mixing.

"That doesn't matter. You can't do something like this in bits and pieces. It's like taking a picture with a camera. If you get what you want in the frame, you take the picture right then, because whatever you're seeing might not be there the next time."

When my grandfather returned to the baptistry, he lined up the different-hued jelly glasses before him like colorful, unlit candles. But it was a carpenter's pencil, not a paintbrush, that he worked with first. Between sky and water he outlined a human head and torso the same way someone at a crime scene might outline a victim. One arm lifted toward the sky, while the other entered the water at the wrist. My grandfather drew outlines of eyes, nose, and mouth. Only then did he dip a one-inch brush into the manila-covered paint. He worked more deliberately now, holding the brush aloft like a dart as he pondered his next brushstroke. The face began to take on details—lips slightly open as if about to speak, a dark-brown beard that gathered under the chin like something woven, the long, angular nose. But the most striking feature was the heaven-searching eyes. They were the same color as the river. I had seen pictures of brown-eyed Jesuses and blue-eyed Jesuses, but never one with eyes of green.

After he finished the face, my grandfather lifted the jar with purple paint and colored the robe, then the manila color for the lifted palm spread out in blessing. The stained-glass windows offered no light, and darkness pooled in the sanctuary's corners, before my grandfather laid down his brush.

"So what do you think?" he asked.

"It's good," I said, "especially the eyes. I never thought of Jesus having green eyes, but somehow it seems to fit."

"Seems that way to me, too," my grandfather said.

"I think you better stop now," I said.

"I hate to, but I reckon you're right," he said. "If I get too tired, I'll get sloppy. Anyway, all we got left now is background. I reckon that can wait till tomorrow afternoon."

My grandfather turned away from the mural. His eyes were red-veined and rheumy, as though the effort to transfer the vision inside his head onto the wall had strained them.

"I don't think Preacher Luckadoo will mind us leaving this stuff in the baptistry," he said. "I wish we could cover the wall with a couple of bed sheets so people couldn't see it till it was finished, but I'm afraid it'll smear some of the paint."

"We could come in tomorrow before church starts and cover it," I said.

My grandfather nodded. "That's a first-rate idea. We'll do that very thing."

The next morning my grandfather stood at the right side of the pulpit as he led our singing of "Will There Be Any Stars in My Crown?" The makeshift curtain we'd taped up earlier covered the wall behind, its bottom draping into the empty baptistry pool.

After the service, my grandfather ate Sunday lunch with my parents and me. He was a man who liked to linger at the dinner table on Sundays, but on this day he did not sip a cup of coffee after dessert or discuss the week's news. He quickly finished his banana pudding and gave me a nod.

"Go get your work duds on. Let's get on back to the church."

We were inside the church by 1:30, and for the next few hours I watched my grandfather reroute the Jordan River through western North Carolina. He began with a red tobacco barn, a barn he was just completing when the front door shut behind us.

"I don't believe they had tobacco barns in Israel two thousand years ago, Deacon Hampton," Preacher Luckadoo said. "I believe that's what they'd call an anachronism."

My grandfather paused but did not lay his brush down.

"The way I see it, folks understand something better when you connect the far away with what's nearby."

"I'm not so sure," Preacher Luckadoo said. "Tell me how you'd argue that."

"Do you believe we're in the presence of Christ, right here in Madison County, right now in 1986?" my grandfather said.

"Yes, I do," Preacher Luckadoo said.

"Well, that's what I'm saying in this here mural."

Preacher Luckadoo looked skeptical as he studied the painting a few more moments.

"I suppose I see your point," he finally said, "but I'm not sure this is the best way to show it. I still think a stone temple would be better than a tobacco barn. And I'd suggest those eyes be brown. After all, Jesus was a Hebrew."

My grandfather listened politely. As soon as Preacher Luckadoo left, my grandfather turned back to the mural and put the finishing touches on the tobacco barn.

"I should have told him what happened to the church man that pestered Michelangelo," he said. "Have you ever heard that story?"

I shook my head.

"Michelangelo was laying on his back from dawn to dusk painting the Sistine Chapel. Most every day this church man named Cesena came around, complaining that Michelangelo wasn't working fast enough, not doing such and such the way Cesena wanted it done."

My grandfather set down his brush and turned to me. "Care to guess what happened?"

"I've no idea," I said.

"Well, when Michelangelo painted his scene of hell he stuck Cesena right down there in the middle of it. Of course, Cesena got all bent out of shape about that. He went running to the pope complaining about what Michelangelo had done and telling the pope that he, as the pope, had to do something about it." My grandfather paused to chuckle. "The pope told Cesena that even a pope couldn't get a man out of hell. You can go to the Sistine Chapel today, and you'll still see Cesena there with the other lost souls."

By the time we had another visitor, it was six o'clock, and all my grandfather had left to do was climb the piano bench a last time and fill in some final sections of blue sky.

"I hope that isn't Preacher Luckadoo with some more suggestions," my grandfather said when he heard a car door slam. My grandfather looked warily toward the door. He stepped away from the mural and stood beside the pulpit, allowing me my first unimpeded look at the painting in hours.

On the riverbank behind Christ's shoulders, deep-green rows of cornstalks sprouted in a patch of dark bottomland. At the field's center, a scarecrow spread its arms as though about to embrace someone. A mourning dove perched on the scarecrow's right shoulder. On a hill in the farther distance, the red tobacco barn rose into an uncompleted sky.

"What do you think?" my grandfather asked, though he was not speaking to me but to Jarred, who stood in the doorway with a cardboard box filling his arms.

"I like it a lot," Jarred said. He shifted the box deeper into his arms and walked down the aisle. He laid the box on one of the bed sheets and lifted from it three foil-wrapped plates, some silverware and napkins, and three sealed jars of iced tea.

"You haven't eaten?" my grandfather asked.

"No," Jarred said. "Momma wanted me to, but I figured I'd eat with you all."

"Well, we're more than glad to have your company," my grandfather said.

Jarred and I sat cross-legged on the floor, our grandfather in front of us on the piano bench. We lifted the tin foil from our plates, and a warm steam rose to our faces. The smell of fried chicken, boiled okra, and biscuits filled the sanctuary.

"Your Momma could always cook," my grandfather said to Jarred after a few bites, "even when she was no more than a child."

The front door opened again, and my father entered.

"Looks like we're going to have a family reunion before it's all over and done with," my grandfather said. He waved my father toward the front.

"You've got school tomorrow, and according to your momma you've got homework yet to do," my father said to me.

"We'll be through in two hours," I pleaded.

"Is that right?" my father asked my grandfather.

"Probably less with Jarred helping."

"Alright," my father said, sitting down beside me. "I reckon your momma and your homework can wait. I'll help so that'll speed it up, too."

My grandfather held a drumstick out to my father, saying "I'm near about full. You eat it."

"I've never been known to turn down a piece of Florence's chicken," my father said, and took the drumstick.

When the plates and jars and silverware were back in the cardboard box, my grandfather picked up a fresh brush to complete his sky, while Jarred and my father and I cleaned brushes. That done, we wiped paint off the outside of cans and jars before carrying them out to the pick-up, then checked beneath bed sheets for paint drops, which we scraped from the oak flooring with razor blades.

We were done by 8:30. I bundled the last bed sheet into my arms, as my grandfather looked over the mural a final time. He nodded to himself before following Jarred, my father, and me up the aisle toward the door. Jarred bent down in front of my father and lifted something from the foyer's floor.

"Look," Jarred said, turning to us. "It must have got in when we were carrying stuff out to the truck."

He held his cupped hands toward us and slowly opened them a couple of inches. A Luna moth filled his palm, its green, silver-tinged wings rising and falling steady as a heartbeat. This was the exact color of the river and Christ's eyes, the color I had seen before but only now could place. It was as if a piece of the mural had flecked off and come alive.

Jarred stepped to the doorway. He opened his hands, and the moth fluttered into the darkness. Jarred stepped back into the foyer and held his right palm under the ceiling light's glow.

"Well, what do you make of that?" he said. A fine green powder spread across my cousin's palm like some rare, beautiful dust.

The next Sunday, the whole congregation saw my grandfather's mural, and the reaction was overwhelmingly positive. Preacher Luckadoo had also dropped any qualms he had about anachronisms, for that same morning he gave a sermon recasting Simon Peter and Andrew as good old boys running trot-lines on the French Broad.

Perhaps if events had turned out differently, my grandfather would have painted more murals, eventually turning Ivy Creek Baptist Church into his version of the Sistine Chapel. But four months later, on a February morning, numerous lives, including my grandfather's, were suddenly and irrevocably altered. It was a Saturday, and the curvy mountain road Jarred drove to work was slick from an ice storm. The Plymouth plunged off the road and tumbled fifty yards into a ravine, catching fire when it hit a tree.

The night of the visitation I sat on a metal folding chair in the parlor of Hendricks Funeral Home in Mars Hill. Sitting with me were my parents and brother and sister, my aunt and uncle, and my great-aunt Edna. Jarred's closed casket lay in the corner, a coffin I would help carry come morning. My grandfather was supposed to come with my aunt and uncle, but when they had gone to pick him up, my grandfather and the truck were gone.

"He shouldn't have gone off like that," Aunt Edna said. "What are people going to think?"

"Nobody that matters could have a doubt how much that old man loves Jarred," my father replied. "Each of us grieves in own own way."

"Maybe you're right," my great-aunt replied. "I do know he loved that boy like life itself."

The visitation ended at eight o'clock, and my grandfather had still not shown up. A light rain began to fall, and my father turned on his wipers as we drove back up the mountain. My mother insisted we go my grandfather's house to see if he was back, but when our headlights splashed across the front of the farmhouse, the lights were off, the dirt pull-off where he parked was empty.

My Uncle Jesse stepped off the porch. Because of his black suit we had not seen him.

"He's not in there," my Uncle Jesse said.

"I'll take you and the kids home," my father said to my mother, "then I'll go look for him."

"No," my mother replied. "The kids and me will stay with Florence and Jesse until he comes back on his own or you bring him back." My mother turned to us in the back seat. "You all get out," she said. "We'll walk over with Jesse."

My sisters got out of the car, but I did not move.

"I want to go with you," I told my father. "I think I know where he is."

It took us ten minutes to get to the church. The pick-up was parked out front, and inside the lights were on. My father and I opened the door and stood in the foyer for a few moments. Bed sheets were bunched and spread across the sanctuary floor. On top of the sheets were paint cans, the lids beside them, one can overturned. Brushes lay on the sheets as well, paint still on them as if thrown down in frustration. My grandfather sat on the front pew, his eyes raised to the mural.

The figure in the river no longer bore Christ's face but my grandfather's, and in his arms he carried Jarred's body. The river was red now. In the distance, orange flames consumed the barn. Christ was in the distance, hanging head bowed on planks that had once held a scarecrow.

"I'm going back to Jesse and Florence's house and tell your mama that your grandfather's okay, but that we're going to be a while," my father said. "Then I'll go wake up Gus Boyd and get us some cans of white paint."

We worked until past midnight that evening, turning the wall into a white blank, while my grandfather slumped on the front pew. He occasionally raised his face, but his eyes were blank as the white wall we were replacing his mural with. When we finally finished, my father insisted my grandfather ride with us back to his farmhouse.

"You can stay with us tonight," my father offered.

"No, I'll be better off here," my grandfather replied. So I walked him to the door, and I went in first to turn on the lights.

"It's been a long night," my father said as we finally pulled into our drive. "You'll likely have few nights that are longer. At least that's my hope."

The next morning, I helped carry Jarred's body into the cemetery. I watched my grandfather carefully. He was exhausted, that was clear, and he mourned fiercely, but he, like all of us, got through it.

My grandfather would live three more years, and during that time he continued to go to church. He led us in song and prayer as before, but the wall behind the sanctuary remained blank. The paints and brushes were stored away in his attic. Instead of spending his days crouched before an easel, my grandfather sat on his front porch, and more often than not his eyes were closed.

Perhaps he felt he had shown us enough, especially of the vision we all shared that bleak February night before Jarred's funeral. My grandfather had taken us, as well as himself, as far as any of us could bear.

The Retired Preacher

BY RON RASH

After years of negotiating
between his squabbling congregation
and the maker he prayed
was not in their image,
he tended instead his
flock of bantam gamecocks
full of strut and preen, hot
tempered as copperheads,
and, on those Sundays
he grew nostalgic, uncaged
two birds, let them peck
and scratch until feathers
swirled like drunk angels, flecks
of blood stained the grass—
and it all came back.

Preacher Malone Considers, Someways, the Lilies of the Field

BY JIM CLARK

Now it says here in Luke, chapter 12,
Verse 27 and following: "Consider
The lilies how they grow; they toil not,
They spin not; and yet I say unto you,
That Sollymun in all his glory was
Not arrayed like one of these." Now, Jesus
Is saying here that we ought to think about
The flowers, we ought to *consider* them.
I'm not sure as I know of anybody
Out here on the ridge that grows lilies, but
Maybe you could think of Miss McGlassen's
Big old purple hollyhocks. Anyway,
Them hollyhocks don't have to work—they don't
Have to *toil*—like Adam and Eve made sure
All us humans have to do all our blessed lives.
Sloppin' hogs and plowin' cornfields, and draggin'
A dead mule down to the Hooter Bluff because
It got into the dadgum feed room and
Foundered itself. No sir, Adam and Eve
They just couldn't be *satisfied* with *Paradise*.
Anyways, who ever heard of flowers toilin'?
And they don't have to *spin*, neither. And brethren,
That don't mean like when they get caught up
In a powerful wind and spin around
On their little stems like pretty toy windmills.

No sir, it means spin like my poor old momma
Used to, on a rickety old spinning wheel,
Her hands a-bleedin' from that thread a-runnin'
Through 'em, tryin' to make some kind of pitiful
Little duds, such as they were, to clothe
Our shameful nakedness. But these here hollyhocks
I'm tellin' you about, well they're so purty,
Through no effort of their own but only God's
Infinite love and compassion, that they put
The fancy purple robes of the great
King Sollymun hisself to shame! I mean,
As God made 'em, these are some kind
Of hollyhocks! Or lilies, to get back
To the actual words of Jesus, which I guess
Is where we ought to end this thing up.

When the Spirit Moved Us

BY TAMMY WILSON

When my older sister, Bonita, brought Cousin Flo back home with her from Akron, I had a feeling we were in for it, but that's usually what happens when you mix city with country. One will always try to outdo the other. Those two girls had always been close, but when Flo's family moved to Ohio in '32, my sister began taking her cues from Flo's big-city ways, and now that Flo had taken up with the Spiritualists, she was determined to show us how to talk to the dead.

Flo asked Bonita to visit her in Akron that July, and it was easy to say yes because it was summer and she wasn't teaching. She had been to Akron once before and had been more than eager to tell us how sophisticated it was. "They have department stores with escalators and automatic traffic lights in *four* lanes."

The way she talked to us, you'd think we never got off the farm. We didn't get to town much, but I wasn't too ignorant to pick up a book. I had read enough to know that Akron was a sooty factory town full of tire plants and foreigners—including Flo's husband, Vince, who had drifted in with the New Deal. After only a few years he had already moved up to assembly line foreman at BF Goodrich. Flo, meanwhile, was a lady of leisure, Bonita said, and she had Vince well-trained. After a full shift, he would come home to cook and clean, while she read love novels and contemplated her Spiritualist meetings. It was hard to think of Flo as a farm girl anymore.

One Saturday, Mama, Bonita, and I were washing another year of dust off Mama's windows. Although I had married and moved out, I saw it as my duty to help since Papa had died. The windows had panes to the floor, four over four with a big cross in the middle. You had to stand on a chair to reach the top of the sash. Mama's poor old joints had a hard time with her regular chores, let alone something this strenuous.

I threw a cotton rag at Bonita, hoping she'd take the hint. Teaching grade school taxed her for eight months out of the year, so by the time May rolled around, she was ready to travel. So far she'd seen most every state bordering Kentucky plus Pennsylvania, which was added last summer when Flo and Vince drove her to the Pittsburgh Zoo where she saw a flock of ostriches. "A couple of those eggs would feed a whole team of threshers," she said.

I mocked a laugh. The only thing she knew about that job was watching Mama feed men from the field. It took the better part of a day slaving over a hot stove. Once during harvesting season, Bonita set the table only after being begged. Mama and I had already baked four pies, boned three chickens, and rolled out enough dumplings to serve seconds. Bonita took her sweet time laying out the silverware, but when she was done, she went back to supervising. It irked me how Mama let her off so easy, but my older sister was fragile and bird-boned, and usually sick with one thing or another. I was taller, stouter, and, as Mama put it, "more mannish." That made me the workhorse.

While Mama and I washed each pane, Bonita related her trip to Akron. "The Madam White lady came out to give us facials, and I felt so deliciously spoiled," Bonita said, chirpy as a hatchling. "About every day, Flo and I discovered this little shop that had the most divine hats—even those straw ones from Italy."

Then, Bonita said, they gorged themselves on jumbo ice cream cones—chocolate and vanilla swirled like a barber pole—and saw a movie at the new open-air theatre and attended Vince's company picnic at Summit Beach. Of course, I didn't know any of the places she was talking about, but I had to admit they sounded more exciting than anything around here.

While Bonita was gone to Ohio, she had missed out on hoeing the beans, picking blackberries, and putting up sweet corn.

As we cleaned the windows, Mama made the mistake of asking that sister of mine what she did for church while she was in Akron.

Bonita shrugged. "Cousin Flo doesn't go to a regular church. She's a Spiritualist."

Mama stopped wiping the glass in mid-swirl and gave her a look as if she had dough for brains. "Bonita Yoakum, nothing good can come from tempting Satan."

My sister laughed as she rinsed a cloth in vinegar water and handed it to me. "They're not devil worshippers, Mama. Flo's coming next week, so you can see for yourself."

That was the first inkling we had of Flo's impending visit, and I'm sure Mama wasn't too impressed with the short notice, but Flo was family. Mama couldn't say no.

Sure enough, that Friday afternoon, Flo called from the depot to pick her up, and Bonita went after her in Papa's old cab. I swallowed hard. I've never cared for Flo much because three can't ever get along.

When Flo had arrived that Monday with her gaggle of valises, I was the one who got the honor of lugging all her stuff inside. Later, I stuck my head into what used to be my room. There stood Flo, still overdressed in her fancy peplum suit and straw picture hat, one with a cluster of cherries on the band. It looked as out of place as wedding cake at a picnic. I could see her nut-colored hair, her penciled eyebrows in the mirror. I'd seen such in magazines, but never in person. Even fashion models looked less ridiculous.

"Are you getting settled in?" I said. Flo had to know I was coming well before I appeared at the doorway. The smell of country was on me from being out at Mama's hen house, though I had a scarf on my head to keep my hair half-ways clean.

She fiddled with a fruit jar holding a sunflower bloom, of all things, and placed it on the bureau. "Lorrine, I don't know if there's enough room in the closet for all my things," she pouted through pinkish red lipstick. At least she wasn't calling me Squirt.

I showed her a couple of empty drawers where she could put her things and that seemed to satisfy her some. Then she opened her little train case full of more jars than Wehrle's cosmetics counter.

"I'll bet things look pretty dull back here," I said.

"Oh, we have farms in Ohio. When Bonita was visiting, we'd go out to the country for milk or eggs. It's a nice drive out past the celery fields." Flo's voice trailed off.

"Celery fields?" I said. We bought a few stalks when the spirit moved us, but I'd never thought of actually raising it.

"They grow things there for the city restaurants. Most people I know don't have gardens. Vince is the only farmer."

She said "farmer" like he was serving a prison sentence tending vegetables. This irked me. Hadn't Flo grown up on a farm? Of course she had, right down the road from where we were standing, until her father couldn't make the payments and took a factory job.

"Farming's honest work," I said.

"It may be honest, but there's no future in it. Dad dug in the dirt most of his life too, and never made the kind of money Vince is making. He was promoted last week. First shift."

"How long are you staying?" I said. That sounded friendlier than asking when she was leaving.

"A week, give or take. I need to get back before Cousin Bonita starts school. She needs some time to get ready."

Sure. A few days to fill out a class roster, count pencils, and drag a broom across the floor. What should take a couple of hours would take Bonita a whole day. Of course, she would make tracks to town to spruce up her wardrobe. The shopping, hemming, and ironing would take the better part of a week.

I let Flo put her things away since there wasn't any use for me to stick around. I hadn't cared for her since the time we were kids playing in the attic. Flo had helped her clumsy self to Grandma Yoakum's wedding gown. "I'll be the bride. Bonita, you be the maid of honor, and Squirt can be the groom." The name "Squirt" was meant to be funny. I was younger, but not smaller.

We rummaged through the pile of clothes from long-dead ancestors, and I was told not to touch the old wedding gown.

"Flo, it won't fit you," Bonita said, trying to squeeze Flo into the aging garment.

"Pull harder," Flo insisted.

The sound of tearing fabric made me sick to my stomach.

Bonita gasped. "Oh no! Mama will have a fit."

"Not if she don't find out," Flo said. She removed the old garment and kicked it across the dusty floor. She hurriedly dressed in her own calico frock and glanced over at me. "If she does find out, say Squirt did it."

When I graduated from high school, I told the folks that I wanted to become a nurse because I didn't mind cleaning up other people's messes too awful much, but Papa insisted that nursing wasn't a respectable line of work because it involved seeing men without their pants on. "It's teaching or nothing," he said. And then Harvey Pendergrass, the long-legged boy from down the road, started turning up on our doorstep regular, and he was a lot more fun than teaching school. He was generally honest, but he had an ornery streak. I knew that when I married him right after high school, which was six years ago this past June. I told Mama and Papa that I loved Harvey, and I believe I did. By then, he was past most of that mischief anyway, and I was looking for better prospects than staying home doing Bonita's chores.

Harvey's folks offered us their tenant house at the bottom edge of the bean field, and we moved there, with me doing the usual farmwife duty—driving a tractor, keeping house, and dressing chickens. Papa and Mama finally came around to liking Harvey, but Bonita and Harvey never hit it off.

"She thinks she's the Queen of Sheba," he said. Harvey had pretty much left her alone compared to what you might expect, though he liked to aggravate her every now and then. He had owned up to leaving a dead fox on the schoolhouse steps one morning, and he stuffed a sweet potato up the exhaust pipe of her coupe. Her car sputtered to the next farmhouse to get help from Mr. Garvin, who discovered the potato. Harvey's pranks were childish, but I couldn't help but find them funny—made even more funny by the fact that he was a big lummox who thrived on rattling my sister's nerves.

Bonita wouldn't have lasted a day as a farm wife. Once, when she came to visit after her school let out for the day, she caught me with a hatchet out at the stump, beheading a tough old Rock hen. She had seen Mama wrestling chickens plenty of times, but the look Bonita gave me was as if she'd happened on a bloody wreck.

She sputtered, grabbed at her throat, and covered her mouth. "My God, what are you doing, the poor thing…you're torturing it."

Between her bleating and that chicken gurgling in half-squawks, I wanted to use that hatchet on Bonita.

A week after Flo arrived, the two of them laid out of church because they'd gone to the pictures the night before. Still, they offered us a Spiritualist sitting that evening. It would be simple, they said. They'd be in charge; all we had to do was sit and listen.

That afternoon, while Flo and Bonita planned the sitting, I happened over to Mama's after church. Bonita had dragged the card table from the hall closet and unfolded its legs. She looked prim enough in her candy-striped Hooverette, a wrap-around she wore around the house in warm weather. Spiritualists, Bonita reminded me, could talk to the dead on any given day. "The medium is the go-between with the special gift, only you can't actually hear the dead person. That's up to the medium conducting the sitting, to interpret what they say."

"Are you it?" I said, like I used to when we were girls.

"No, Flo's the medium. The spirits will give signs."

I carried a folding chair up to the card table and pulled down the seat. "What makes her so special?"

Bonita said it had to do with being anointed.

"Don't be silly. Dead people can't talk."

"Oh, don't be so sure. It says in Matthew that on Good Friday the dead got up and walked all over the place." She pulled Mama's Bible off the top of the piano and thumbed through the onionskin pages until she came to the passage. "See? 'The graves were opened; and many bodies of the saints which slept arose and came out of the graves after His resurrection, and went into the holy city, and appeared unto many.'"

I waved Bonita off. "That was back then. It doesn't mean you can call up dead people nowadays, and even if it does, they don't preach that in *our* church."

"Well they do in Flo's, and if you ever went to a sitting, you'd believe."

She said "believe" like Brother Daniels in his morning sermon. I rolled my eyes and wished Mama was here to rescue me. She wouldn't stand for such nonsense. She'd brought us up as God-fearing Baptist girls.

"Does Vince know Flo's a Spiritualist?" I asked.

"Of course. He goes to the meetings." Bonita's eyes flashed as dark as walnuts as I followed her into the front room. "They meet in this big lecture hall. A medium comes on stage, lights the candles, and when things get very quiet, she calls up the dead. That's when the table moves around. One time it nearly flew off the stage."

"That's just a Houdini trick," I said.

Bonita looked hurt and snotty as she smoothed dark cloth over the card table. "The trouble with you is that you're closed-minded. If you ever went someplace, maybe you wouldn't be so dull."

I put my hands on my hips. Who did she think she was, calling me dull? We're farm folks who mind their own business, tending our God-given land. I knew then that Mama had been right all along. She says the more you see of the world, the happier you are to stay put. Nothing good comes to folks who forget where they're from. Like those actresses who run off to New York or Hollywood. They pretend to be glamorous, though they're just farm girls with chicken manure under their painted nails and with flour-sack britches covering their behinds. And if they don't wear homemade drawers, they should, because it's honest underwear. People in cities are crazy-acting, Mama says, running around like rats, living in little compartments way up off the street. It isn't natural. You don't see us living up on top of a silo.

Why would a sensible person try to talk to dead people when they've gone to live with the Lord? I thought of Papa, caught in his corn picker, struggling till he bled to death. That was three years ago. If he'd been in Heaven all that time, why would he wait this long to contact us? That kind of thing couldn't be part of God's plan, as Brother Daniels would say. It wasn't right for us to bother souls up in Heaven.

"I can hardly wait for tonight's entertainment," I said.

Bonita puffed up like a toad ready to spit, and, before either of us said more, I marched into the kitchen where Mama was rolling out biscuits for supper. Even on Sunday she knew no rest, the only Commandment she chose to ignore.

"Mama, do you think we can talk to dead people?"

She slapped the biscuits hard with her rolling pin. "Sounds like you've been talking to Bonita. Since that girl went to Flo's, all she wants to do is talk about Spirits." Mama wiped her brow. "They've already come to borrow candles."

"Why don't you tell them to go someplace else?"

"Flo's company," Mama said.

The plan was for Harvey and I to get our chores done and come back over to Mama's for supper. When Harvey heard that we were going to talk to the dead, he was bent over the kitchen sink, working soap into a good lather. Even though it was Sunday, he'd had to feed the livestock, ignoring the Eighth Commandment like Mama.

"Are you sure you want to go to Flo's sitting?" I asked.

He shrugged. "It beats watching the corn grow."

I warned him not to breathe a word of it to Brother Daniels or anyone else from church. Harvey looked over at me like a hound grinning at a coon run up a low-slung sapling. "This ought to be fun."

I wasn't exactly sure what he meant by fun, but knowing Harvey, he'd see that we had plenty.

He insisted we arrive at Mama's early so he could get the full benefit of hearing about Flo's new church. Mama did the serving as usual, and held her tongue about the Spiritualists since it isn't nice to argue with guests, even if they're family. Harvey didn't say much, either. He was drinking it all in, along with Mama's iced tea. He swatted flies beside Mama, who sat there with her dust-gray hair pulled up on her head. Her face was pained and tightened as if her underthings had soaked overnight in boiling water.

"Flo, I hear you've changed churches," he said.

"Yes. Vince and I are part of the Spiritualist community. We attend sittings at least once a week," Flo said.

Harvey swiped his plate with a half-eaten biscuit as Mama asked, "What do you believe in, other than talking to dead people?"

"We believe in infinite Intelligence, the natural law that extends to this world and the spirit world," Flo explained. Her voice twisted like a dust devil in a plowed field. Before she was done, she had covered belief in Jesus, Mary, the Jewish God, Mohammed, Buddha, Mother Nature, and Indian deities.

Mama had stopped eating and looked as if she might have to call Brother Daniels.

Harvey folded his arms. "Sounds like you folks believe in pretty near everything."

Flo sidestepped. "We have open minds."

As if we didn't! It was all I could do to hold my tongue.

Once the dining room table was cleared, Bonita and Flo pulled the window shades, lit a couple of candles, and beckoned us to take a seat at the card table. With the breeze blocked by the drawn shades, we would've roasted if it wasn't for the electric fan. Mama was on one side of me, and Harvey was on the other next to Flo. Bonita sat opposite him. We gathered around the draped card table and spread our fingers flat as if we were about to have a group manicure.

"Now relax," Flo said. She held up that very same sunflower I'd seen on her bureau. It was wilted now, bent over on its chin like an old person fallen asleep. "This is our symbol. As the sunflower turns its face toward the light of the sun, so we turn the face of humanity toward the light of truth."

Harvey muttered something under his breath as Flo instructed us to close our eyes and concentrate. For the better part of five minutes, she droned on like a radio announcer listening to silent Morse code. She claimed to hear a messenger called Remus, one of the old souls on the Other Side who included Grandma Yoakum and Vince's Aunt Sophia and his father, Julius. "They say they are doing fine and not to worry."

Since I never knew any of those people in the first place, it was easy not to worry about them, but I couldn't help but wonder if Grandma Yoakum knew Flo had ruined her wedding dress. Maybe that's why she had made a point to get in touch.

Flo talked faster as she mentioned Uncle John, our Papa. "He says he's all right," she said in a voice that had taken on a peculiar accent. I couldn't imagine my Papa being all right, knowing he'd been chewed to pieces by that corn picker. He sure hadn't looked all right lying there at the funeral parlor. His right shoulder was twisted where the machinery had gnawed his arm to a stump before Harvey and Mr. Garvin found him. I wanted to kick myself for not going to nurse's school, though they said not even a doctor could've saved Papa. In death his face looked as waxy as a doll's, her eyes glassy and peaceful, but not blissful. Mama had shored up like she always does in such cases, but frail Bonita shielded herself with an ailment that kept her bedridden until after the funeral.

The electric fan rustled the shades as insects buzzed their evening racket. I thought sure that mention of Papa would set Mama off, but she sat there calmly with her eyes closed.

"John said that he has found peace on the Other Side," Flo said. She rambled on, telling us nice things preachers say at funerals, about how happy we should be for the deceased, how he's over there waiting for us.

And then, about the time I figured we'd had enough of the heat and Flo's séance, the table budged slightly. Bonita gasped. I opened my eyes again. Mama's brows were arched, and I knew mine were too. Harvey's eyes met mine and gave me a slight wink.

"Listen to the spirits," Flo said.

Our hands wobbled around along with the surface of the table that bobbed like an acorn in a horse trough. Finally, the table settled down for a short while, when suddenly it began to move again, its legs making a scraping noise until one leg finally came to rest on the edge of the rug.

After several minutes of quiet, Flo declared that the sitting was over. She blew out the candles and turned on the floor lamp.

"Whew! That was quite a ride," Mama said, opening her eyes.

"Are you all right?" Bonita leaned toward her.

"Heavens yes! Harvey is keeping me straight." Mama gave him an odd grin. She knew.

"We've seen this kind of manifestation fairly often," Flo said. She looked around the table to get my reaction, but I darted my eyes toward Harvey, who was still squinting from the sudden light.

"Who's this Remus?" he asked.

"Why, he's my spirit guide. He puts me in touch with the Other Side. I've only begun to use my gift. He's the guide to channel my thoughts. He picks them up and speaks to me."

She had the language down pat. I had to keep reminding myself that this was Flo, not some hocus-pocus medium. This was the girl who had once lived up the road.

"Oh," Harvey said, his lips half-smiling. "Has Remus ever put you in touch with Bre'er Rabbit?"

Mama and I chuckled.

Bonita frowned. "Harvey, be serious."

"Have you ever actually heard Papa's voice?" I said. But the second I spoke, I wished I hadn't—not with Mama sitting there. Lord knows what she would do or say if Papa started to talk. She had never said much about the accident, not since Mr. Garvin had run up to the house that cold October day to tell her that he and Harvey had found Papa in the field. Not since Mr. Garvin had run back to see Harvey pulling parts of Papa's right arm out of the picker and giving it to the undertaker. I wondered how Harvey was able to do a gruesome job like that. "I didn't think of it more than skinning a rabbit," he had said. "I wouldn't let myself." There had been tears in his eyes when he said it.

"I don't believe Uncle John's spirit has ever manifested itself," Flo said.

Neither she nor Bonita would let on that Harvey was the real spirit, and I wasn't going to tell them and he wasn't either. He'd leave them guessing, and, of course, Mama wouldn't tell. So we sat there like rocks, letting Flo go on about how Remus had told her, about how her husband was missing her these past few days and how she should go home pretty soon. My only worry was that her train might be late and she'd have to stay here a minute longer than necessary.

"I hope you have a nice trip," Mama said. She excused herself to serve a round of lemonade.

Harvey gave me a hard wink and followed her to the kitchen.

Bonita started her lamentations about Flo's leaving. "It's going to be so dull around here, I don't know what I'll do with myself," she pouted.

I took my cue. "How about helping out around here? You're the one who lives here with Mama, so the least you could do is help out instead of playing games."

Bonita stared at me like a stunned animal. "You think Flo's religion is a game? Is that what you think?"

"If the shoe fits," I folded my arms across my chest. "Why don't you grow up and do some real work for a change?"

"Real work? The trouble with you is you're jealous that I've got a paying job and you don't."

At that moment, Harvey appeared with a sweating pitcher of lemonade, followed by Mama carrying a serving tray I hadn't seen since Papa's receiving. She set the glasses down along with a sugar bowl, curiously surrounded by three bristling women, myself included.

"What's the matter?" Harvey said.

"Your wife is being rude to Cousin Flo," Bonita said.

"Rude? She was moaning about what to do after Flo leaves. I suggested she help Mama," I said.

Flo cocked her head to one side, then another, her lips grinning widely like they usually do when she thinks she's being fought over.

"She's saying I'm lazy. I'm not lazy, am I, Mama?" Bonita asked.

Mama motioned for Harvey to sit down. Then she painted each of us with a hard gaze and folded her hands. "I'm too old and tired to take a stick after you girls."

Harvey took a sip of lemonade and remained oddly silent.

"I think it could use more sweetening, don't you?" Mama said as she took the lid off the sugar bowl.

"Do you think I'm lazy?" Bonita repeated.

Mama stirred her lemonade, dissolving a healthy measure of sugar into the sour drink, as the rotary fan cast a slight ripple across the tablecloth.

What Color is Vermilion?

BY ROGER SHARPE

Not long ago, I convinced my brother and sister-in-law to consent to our building a Japanese *torii* for a 2-acre spring-fed pond by their cabin at Sandy Springs. I think it is the first one in North Carolina. The red, gateway-like structure of a *torii* can be seen in Japanese gardens at some of America's finest botanical gardens. It's a kind of "Heaven's Gate." Brooklyn has one in its beautiful Japanese Garden, as does the Art Center at Muscatine, Iowa. So does the Birmingham Botanical Garden in Alabama, and the Osaka Garden in Jackson Park, Chicago. Our Canadian neighbors in British Columbia have one in Victoria's Butchart Gardens. All of these examples of *torii* may be considered imitations of the eighth Torii of Itsukushima at Miyajima, Japan, the first one having been constructed at that site in the twelfth century and built to stand above the sea 16.8 meters (about 52 feet) high. But the aesthetic beauty of smaller American renderings inspired by the original is no less wondrous. I learned this when I first saw Peter and Nora Lejins' *torii* at College Park, Maryland. Theirs, which is not much larger than a typical doorframe, accented a small water-lily pool at the "Apollo path" entrance to a 5-acre garden in their back yard. During more than fifty years of marriage, the Lejins had collected 6000 azaleas from the many countries where their lifetime work had taken them—Peter's, as an internationally-renowned criminologist, and Nora's, as a US State Department official.

Traditionally, the *torii* points the way to a shrine, a holy place, the path to which is designated in many instances by large, carved stone Japanese lanterns, like the ones to be found among the cherry trees between the Lincoln and Jefferson Memorials in Washington, DC's Tidal Basin and beside the Swan-boat pond of Boston's Public Garden and Commons. Columbia University in New York City has one of the pedestaled ancient lanterns on its Morningside campus on Broadway Avenue, and the Atlanta Botanical Garden displays such a lantern at the entrance to its petite Japanese garden. Harvard University's Arnold Arboretum has one, too, standing among its famous Larz Anderson collection of *bon sai*.

The various reproductions of the Japanese lantern have become an icon almost as familiar as birdbaths are in the suburban American yardscape. Many of the lanterns are copied after the Kasuga lantern of Nara, Japan, and contain stone-carved or concrete-molded images of deer on their casing-panels. Legend holds that deer in ancient times served as messengers of the gods carrying news from Paradise. My sister-in-law in Harmony, North Carolina, has a short, square-legged, snow-viewing Kodau Yu Kimi lantern in her iris garden, and my second cousin, an octogenarian and veteran of World War II, has a large Kasuga-like lantern in his rose garden nearby at Union Grove, North Carolina. I noted that my neighbor, whom I welcomed back from his fiftieth anniversary reunion with Korean War veterans traveling to Seoul, displays a very attractive concrete Rankei-style lantern with an out-stretched and welcoming-arm base. It is thoughtfully positioned among ornamental shrubs at the entrance to his driveway. Perhaps some of the people who appreciate these lanterns, upon seeing the *torii* at Sandy Springs, will be inspired by the difference?

Rather than designating a shrine per se, our *torii* designates the location of springs as a source of the life-sustaining water that creates the pond. Our *torii* marks the source of new beginnings, as it were. I would like to think of the *torii* not just as a landscaping accouterment, but as symbolic of a decisive *kairos* moment in our changing lives, in which we are ready to pass through a gate, to let go of something old and to embrace something new in its place. As descendants of pioneer farm families, who first migrated here over the Great Wagon Road through the Shenandoah Valley from eastern Pennsylvania and who fought for our country's independence in the Revolutionary War, my family is among thousands of families in Southern Appalachia who, after several generations of immersion in tobacco culture, are in reluctant transition to alternative cultures in nursery crops and vineyards.

The Torii of Sandy Springs is emblematic of a transformation from the old to the new that is taking place with farmland and within society in the Yadkin Valley area of North Carolina, which is west of Winston-Salem and north of Charlotte and at the western edge of the Old Flue Cured Tobacco Belt. Two big tobacco growers in our community have begun to grow ornamental trees as an alternative crop, and another grower is using his greenhouses for hothouse tomatoes, reserved ordinarily for tobacco-slip beds. Moreover, the number of vineyards in the Yadkin Valley has quadrupled in the past decade in a state that still leads the nation in flue-cured tobacco production. In former tobacco fields on my family's land grow a young nursery of Japanese maple trees and a small orchard of apple trees (some of the latter's varieties were known in Shakespeare's day). Seedlings for the nursery came from a red-leafed Japanese maple tree that my late father planted in our rural community. After his death from smoking fifteen years ago, I became a public advocate for transition from tobacco to arborculture and viticulture.

This break with tradition, I can assure you, has not been without difficulty. A twice-removed cousin of mine is president of the state's tobacco growers. Our last governor, known for his education provisions for the state's youth, stood in a tobacco field before cameras and pleaded with the federal government not to label tobacco a drug. Since 1991, that same government has reported a third- to a half-million deaths annually related to tobacco consumption. The economic security of many families is tied to the "gold leaf," while North Carolina's government has been equally addicted as smokers are to *Nicotiana tabacum*, depending upon cigarette taxes to fill their state coffers. Many growers have avoided changing their crops in part because consumers are unwilling to pay as much for an apple as for a pack of cigarettes.

The Torii of Sandy Springs is 14 feet high and about 10 feet wide and deep. It is constructed of lumber from the black locust tree, *Robinia pseudoacacia,* a native mountain hardwood that long endures in the elements. The structure's large finished beams are connected to each other as a thread is fed through an eye of a needle. It has a "roof" of rough-hewn locust planks, which in its design resembles the wingspan of a brown pelican, considered to be suggestive of long life. An attached wooden plaque, about 2 by 4 feet and painted with black letters on white, features two Japanese sumi characters that read "Sandy Springs." An artist friend of mine, Kaneko McNeil, a survivor of the atomic bomb dropped on her childhood home in Hiroshima, painted the calligraphy on rice paper, which I then engrossed for the sign. It is especially fitting that this majestic gateway to things lasting be placed here in the foothills of the Blue Ridge Mountains: our now-deceased neighbor downstream on Hunting Creek, Thomas Ferebee, at the age of twenty-seven was the bombardier on the B-29 plane *Enola Gay*, which dropped the bomb on Hiroshima to end World War II.

The main vertical and horizontal locust beams of our *torii* are painted with a vermilion-colored lacquer. This was the second coat of paint. While

I gladly accepted my brother's practical offer of surplus barn paint he had on hand for the first coat, I found that the color of barn-red paint was lost in its surroundings. The paint was more brown than red. About the time the barn-red paint had dried well, Wal-Mart offered a special sale on high-quality oil-based paint. Its color chart designated one color "vermilion," the name of the color attributed to the Torii of Itsukushima. I had been certain that vermilion contained some yellow pigment but noticed that no yellow was added by the paint specialist as he squirted other precisely-measured portions of red, magenta, and bright white pigments into the paint-base. Perhaps I was mistaken.

After I returned home, I decided to look up the color *vermilion* in my dictionaries. *The American Heritage Dictionary* defined *vermilion* as a bright red pigment or color, a vivid red to reddish orange. A preconceived notion of yellow in vermilion was justified in that dictionary's inclusive reddish orange definition, though my second coat of paint for the Torii of Sandy Springs had none. *The Oxford English Dictionary* offered alternatively a wide variety of descriptions: the ore cinnabar or mineral mercuric sulfide; a bright red or brilliant scarlet; the color of red earth; an earthworm; the rouge-colored cheeks of babies and brides; and the war-paint of American Indians. Even one early translation of *Isaiah* 1:18 from the Hebrew Bible was mentioned: "[T]hough your sins are like scarlet; they shall be white as snow; though they be red like vermilion, they shall be as wool." Upon reading this, I immediately recalled Nathaniel Hawthorne's great American novel *The Scarlet Letter*, which if in his concern for sin, alienation, and redemption, he had named his work *The Vermilion Letter*, we might know more precisely what color this variation on red is today!

Our scarlet-lettered sins not withstanding, I could easily identify with other examples of the vermilion-red color, ranging from crimson to brilliant yellow-red offered up by the dictionary's examples. As a boy, I had hoed tobacco with my siblings in the rolling, red clay fields of piedmont Carolina. At our Sandy Springs farm, I had fished for brim and large-mouth bass in the red-banked pond with hundreds of the reddish-pink worms unearthed from damp soil beneath an old Limbertwig apple tree. We identified this type of invertebrate then as we do now as either "red" worms or "fishin'" worms. Because of my ties to the red soil, I also knew exactly what Edwin Markham meant in his poem "Lincoln, Man of the People": "The color of the ground was in him, the red earth; The smack and tang of elemental things." If he were alive today, would Abraham Lincoln, the rail-splitter, be considered a "redneck" by the same Americans who use that word to label disparagingly tobacco farmers and other agricultural laborers?

I decided to take an inventory of other examples of vermilion about me. Let me cite a few examples observed over four seasons, mostly out-of-doors. On a trip to Raleigh, I noticed that flowers of several redbud trees (collected from a world plant search by horticultural students for the J. C. Raulston Arboretum) were vermilion-colored. Azalea lovers will quickly identify as being shades of vermilion the varieties of Hinodegeri and Red Wing—the latter grown in greenhouses nearly as often as potted lilies and poinsettias by commercial florists for Easter and Christmas. The bright, almost electric reddish-pink color of the fruit of the grand magnolia tree as it ripens in summer is really vermilion, as are the red markings of the gray Box-elder bug. On a trip to Garden City near the Atlantic coast in South Carolina, I noticed a vermilion oleander in resplendent flower. When my grandmother Ollie Chamberlain Sharpe's favorite peony bloomed last May, I realized that its color was vermilion. Her devoted middle son and my father, Woodrow, had planted at Sandy Springs a winter-hardy camellia bush that now flowers profusely from Thanksgiving through Easter with large vermilion blossoms the size of desert plates. In fact, I have observed that nearly every genus of plant-life possessing a perceptive scale of red blossoms is likely to have one that may be said to be vermilion.

Before last winter turned to spring, I realized that my elderly mother's favorite sweater and tam were woven in bands of black and teal interspersed with wide strips of the vermilion color whose definition had once so eluded me. On the last anniversary of my father's death, I photographed Hattie Bell Shore Sharpe, aged eighty-eight, wearing her sweater and tam and holding a bouquet of those vermilion-colored camellia blossoms in front of the Torii of Sandy Springs. Anyone seeing these pictures would think that this *torii* was painted by nature from the same paint bucket as were the blossoms Mother held to her bosom. Bathed in amber rays of a late afternoon sun, the *torii*'s second coat of paint gave the impression of containing yellow pigment that it does not show in morning light when it looks the reddish-pink of fishing worms and ripened magnolia fruit.

Why all this fuss about definitions of color in the first place? There's a good reason. About twenty years ago in Washington, DC, I was told by a Peace Corps volunteer just returning from teaching in West Africa that he had met members of an indigenous tribe who used only three words to describe color. I had filed this information away in my mind with every intention that someday I wanted to pursue the matter. Restricting color labeling to three terms seemed to leave a lot to be desired. My own life has been immeasurably enriched by several teachers and artists, who have taught me to recognize the spectrum and glory of color in everyday settings. From those mentors I learned some of color's extensive vocabulary. Allene Rose Boone, an artist friend at Wrightsville Beach, North Carolina, once identified for me more than a dozen different blue colors by name in one of her seascapes. Peter Walker's photography exhibition, which I saw last spring in Chester, Connecticut, was a testament of this former Marlboro Man model's dedication to color. I once read published letters of Ranier Maria Rilke, who after viewing an exhibition of Paul Cezanne's paintings in Paris in 1905 observed that that artist had demonstrated the extent to which painting takes place among colors themselves. "Art is a matter of conscience," Rilke wrote. "In artistic work, one needs nothing so much as conscience: It is the sole standard." At the Library of Congress, I delighted in reading Sir Winston Churchill's thoughts on color's palate. Churchill, who practiced oil painting at his country estate in Chartwell, England, wrote: "The greatest landscapes were painted indoors, often long after first impressions were gathered." My selecting paint for the vermilion-colored Torii of Sandy Springs echoed such earlier queries about the difficulty of defining color. My task at hand was not to be taken lightly.

There is a body of knowledge regarding color. Organizations dedicated to promoting understanding of color include the Reston, Virginia-based

Inter-Society Color Council, and the Association Internationale de la Couleur, located in Vienna, Austria. My inquiry on whether or not vermilion paint should contain a yellow pigment could perhaps be answered by the Committee on Paints and Related Coatings, Materials, and Applications, which is sponsored by the American Society for Testing Materials, in West Conshohocken, Pennsylvania. I learned that Brent Berlin and Paul Kay of the University of California at Berkeley, among other research scientists, had studied the universality of color terms and of their evolution in ninety-eight languages. Those researchers concluded that there exist eleven basic perceptual color categories, which serve as psychophysical referents of eleven or fewer basic color terms in language. The order of naming a basic color in any language follows a pattern of encoding: white, black, red, yellow, green, blue, brown, purple, pink, orange, and gray (some languages insert the color green in their sequence of colors before naming yellow). Berlin and Kay also observed that the order of naming a color in a given society was an evolutionary one: historically, simple cultures with simple technologies have developed few terms for color, while complex cultures and complex technologies have tended to have many terms. Thus, any culture with only three words for basic colors would differentiate color in terms of white, black, and red—such a labeling of colors emanating from seeing objects that appear to the observer to be light or dark or resembling the color of human blood.

About the time I undertook the *torii* construction project, I was named a Guthrie scholar at Columbia Theological Seminary, in Decatur, Georgia. I went there to engage Presbyterian-affiliated scholars and students in the prospect of seeking reconciliation with poor whites in American society—those people too often dismissed as "rednecks"—just as I had done with the Episcopalians not too long before as a Visiting Fellow at the University of the South, in Sewanee, Tennessee. While studying religion, politics, and the media in my recent past at Union Theological Seminary and at Columbia University's School of Journalism, both in New York City, I was appointed seminarian with Episcopalians at the Cathedral of Saint John the Divine and with Presbyterians at Fifth Avenue Church. I discovered that, more often than not, worshipers on Fifth Avenue and Cathedral Heights read from the same page of King James scripture as some of their worshiping counterparts in the hinterlands, including many who identified themselves as born-again Christians. While in Georgia, I used part of my time to access the resources of a consortium of public and private university libraries on the topic of color, and in the process of my research I came to understand that the diversity of people and religious views is as consistent within creation as is the presence and variety of color. Josef Albers in his book *Interaction of Color* argued that a color has many faces. "If one says red and there are 50 people listening, it can be expected that there will be 50 reds in their minds, and one can be sure that all these reds will be different." Poor, working-class whites, who are often stereotyped as Rednecks and who are frequently identified as Christian Fundamentalists, are not necessarily a monolithic group in their faith or in their politics.

When I was young, I attended a fundamentalist Christian church at Sandy Springs, where I learned a children's hymn, "Red, yellow, black and white, they are precious in God's sight," which referred to our Creator's love for all the little children of the world, and it turns out that that hymn was not bad theology after all. Just as the *torii* signifies a gateway to something sacred, the hymn points the way to the great diversity in the human family by "color and size and other accidents of appearance" (as Ralph Waldo Emerson described surface differences) and underscores the importance of our recognition and appreciation for that diversity in the world about us.

To paraphrase Alexander Pope, hope for reconciliation within our divided American family and society springs eternal in this human breast. Maybe the vermillion-colored Torii of Sandy Springs will serve as a reminder for its viewers to recognize the unity of cause in our human family.

Sylvia's Story

BY NANCY GREGORY McLENDON

The light filtering through the iron bars of the old jail's tiny window cast an eerie glow around the slender black woman seated on the plank bench. A worn cotton dress enveloped her delicate frame, while black hair, held in place by a faded kerchief, framed her small face. A noise at the cell door startled her, and she stirred briefly from her thoughts, as the jailer slid an unappetizing bowl of cold greens under the door. She glanced briefly at the dish, then turned away. In spite of tear stains on her cheeks, her almond eyes, pointed chin, and high cheek bones revealed a natural beauty not dependent on expensive clothes or paint.

Seemingly oblivious to everything around her, she was deeply immersed in thought. She realized that, in less than an hour, the jailer would appear again at her door and lead her from the narrow room, down the stairs, and through the front door to the wooden porch of the old building. From there, a short walk to the portico would take her to the gallows, where a stranger would place a hood over her head and slip a noose around her neck. Then...she shook herself free from the disturbing vision. Her thoughts turned instead to her mother and to other family members, and she was moved by their unwavering faith in her innocence.

⁂

As far back as I can recall, Sylvia's name was mentioned in our family with loving fondness. My grandmother often measured events in the lives of her children by whether or not they occurred "before Sylvia's time" or "after Sylvia." My mother, born in 1916, often said that she felt cheated because she did not know Sylvia; the family members who knew Sylvia have recalled certain facts, each from his or her perspective. My Aunt Bonnie recalled the good times when Sylvia went to town on Saturdays to spend the nickel my grandfather had given her and to meet with her friends. Sylvia always brought back candy and shared it with the Glover children, fourteen-year-old Bonnie and thirteen-year-old Lester. But the events regarding Sylvia most remembered by my aunt and my grandmother alike revolved around how they dealt with Big Bertha. A large black woman, Bertha often came to the well near the Glover house to get water, and she never failed to pick on Sylvia, sometimes going so far as to attempt to beat her. Petite, small-boned Sylvia was no match for Big Bertha.

The first line of defense against Bertha's onslaughts was my Aunt Bonnie, who frequently came to Sylvia's rescue holding the nearest weapon at hand, usually a large yard broom. In those days, yards around houses generally had no grass, only dirt, and one of Aunt Bonnie's duties (and in later years, one of my mother's) was to sweep the yard with a large stiff broom made of long twigs. Each housewife tried to make nice, curvy strokes with the broom in the dirt. It was a matter of pride to make sure one's yard had the smartest, fanciest-looking broom strokes. Hence, the yard broom was Aunt Bonnie's most convenient weapon.

At times, Bonnie's screams would bring thirteen-year-old Lester from the field behind the house, where he would plow the garden with Joy, the family mule. The animal would wait patiently, reins dangling, while Lester would help Bonnie chase Big Bertha away from Sylvia and back to her own turf. Many times, my grandmother, Dolie Glover, would hear screams coming from the vicinity of the well and would run outside to see Big Bertha fleeing and Bonnie's yard broom flying after her. But Bertha never stayed away for long; she always returned to stir up trouble again and again.[1]

---

[1] Bonnie Glover Shirley to Marian Glover Leonard, April 1982, Marian G. Leonard private papers, Abbeville, Alabama.

Upon realizing that Big Bertha was going to continue tormenting Sylvia, Dolie determined to put an end to Bertha's shenanigans once and for all. Taking some twigs, she wove them into a minuscule doll-like figure with life-like arms and legs on the trunk. Scraps from her sewing basket became a miniature dress complete with apron and sash. With determination, Dolie placed the tiny form strategically on the well for anyone to see. The next morning, Big Bertha sauntered into the yard as usual and strode confidently toward the well. However, crossing the last 5 or 6 feet to the well, she stopped short. Taking in the sight of the life-like twig figure, a perfect voodoo doll, Bertha's eyes grew wide. In an instant, she threw her watering pail through the air, letting it land wherever it fell, and she took off running for her life, never once turning to look behind her. My grandmother and Aunt Bonnie recalled with fond memories the sight of Big Bertha fleeing from the yard, never to return. How she managed to get the water she needed in the future, no one can say. Maybe she sent someone else or maybe she went to another well. At any rate, she never bothered Sylvia again.[2]

My grandmother's fondest memory of Sylvia was the day she felt she really came to know the young woman. The event that brought about Dolie's epiphany was a rather ordinary one. She and Sylvia had been working together in the house, and Sylvia stopped to eat lunch, or *dinner*, as the large noonday meal was called in those days. Sylvia, almost finished eating a piece of steak, suddenly began making strangling noises. My grandmother turned from the stove to see Sylvia bent over, obviously unable to breathe. Rushing across the room, Dolie took Sylvia's face between her hands and reaching her fingers down her throat, pulled out the offending piece of meat. In that moment, the younger woman's eyes met those of the older woman; the two women locked gazes—neither able to turn from the stare of the other. Dolie later said that she knew instantly the talk about Sylvia could not be true. 'Lige was right after all; the others had been wrong. She would now stake her life on Sylvia's innocence. Sylvia, unaware of what

[2] Dolie Godfrey Glover, interview by author, April 1970.

Dolie was thinking, sobbed her thanks, "Mrs. Glover, Mr. 'Lige saved my life once; now you have saved it a second time."[3]

The first saving of Sylvia's life occurred two years earlier in 1912. In those days, black people were not allowed to serve on juries; in fact, no women were permitted on juries, nor could they vote. So when young Sylvia was accused of poisoning a man whose house she had visited on the day of his untimely death, she and her family knew she would be facing an all-male, all-white jury. In the minds of the community, circumstances pointed to Sylvia's guilt because, as far as anyone knew, she was the only person in that house on that particular day. Sylvia needed a miracle.

When Elijah Glover—known as 'Lige to many people in southeast Alabama—raised his head from the mound of paperwork on his desk that April morning in 1912, he was not surprised to see Sylvia's mother standing in the doorway. Well known as a competent lawyer in the small town, he often defended its citizens, black and white, when they needed an attorney, regardless of their ability to pay. He was, however, surprised to see that Sylvia's mother seemed to have an unwavering faith in his ability to exonerate her daughter. "Mrs. Williams, "'Lige protested, "you know I will represent Sylvia, and I'll do my best, but I can't promise anything."

'Lige's preparation for Sylvia's case began years before on his family's farm near Haleburg, a tiny community located in Henry County, a few miles from Abbeville, Alabama. He and his five brothers farmed their 400-acre place with their father Eli Frank. 'Lige, accustomed to hard work, found that getting an education was not an easy feat. His clients often found him to be a sympathetic, caring man who, much to Dolie's disconcertion, frequently did not ask for payment for his services.[4]

Soon after the visit of Sylvia's mother, 'Lige set about preparing for her daughter's trial. He first talked with everyone he could find who was anywhere near the victim's farmhouse at the time of the poisoning, but he had no luck. Those who might have known about the comings and goings at the

---

[3] Ibid.

[4] Marian Glover Leonard, interview by author, April 2004.

place seemed to know nothing—except that Sylvia often helped prepare meals for the farmer in question, and that she cooked a meal for him the day he died. 'Lige knew, however, that even worse than the circumstantial evidence was the fact that everyone in the county talked constantly of the murder, and, according to the talk, Sylvia's guilt was assumed to be a fact. The trial had not yet begun, but Sylvia was already standing trial in the town's barbershop, streets, and stores.

In spite of constant talk, the young attorney conferred almost daily with his client, and came to the firm realization that, under no circumstance, could she be guilty of this crime. Other than Sylvia's family, 'Lige seemed to be alone in this belief of her innocence. Nevertheless, he continued diligently preparing for a presentation he hoped would prove Sylvia's innocence to the twelve men who held her life in their hands.

In retrospect, those who remembered the trial and the events that soon followed would realize that words from the United States Constitution—which assured all Americans of "the right to a trial by a jury *of one's peers*"—did not have the same meaning for black people in 1912 as today. Those twelve white men were not the "peers" of the young woman standing in that courtroom on the opening day of the trial. In fact, if the talk of the town and countryside was any indication, the words "innocent until proven guilty" did not seem to apply to Sylvia either. And so, the trial of a young black woman proceeded to take place as a semblance of justice, rather than as its essence.

On the opening day of the trial, the town's citizens awakened to a beautiful sun-drenched morning. Shortly after dawn, wagons surrounded the old two-story courthouse on the square in the center of town, and the harnessed mules drank thirstily from wooden water troughs. Inside the courtroom, fanning spectators filled the oak chairs and soon spilled into the anteroom of the old building. As the eight o'clock hour drew near, latecomers stood on the outside steps or in the dirt yard around the building talking with neighbors as though enjoying a long awaited church picnic.

PHOTOGRAPH OF HENRY COUNTY COURTHOUSE, ABBEVILLE AL.
Courtesy of Abbeville Memorial Library and T. Larry Smith, Henry County's official historian.

Inside the courtroom, though, the ominous atmosphere was becoming heavier. In spite of the early hour, the air was muggy. Open windows brought in no cooling breezes; in fact, the only stirring air in the packed room was produced by small hand-held straw fans. Every chair and bench was crammed. The men of the jury, twelve very solemn figures, were positioned behind the oak rail of the jury box waiting for the judge to appear. To the left and right behind the judge's bench were two large closed doors, and above each door was a large sign that read "Five Dollar Fine for Spitting on the Floor or Walls of This Building." However, the brass spittoons placed around the outer edges of the courtroom were impossible to reach because of the mass of spectators. By the day's end, there were more tobacco stains on the pine floors.

Finally, one of the wooden doors opened, and the robed judge entered as the bailiff cried out above the noise of the crowd, "All rise!"

The audience grew quieter as the judge nodded. "Be seated." He called the court to order with several loud raps of the wooden gavel.

The prosecution called one witness after another who all testified to seeing Sylvia enter the farmer's house on the day of the poisoning; others testified that they had knowledge of her working at this farmer's house on a regular basis. But no witness offered testimony that could prove, or even suggest, that Sylvia had any motive for this crime. In fact, no witnesses could testify as to the possibility of any evidence connecting Sylvia to the murder—just her presence in the house on the day of the man's death. By early afternoon of the first day of the trial, the judge called a recess until the following day, and the jurors were dismissed to go home. No one cautioned the jury not to discuss the day's testimony, and under the circumstances of this trial, such an admonishment would probably have been in vain. Perspiring men and women piled out of the stifling courtroom discussing the day's events, clearly disappointed that the day had not yielded some startling new revelation.

Day two continued much as the first. On day three, the defense completed its questioning of witnesses, none of whom testified as to any guilt-proving evidence. Character witnesses testified to Sylvia's trustworthi-

PHOTOGRAPH OF OLD COURTROOM AS IT APPEARED DURING SYLVIA'S TRIAL. SIGN ADMONISHING CITIZENS NOT TO SPIT ON FLOOR OR WALLS OF THE BUILDING IS ENLARGED IN THIS PHOTOGRAPH.
Courtesy of Abbeville Memorial Library and T. Larry Smith, Henry County's official historian.

ness, but the jury only stared impassively at those witnesses, apparently unmoved by the attorney's plea not to convict an innocent young woman for whom no evidence of guilt could be found. Day four dawned brightly, and the courthouse again filled with spectators, curious bystanders as well as malicious gossipers who yearned for a little excitement in their otherwise dull existences.

If any onlookers hungered for excitement, they were not disappointed. The jury reached a verdict within minutes. Just as expected, the judge read aloud: "Guilty as charged of committing first degree murder by poisoning." In those days, sentencing often took place right away, and Sylvia's sentence, read within minutes of the verdict, was heard by all: "Sentenced to die by hanging from the neck until dead." Pandemonium erupted in the courtroom as Sylvia's family and close friends, seated in the balcony with the other black citizens, sobbed loudly. A cheer went up among another group of people, who possibly looked forward to the excitement of the social goings-on of a public hanging. The remaining observers talked loudly with friends as they emerged from the courtroom, ignoring the rapping of the judge's gavel.

And so a mere two weeks later, Sylvia found herself in the barren jail cell staring at cold walls as she listened for the footsteps that would signal her death knell. The last moments of her life approached quickly, and she would die as she lived, bravely and knowing the love of God was firmly in her heart; no one could take that from her. As dire as her situation was, Sylvia realized that for a black person in 1912, things could be even worse. The victim in this case also happened to be black; had the dead man been white, she could very well have experienced the horrors of a lynching, all-too-common in those days.

The gallows, with its rough hewn lumber, waited for Sylvia at the east end of the jail porch. She saw hemp rope in the hands of the waiting official as she approached. Her last glimpse before the attendant placed the hood over her head was of the heavy trap-door beneath her feet. She stepped onto the spot marked *X*, and then darkness enveloped her. She realized that when the noose tightened around her neck, the door would fall away. She bowed her head, both in prayer and in submission to the pain soon to overwhelm her. She hoped it would be quick. As she prayed silently, she could hear the sobs of her mother and sisters who hovered close to the porch's edge. Always a devoted daughter, Sylvia grieved to know she could not comfort her mother now.

Listening intently, her eyes seeing only darkness, Sylvia heard the muffled sobs of her mother. The crowd grew quiet as they waited expectantly. Sylvia's mind became blank as she anticipated her executioner's next move. She realized she could no longer discern her mother's voice from those of other spectators near the gallows, as the mumblings grew louder. Her family saw the cause of the commotion—all eyes fixed on the looming figure of a man running, waving a paper above his head. He soon could be heard above the din as he shouted, "Stop—stop the hanging…a pardon…the governor's pardoned her! Stop immediately!" The amazed spectators watched as a panting 'Lige Glover collapsed on the porch railing; at the same time, he thrust a telegram into the face of the incredulous official. The executioner hesitated but a moment, then read: "Request for Pardon for Sylvia Freeman—Granted—signed Emmett O'Neal, Governor of Alabama."

A dumbfounded sheriff hesitated only a moment. A deputy examined the priceless paper, while others crowded around. The hood off her head, a stunned Sylvia stared at the paper and at her lawyer. "Go on, Sylvia, go to your mama; you're free to go home now," 'Lige said softly to an incredulous young woman.[5] Sylvia hesitated but a moment; then, she turned and walked quickly down the porch steps, a free woman, into the waiting arms of her mother and family.

Years later, Henry "Hamp" Herring, a Henry County native recalled attending the hanging that never took place when he was seven.[6] He recalled the large crowd gathered at the old jail, waiting to see a hanging only to have it stopped at the last minute.

---

[5] T. Larry Smith, "Black Lady's Hanging Halted," *Abbeville* (AL) *Herald,* March 14, 2002, 6.
[6] Ibid.

Many years later, a guilt-ridden man on his death bed confessed to the crime for which Sylvia almost paid with her life, proving what her family and friends already knew—she was an innocent victim of a justice system that almost failed her.

When a young woman in her twenties, Sylvia became ill while visiting relatives near Montgomery. She caught a cold, which developed into pneumonia. Unable to get home because the Alabama River had flooded, she contracted tuberculosis and died. She had cheated death twice in her young life, but she didn't survive the third strike.

Sylvia's spirit affected all who knew her; the Glover family was especially close to her during her final days. The final parting of Sylvia from her parents and her friend, 'Lige Glover, took place at the train station in Abbeville on a February morning. Earlier, the day had dawned colder than usual, and a light mist hung over the entire scene. Since Abbeville was a small southeast Alabama town only a few miles from the Gulf Coast, its residents often experienced winter dampness that made old bones ache with rheumatism and young children whine miserably with boredom and cabin fever. The fog normally lifted by mid-morning because of the town's elevation, but on that particular day in 1914, a shroud of dank air hung over the depot on the outskirts of town. The dampness clung to the clothes and hair of the solemn group as they waited expectantly.

Each face in that group bore the same look of tired resignation. A middle-aged black woman, a dark-colored coat wrapped snugly around her thin body, spoke softly to the two children who clung to her skirts. An elderly black man stood close to her and occasionally put his arm around her shoulder to offer comfort, but slowly he let his arm fall to his side, realizing that nothing could console the sad-faced woman beside him. The white man, possibly in his late thirties, waited with the couple, occasionally breaking the silence as he spoke in a low voice to the other two adults. The two children, quiet at first, began to whine and pull at their mother's skirts; the woman bent and softly shushed them.

"Here's my baby; here she is," the woman said, as she stood upright watching an approaching train chug into the station. At these words, the elderly black man put his arm around the woman's shoulder again. "My poor baby, my poor Sylvia," sobbed the woman. The children by her side fell silent, looking at their mother, as though unaccustomed to the sight and sound of her tears. The train came to a stop, and seven or eight travelers stepped to the ground, glancing curiously at the group, now standing very close to the tracks. Finally, the last passenger disappeared into a waiting buggy, and the impatient horse trotted down the dirt street toward the main part of town. The conductor and two other men carefully lifted a crude pine box from the back of one of the last cars in the line and hoisted it onto their shoulders. The woman's composure broke, and she sobbed uncontrollably as the coffin was loaded onto a waiting horse-drawn cart.

Softly, the elderly man spoke to the white man, "Mr. 'Lige, my baby, she's with Jesus now, and one day we'll all be there together—Sylvia and all of us."

"That's right, Mr. Williams, we'll all be there, and we'll all be together," 'Lige nodded in agreement. The horse pulling the cart slowly ambled down West Washington Street. It continued through the town onto East Washington, making its way toward the churchyard at the old St. Peter Church[7] on the outskirts of Abbeville and the final resting place for the young woman whose body rested inside.

EPILOGUE

Years after Sylvia's death, an older black woman, Nunnie Jordan, told my mother that she knew the exact location of Sylvia's grave in the old St. Peter Church Cemetery. However, somehow this lady and my mother never got together to find the grave.

'Lige Glover lived until 1946. Before he died, he served in the Alabama state legislature for twelve years; he introduced the first bill providing Alabama school children with free textbooks[8] and was listed in the *1926 Philadelphia Sesquicentennial* as one of four outstanding Alabamians.[9]

---

[7] Marian Glover Leonard, interview by author, January 2002.

[8] A. B. Moore, *History of Alabama and Her People II* (American Historical Society, 1927) 634–35.

[9] Anonymous, *The Philadelphia Sesquicentennial* (n.p., 1926).

Daddy and Dudley

BY EDWIN C. KING

I have studied the issue of race for many years now and have tried to learn why those of us with light skin discriminate against those with darker skin; why those of us in the majority discriminate against those in the minority. I have never learned. One book tells me it is because the group discriminating feels threatened by the discriminated group. Another book informs me it is because one group was taught to be superior, and the other group was taught to be subordinate (I wonder who decided which group would be superior). I decided to stop trying to learn why, and just stop doing the discriminating. I haven't learned how to do that yet either, but I'm making progress.

It was clear to me even as a little boy that "we" were different from "them." I knew very early that "we" were white, and that "they" were not white and had dark skins. "They" did not come in our house; "they" stayed outside, and were only allowed on the back porch. "They" were very careful to say, "yes, ma'am" and "no, ma'am," "yes, sir" and "no, sir," to Mama and Daddy. The very old among them were always called "aunt" or "uncle" so-and so—Aunt Emma, Aunt Polly, Uncle Gardner, or Uncle John. To my "aunts" and "uncles" I said "yes, ma'am" and "yes, sir." I really don't remember exactly how my "aunts" and "uncles" addressed me. I'm quite certain it was in a very respectful way, though.

As a little boy, I did not know to discriminate against other minorities. I remember there was a pretty little Jewish girl in the first grade with me. I did not learn she was Jewish and "different" until some years later. Her name was Betty, and I thought she was my girlfriend. I didn't understand that I was supposed to discriminate against Jewish people until I was told so as an adult.

I was slow in learning to discriminate against the Catholics, also. I really did not know about Catholics until I was about twelve years old, and I did not learn until later that I was supposed to discriminate against them. At age twelve or so, I saw the sign in front of the Catholic Church in Quitman. I knew about Baptists, Methodists, and even Presbyterians, but not about Catholics until I saw the sign. I was not told to discriminate against them then. This, too, I learned after becoming an adult.

Our way of viewing race did occasionally generate a laugh. Once, a watermelon buyer came to Boston, Georgia, from New York City and was coached on how to treat both races. A local man named Jack McNeill came to town to sell his melons, and since this man was quite dark, the buyer called him Jack. A knowing farmer quickly told the buyer to call Jack "Mr. McNeill" since he was really white. Shortly afterwards, a very light-skinned black man, Bud Johnson, showed up to sell his melons, and now the buyer, certain that he understood the race issue in south Georgia, called Bud by the name Mr. Johnson. The same farmer who had corrected the buyer before did so again, advising the buyer to call the man Bud since he was a Negro. The buyer, now totally confused, said, "I don't think I can do it; I'll never learn. Here in south Georgia, you call the black ones white and the white ones black. I think I will go some place else where I can tell what people really are."

I learned most of what I know about race relationships from observing Daddy and his friend Dudley. The latter was black, and it seemed to me that both men felt an unsure tension while together. As a little boy I did not know who Dudley was. Oh, he was a man with dark skin and Daddy's friend, but that doesn't mean I knew who he really was. No other human being, except for my Mama, was closer to Daddy, and no one else could get from Daddy what Dudley could. They would sit in their chairs on our back porch or under the huge pecan tree that stood only a few feet from our house, talking or just sitting for hours. It was clear, even for me as a little boy, that to each of them the other was special. I didn't know how special until years later.

Dudley had been born on either my granddaddy's or my great-granddaddy's farm (I just don't know who actually owned it when Dudley was born—I think it was my granddaddy). I know that Dudley and Daddy were nearly the same age; one was born a week or two before the other. I know they played together, fished together, hunted together, and did all kinds of boys' things together. I don't know exactly how or why this friendship developed. Daddy had brothers—six of them, all close in age—so why did he spend so much time with Dudley? I knew enough about Dudley and Daddy to want to know more. I didn't ask either of them about their friendship, though. I wish I had—it must have been an interesting story.

I remember, as a very early memory, Dudley being at our house. I think I was only three or four years old, and Dudley would hold me in his lap. When I was a bit older, but before I went to school, I remember Dudley coming to our house early on a Christmas morning. He always did this, and Mama and Daddy always had something for Dudley's children, usually fruit or candy. On this particular morning, Mama, as she often did, fixed Dudley breakfast, and he ate off the stove's oven door. He never came near our table. I had gotten a water pistol for Christmas. While Dudley ate, I got him good, a full load of water in the face. Dudley slowly wiped the water from his face, turned to me, and said, "When your brother and sister grow up I will call them Mr. Raymond and Miss Kathryn, but you, I won't ever call you mister, Little Boy."

Dudley's arrival at our house was always a bit strange. He would walk to our house, since he had no car, and his older boys would be working his mules. He would never stop at the front gate. He would take off his hat and hold it in his hand, walk around the house to the back door. He would then knock and stand there until someone came to the door. Dudley would speak very politely and just stand until asked to come up on the back porch. Then, when asked, he would take a seat in the same chair he always sat in. If Daddy was home, he would come out and either sit by Dudley's chair or they would move together to their seats under the big pecan tree. Only on special occasions—or to do some work in the house—would Dudley enter the house. If he had a meal at our house, he either ate on the back porch or sat by the open oven door on the stove and used it as a table. It was just not right for him to be in our house: he recognized it, and Daddy knew it.

Dudley was a deacon in his Baptist church. He did lots of work for the church and was chairman of a committee that provided hospitality to visiting preachers. There were many such visitors, and Dudley had to "feed the preacher" often. Mama raised chickens, and I am sure that over the years Dudley bought hundreds of Mama's chickens to feed visiting preachers.

My very favorite memory of Daddy and Dudley together involves chickens. It was in early 1955, shortly after Mama died of cancer. At the time of her death, Mama owned hundreds of laying hens, as she sold eggs. Daddy soon made arrangements with an interested buyer and sold as many of the hens as the buyer could catch. Naturally, some hens remained, and these were now out of the chicken lot and running free about the place. They were bothersome to Daddy, and he immediately began to try to sell them. He put out the word that there were "hens for sale, catch your own for $1.00 each." One Saturday afternoon after Daddy started selling the hens, Dudley came to see him. Following his normal routine, Dudley took his hat off at the front gate, walked around to the back door, and knocked on the door. Daddy went to the door, greeted his friend, and they sat on their back porch chairs. Shortly, Dudley got to the point of his visit. "Mr. Raymond," he said, "if you still have some hens to sell, I needs to buy two of them to feed the preacher tomorrow." Daddy said that there were some left and that Dudley could buy two. Dudley said, "Now, Mr. Raymond, I know that the hens are $1.00 each and that you don't sell them on credit. You can't sell them on credit, and no one should expect to buy a chicken on credit to eat. I agree with you, but, Mr. Raymond, I gots to feed that preacher tomorrow. Now, Mr. Raymond, if you will lend me two dollars, I will pay you cash for two of them hens." Dudley got the two hens. But did he repay Daddy the two dollars? I don't have any idea, yet I'm quite sure that neither Dudley nor Daddy was concerned about it. What was important was maintained, the special and peculiar relationship between one white man and one black man in the pre-civil-rights-era Deep South.

I last saw Dudley at Daddy's funeral. Dressed in his Sunday suit on the back row along with his wife Sue and several of their children, Dudley sat sadly through the service. Before the casket containing Daddy's body was taken from the church, Dudley and his family all knelt around it and prayed, then they filed out of the church. I never saw Dudley again.

The Burying

BY KYES STEVENS

"The toiler who has laid away his tools at last and come to rest."
—Ruby Pickens Tartt

After Great Grandma died, all the neighbors and family left in Sumter
gathered at the old plantation on the south of town.
Great Grandma wanted to be buried where she was born.
Lots of kin didn't want to plant her under trees
that kept her slavery bound. But we stood there on Sunday
singing and praying as the men folk dug hard into limestone.

We stood there singing and praying 'til you couldn't see
Uncle Jack's shoulders anymore. They laid four
skint gum trees over the hole to help lower the casket.
Aunt Manny started soulful wail as dirt fell back in the ground.
After the soil was heaped, men stuck the skinny end of shovels
into the mound. A circle of spades surrounded the fresh earth.

Memories of a Georgia Convict Camp

BY HUGH M. (MAX) THOMASON

My dear Father & Mother

Just a line or so to let you know that I'm here and think I'm going to like [it] very well. Came up on the first. The Com. [County Commissioners] all are mighty nice and seem to want to back me to the limit but say they are looking for results. Haven't moved yet but hope to this week some time. Can get a place out about a mi[le] from town that has all conveniences and 15 acres of ground for 15.00 or the house garden and barn for 10.00 Believe the Com. have an idea of building a house on the county property for the Warden and if I stay here I hope they do. The salary is small but we can live cheap. Meats 42¢ per lb.[,] chickens for 12¢[,] and vegetables nothing almost.

Had to buy a car which I hated like smoke to do but couldn't do otherwise as they won't furnish one but will keep it up.... Times are sure tight for jobs and I believe it's going to be even worse yet in the construction line. That's the reason I thought best for me to get this to be sure of something.

This is an extract from a July 4, 1932, letter my father wrote to his parents from Sylvania, Georgia, in his neat and spare handwriting. In few words, the letter expresses his reasoning for accepting the position of road superintendent and Warden of Screven County, Georgia, a career change that took him out of the business of being an independent contractor and into the role of being a hired overseer.

Located between the cities of Savannah and Augusta, Screven County is one of Georgia's oldest and largest counties. Although bounded on the east by the Savannah River, Screven County never benefited significantly by the traffic on that water artery. The 1940 WPA guide to Georgia counties identifies that county's chief industries as being "lumbering from which fortunes have been made" and cotton cultivation. In his letter to his parents, my father described it thusly: "This sure is a fine farming section and a big county.... [T]here's farms here as large as 17,000 acres in one body with 8 or 10 overseers under a supt. [superintendent]." The Guide related that Screven "has one of the highest production rates [of cotton cultivation] in the state" and that there were twenty cotton gins and eleven cotton warehouses in the county at the time of that book's publication.

Sylvania was established and identified as the county seat of Screven County by Georgia's legislature in 1847. Prior to that date, Jacksonboro had been the county seat and population center. Ill fortune had befallen Jacksonboro, however. In his 1849 book *Statistics of the State of Georgia*, George White said of that town: "The place had formerly a very bad character. It was reported that in the mornings after drunken frolics and fights you could see the children picking up eyeballs in tea saucers." But it was the visit of Lorenzo Dow, an itinerant preacher, that presumably led to the demise of Jacksonboro. Dow visited the town circa 1830, and his poor reception there led him to place a curse upon it. Thereafter, Jacksonboro withered.

The guide of 1940 listed the population of Sylvania in that year as being 1,781, and that figure was little changed from the town's population when we moved there in 1932. The town is located on the main highway between Savannah and Augusta (Georgia 21), paved at that time in contrast to the numerous red clay or sandy soil roads in the county. Downtown Sylvania at that time featured several grocery and dry goods stores, at least one furniture store, a hardware store, car dealerships, at least two filling stations, and one movie theater. There was a 5-and-10-cent store

(Woolworth's, if I remember correctly) and three drugstores. A block away from the main street were a few stores serving mainly a "colored" clientele. The Georgia of 1932 was a state in which races were strictly segregated and all the town's businesses adhered to this custom. The town also harbored a "colored section" where blacks lived. In contrast to the several "white" public schools located in outlying communities of the county (Rocky Ford, Bay Branch, and others), only one school existed to serve the entire county population of blacks, and that was located in Sylvania. The town also had a few black churches and one black medical doctor.

When we moved to Sylvania in the summer of 1932, I was eleven, a boy about to enter the sixth grade. I lived in the town through my high school graduation in spring 1938, then went off to college. Not long after I returned to Sylvania following my freshman college year, my father fell ill; our family relocated to Atlanta, near the home of Dad's parents, during the summer of 1939. My recollections in this narrative reflect most of what I remember about the convict camp during the years of my boyhood, 1932–1938.

As warden, Dad was in charge of the "convict camp" as it was commonly called. This was the place where people, both blacks and whites, were incarcerated who had been convicted in Georgia courts for various misdemeanor and felony crimes. As road superintendent of the county, Dad was expected to use these convicted persons as his work crew to construct or to maintain the county roads. In his role as warden, Dad had to run the convict camp—that is, he had to carry out policies which would assure the orderly and peaceful business of the camp itself, to feed and take care of the prisoners, to demand their good behavior and to prevent their escape, and to oversee their work in jobs they needed to perform.

To assist him in all of this, several guards—all white males—were employed, as well as a person whose job it was to maintain and distribute foodstuffs and other supplies and see to the other internal business of the camp on a day-to-day basis. At least three guards accompanied the work crew away from the camp and were armed with one or more guns, whether a pistol or a shotgun. These men had limited formal educations (not

CLYDE THOMASON, SR. (LEFT) WITH CLYDE, JR. AND SARA, 1926.
Photo courtesy of Hugh M. (Max) Thomason.

uncommon in those days). These three differed in appearance, and Mom considered one guard in particular as being somewhat corpulent; she referred to him as "pus-gutted." Dad inherited all of these persons when he was hired. The camp head man, responsible for the internal workings of the camp, was an ancient who on his occasional forays into town always rode in his horse and buggy.

Our family lived in a rental house located about a quarter mile from the camp itself, between the camp and Sylvania. This was, of course, a convenient location. In our home, we had an old-fashioned (we would now say) telephone, a wooden-boxy sort of instrument, mounted on the living room wall, with which we could communicate directly with the camp by turning its crank handle two or three complete revolutions; this rang the telephone in the camp office, and if we were lucky someone might answer it. Because this was a party line connected with the central switchboard in the town telephone office, we knew that the call was for us if the telephone rang only once; if it rang twice, someone was calling the camp. The operator at "central" in town could be roused by our turning the crank handle one revolution. We were careful about using this telephone during a storm as lightning could strike nearby, and, if so, the telephone's bell would go "ding!" and the user might run the risk of getting an electric shock.

The convict camp was perhaps 6 to 8 acres in size and was divided into two parts: 2 to 4 acres used to grow crops (corn, other vegetables, watermelons, etc.) for the camp, the remainder of the acreage being the camp compound. I never gave thought as to who worked the crops, but I assume now that "trusties" among the prisoners did so. On some of the outer land, hogs were likely raised, and perhaps even cows for milk and beef. This land lay behind the camp compound, and I never really paid attention to what was there.

During the more than six years that Dad headed the convict camp, I became quite familiar with the camp compound. Its grounds—sandy soil kept clean of debris—was enclosed within a high wire fence topped by one or more strands of barbed wire. Entrance to the camp was gained through a gate made of this wire, the gate being large enough to permit the entrance and exit of trucks and other vehicles. There was a second, smaller gate that permitted access to the camp's water source; this was a deep well from which water was drawn by a pump powered by a windmill (There may have been an electric motor as well.) located atop a tall steel frame. Such devices were then fairly common for supplying water in rural areas across the South. The water was stored in a large wooden tank built perhaps 30 or 35 feet off the ground and was distributed throughout the camp via underground pipes.

Within the compound were several wooden buildings. Near the front gate and to its right was the camp office, which also contained one or two separate rooms that served as sleeping quarters for night guards. The largest structure was the prison itself, a single-story dormitory (perhaps 50 feet wide by 100 feet long) built on a concrete slab. About half the building was the black prisoners' "bull pen"; adjacent to that was an open space with wooden bench tables for meals. Also located in this space were "stocks" and a smaller "bull pen" for the white prisoners. To the left of this open space was a wall with a door opening into a dining room for the guards; beside that was the camp kitchen. A door from the dining room led to an outside covered area perhaps 8 by 10 feet, one side of which was walled with a long, narrow table built on its interior side.

Another structure on the grounds of the convict camp was a long, wide shed with a tin roof under which trucks, other vehicles, and miscellaneous pieces of equipment were parked; adjacent to it was a gasoline pump. Nearby was a small wooden storage building for canned food, beans, salt pork, flour, meal, and other foodstuffs. Next to it was an iron latticework cage slightly smaller than a railroad boxcar; it contained double- or triple-decker bunks, perhaps six in total. I believe this odd structure could be hauled to a different location if necessary, but it was never moved while Dad was there, nor do I recall seeing it housing any convicts.

At the water tower end of the main prisoner building was a punishment facility, a steel or iron cage intended for one person. My recollection is that the person confined therein could only stand up; this metal cage was situated so that it would receive a heavy dose of daily sunshine, so anyone placed within that cage would suffer from South Georgia's usual hot weather, furthering the misery of the confined person. I have earlier mentioned the "stocks." This wooden structure was constructed so that it could accommodate (if that is the right word) two persons at once. An offender would sit on a wooden plank with his arms and legs stretched before him; these limbs would be enclosed within a wooden frame, the arms pinioned above and the legs pinioned below. I never observed anyone in the metal cage and seldom saw any offender immobile in the stocks. I think Dad doled out punishment as infrequently as the circumstances permitted.

Another structure on the grounds was a long, covered shed at the rear of the camp compound; this was probably used as a hog-killing and -rendering shelter. If I remember correctly, the vehicle shed harbored a Pierce-Arrow touring car—which was top down, dusty, and hors de combat. That car had a sixteen-cylinder motor and two gear shifts, one of which was short and on the floor with a brass floor plate; the plate was inscribed with words warning the driver to engage that short gear shift for speeds above 80 miles per hour. I believe that normally only eight of its sixteen cylinders were operated and the other eight cylinders came into play for the higher speed. I marveled at this monster, for it was a long, heavy vehicle, and when I was age twelve or thirteen, I liked to sit in the driver's seat and pretend to go like the wind. Whose car this was, or had been, and how it came to be under this shed, I never inquired or learned.

Outside the wire compound was an open area among the small pines in which were jumbled together a small road grader and miscellaneous pieces or parts of equipment, mostly junk or salvageable discards for which there was no alternate means of disposal. I never observed anyone from the camp searching for anything there.

As the warden's son, I had the run of the camp, with the exception that Dad forbade me to enter either of the "bull pens." Over the six-year period that Dad was "the Cap'n" (as he was referred to by all, prisoner and guards alike), I was both a frequent visitor and a thoughtless observer. Would that I had had sense enough, and a feeling for history, to have kept a journal or diary recording my observations and conversations, and so forth! Alas, such an idea never occurred to me, being a youth at the time. I thought then that all I saw and heard was a part of the natural order of things, and I never gave a second thought to anything about my small world. The idea that one day that world would exist no more and that I would be writing about my memory of it never occurred to me back then.

The ordinary prisoner wore a uniform of alternating black and white stripes, a jacket and trousers made of cotton cloth. "Trusties"—those prisoners deemed unlikely to try to escape and who therefore could be "trusted"—wore a solid gray jacket and solid gray trousers. Trusties were used for the kinds of jobs that could not be assigned to other prisoners. In fact, for the first couple of years of Dad's tenure, a black trustie we called "Speed" worked around our home and minded the livestock (a milk cow and a mule) that Dad owned and kept in the barnyard located behind our house. Eventually, Dad decided there was no need for this arrangement, so "Speed" was returned to other camp duties and we sold the livestock.

Very few prisoners either escaped, tried to escape, or were thought to be a possible escaper. Most, if not all, of those who escaped were caught at some subsequent time and were returned to the camp. I have documents confirming that escapees were apprehended in New York state and in Kentucky, and that the governors of those states approved their extradition to Georgia. Dad usually made the trip to bring back the captured escapees. A prisoner's running away (usually from a road work crew) necessitated a search with bloodhounds and a sense of urgency; Dad would head the search effort, carrying his revolver (a .38 caliber Smith and Wesson). Returned escapees—those who tried to run without success—and "possibles" or troublemakers might be punished by having metal shackles locked around their ankles, those shackles being connected by a short chain. A more severe and cruel form of shackle was shaped like a small sharp metal crescent, which was very heavy and cumbersome to lug around and which could seriously impede a prisoner's walking. My recalled impression is that there were very few prisoners who were ever shackled.

The prisoners' work week was from Monday through Friday, with a half-day of work on Saturday. Sunday was a leisure day except for the prisoners who were cooks. Days off from work were offered to prisoners for such holidays as the Fourth of July, Thanksgiving, and Christmas. Some of these holidays prisoners celebrated with a barbecue of hog meat, for which large ham shoulders and other pieces of hog meat would be placed on a wire grate of fencing and then cooked over the coals of a large outdoor pit fired by oak or hickory logs. The meat was frequently basted with a mixture of vinegar, salt, pepper, and other ingredients, and would be cooked all through the night. Dad usually asked Mother to make a large container of Brunswick stew. This, plus the barbeque and loaves of white bread, would be the prisoners' fare for the holiday.

Mother was given the task of writing the required account of the convicts' names, their crimes, the length of their sentences, and other essential facts, which she faithfully recorded in large red leather-bound ledgers at the end of each month. Most of the time I assisted her in this chore, reading to her all pertinent information from other records while she wrote it down at the roll-top desk in our living room. As I recall, this information had to be sent monthly to the State Department of Corrections (or whatever it was called then) in Atlanta. As a consequence of this monthly duty, I became quite familiar with the names of all the convicts (black and white, felons and misdemeanants), as well as the crimes they had committed, and so forth. This duty was edifying, but there were many other things I would have preferred to do, and doubtless Mother must have felt the same way.

Over time, I learned to associate names and faces, so that I came to recognize and could call by name a few of the convicts. It was not unusual for a prisoner, when speaking to another prisoner, to call him "Doubler." This term was used, almost without exception, when one sought a favor from another, such as asking for the cigarette the other was smoking. "We're just alike, so give me a break" seemed to be the term's implication. It wasn't within my power to grant any favors, but as the Warden's son the prisoners thought that maybe I could do something for them—more than once in my contacts with those individuals, I was addressed as "Doubler."

During the six years Dad was warden, I came to like some of the convicts better than others. The only prisoner that I recall with any clarity was called John Henry. I forget both his last name (it may have been Brown) and the crime for which he was incarcerated. John Henry, a tall, intelligent, muscular black man with a fine-featured face, was the camp blacksmith. On major jobs requiring considerable road machinery or jobs that used wheelers (a wheeler was a large steel scoop drawn by a team of horses or mules, usually the latter), John Henry set up shop to repair anything metal that might break. Additionally, of course, there was a constant need to shoe the mules, so he would have to hammer out horseshoes from time to time. John Henry also fancied himself to be a singer, and on occasion—mainly Saturday afternoons or Sundays—he and two or three other convicts would sing a range of songs as a trio or quartet. I remember one such song, whose lyrics went something like this:

Lead singer: "Dey calls me Mister Tenor."

All except the lead singer: "How do you do, Mister Tenor?"

Lead singer: "Calls me Mister Tenor."

All except the lead singer: "How do you do?"

All singers: "It's gettin' late, late, late, up in de evenin'. Lawdy, how do you do?"

Another singer would sing the next verse:

Another singer: "Dey calls me Mister Alto."

All except that singer: "How do you do, Mister Alto?"

Another singer: "Calls me Mister Alto."

And so on, repeating the tune and words of the last three lines above, with "Mister Baritone" singing next, then finally "Mister Basso." John Henry was usually the lead singer on performances of this song.

During summer vacations, I would often accompany Dad when he would drive out to spend time where the work was going on. By around 1935, the county commissioners were providing him with official county transportation in the form of a small, uncomfortable Dodge pickup truck. Frequently, roadwork called for moving dirt by hand shovels wielded by the convicts, and on occasion I heard "work songs" one of the prisoners would start and many other prisoners would join in singing. Not that such singing was an outcome or manifestation of a carefree existence, but the prisoners likely felt that singing a "work song" could help a shoveler settle into a rhythm of "dig—pitch—dig—pitch—dig," and so on, making a hard, back-breaking burden just a little more bearable. On most of these work crews, a "water boy" would carry a tin bucket of water brought from the camp (or more likely obtained from a nearby house's well) complete with a tin hand-dipper, to be shared by all. Few jobs back then were not hot, dusty, tiring, and stressful, so plenty of water was needed, especially during the summer months, but I never saw anyone who had fallen out of line for any reason.

So ends my recollections of a bygone day. I know my father was a skilled road builder, and I believe he was a humane warden. In the other 153 counties of Georgia, there were other humane wardens, I have no doubt, and there were also likely cruel and sadistic wardens. I am sure that Dad would have preferred to work solely in his former profession as a road builder, but in 1932 one had to make the best of whatever work one could find. We were fortunate that Dad found this job, for it brought our family the security of a steady income (approximately $125 each month), which was enough for us to live on and which was more than many a family had in those economically desperate times.

Angola Blues: The Prison Songs of Robert Pete Williams

BY MARK ALLAN JACKSON

In early 1958, folklorist Harry Oster, a professor affiliated with Louisiana State University, visited Angola state prison to collect traditional work songs, spirituals, and blues. There, warden Maurice Sigler asked convicted murderer and musician Robert Pete Williams to perform his original, eclectic blues for Oster. The first song Williams performed was "Prisoner's Talking Blues." Backed by Williams's haunting twelve-string guitar work, this improvised, spoken-word lament confessed the bluesman's state of body and mind since being sent to Angola. He moaned, "You know begin to get gray since I got here. / Well, a whole lot of worrying cause that. / But I can feel myself weakening. / I don't keep well no more. I keeps sickly." After expressing doubt that he would see his children again and stating that it was a blessing that his mother died before he committed his crime, Williams admitted, "Sometimes I feel like, Baby, committing suicide. / I got the nerve if I just had anything to do it with."[1] According to Williams, the song was so persuasive that it "got the prison kind of worried" about his state of mind.[2] Music critic Peter Guralnick believe that "you listen to a man's naked suffering in this song."[3]

---

[1] Robert Pete Williams, "Prisoner's Talking Blues," *Angola Prisoners' Blues*. Arhoolie 419, 1996.

[2] Chris Strachwitz, "Robert Pete Williams," *Robert Pete Williams: When a Man Takes the Blues*. Arhoolie 395, 1994.

[3] Peter Guralnick, *Feel Like Going Home: Portraits in Blues & Rock 'N' Roll* (Boston: Little, Brown and Company, 1999) 137.

Guralnick also argued that Williams's songs are "tinged with a fundamentalist, almost holy fervor that has little to do with politics or political realities."[4] But Guralnick was wrong about this bluesman's work. Given Williams's place within Angola, with its white-dominated administration and its majority black population, many of his blues not only documented the feelings and observations of a one man held in prison but also the experiences of many African Americans locked within a strict, white-controlled political, social, and economic system in the deep South. In light of this historical perspective, a discussion of Williams's songs reveals as much about the 1950s-era black experience across the South as it does about the man himself.

Long before ending up in Angola, Robert Pete Williams endured a difficult and hardscrabble life. Born on March 14, 1914, in Zachary, Louisiana, the seventh of nine children, Williams grew up in poverty and under the shadow of racism. His father was a sharecropper, and the whole family—to help increase yield and profitability—had to help in the fields, leaving no time for a formal education for the children. Williams admitted to Guralnick, "I can't read, I can't write. I never been to school in my life."[5] As the bluesman reached manhood, his life did not get easier. He held a number of menial jobs: dairy farmer, barrel maker, highway crewman, and levee camp laborer among others. The hard work Williams endured and the disregard his white employers directed at him would find voice in one of his non-prison songs: "[The man] hear me blowin', he say, What's the matter? / I say, Man, I tired and hot. / He say, Let's get it, boy."[6]

Throughout his life, Williams felt the burden of being a black man in the Deep South, where he had to defer to whites simply because of their race. An example of the subservience with which the black man treated his white boss was communicated in Williams' song "Yassuh an' Nosuh Blues." Here, Williams remembers previous times when he walked into "my boss-

[4] Ibid., 126.
[5] Ibid., 133.
[6] Ibid., 131.

PORTRAIT OF ROBERT PETE WILLIAMS, 1968.
Photograph by Chris Strachwitz. From Arhoolie CD 395. www.arhoolie.com. Used by permission.

man' house" and "forget [sic] to reach for my hat." His white boss would tell him, "Nigger, what's wrong with you'" and then would yell, ""I want you to get that hat off yo' head!,'" but he was also "likely to get him a club an' knock it off my head." The song continued, noting that only race, not age, would determine the treatment of black people: "[A white person] may be young, he don't have to be no more than sixteen or seventeen years, / You got to honor him at the groun'."[7] Another Louisiana bluesman, Willie Thomas, told Oster, echoing Williams, "You sho' had to be obedient to white people. That's taught from the fire hearth trainin' up. You see, when a white man walk up, you surely had to get plumb out the way."[8]

Williams performed music to offset his troubles and hard life. As a child, he would "get tin buckets and beat on them…and sing." He would also pick up a rubberband, "put it in my mouth and make it sound like a jew's harp." In his late teens, Williams crafted a crude guitar from a cigar box and copper strings and "put nails on it for the keys. Tighten[ed] these strings up and went on…started hitting on it, and it kinda sounded good to me." Later, he bought a cheap factory-made guitar, but "it was an old box, strings about an inch from the neck." But he "worked with it and worked with it 'til I learnt." After he had improved his performing ability, he looked around for a better instrument—and made a surprising acquisition. A local white woman had an expensive guitar that she had bought for her son, who showed no interest in the instrument, leaving it to languish. When Williams heard about the instrument, he asked her if he could buy it: "She said, 'Yeah, I'll sell it.' And that guitar she sold me, it was worth around $40 or $50. She sold it to me for $4! Late at night you could hear that guitar ringing for miles."[9]

Initially, Williams played and sang through the influence of musicians within his family. Several of his siblings played guitar and piano, and his uncle Simon Carney played guitar, using a knife slide to fret the instrument. Other influences came from such local performers as Solomon Bradd and

---

[7] Harry Oster, *Living Country Blues* (Detroit: Folklore Associates, 1969) 141.
[8] Ibid., 142.
[9] Pete Welding, "Haunted by the Blues," *Downbeat*, 37/16, (6 August 1970): 16.

Dan Jackson, both guitarists who also used slides and played down-home country blues. Williams was also greatly impressed by the music of Texas blues legend Blind Lemon Jefferson. Williams once said, "I used to listen to Blind Lemon's records, more than I did anyone's records that was ever put out, because I was interested and I loved to hear him."[10]

Williams eventually developed his own sound to fit his own aesthetic, his own mood. As Guralnick observed, "It was some time in the forties…that he developed the style by which we know him today, an arresting, absolutely unique blend without apparent influence or precedent."[11] Often, Williams's blues—blending a unique guitar style with evocative, emotion-driven lyrics—were a means for him to deal with his personal hardships, helping him to lessen the suffering detailed in the words themselves. As Williams said in a 1970 interview, "Some people say you take the blues if you're worried or you're broke. Well, I guess that is true, 'cause I have been broke plenty of times, and I have been mistreated a lot of times. Well, that gives me the blues, more so. Things that I want and I don't have the money, or something like that, and I get aworrying, and I just get it off my mind going up somewhere, and I sing the blues." According to Williams, by singing the blues, a kind of catharsis occurs: " I've had sad feelings to come on me. Know what I mean by sad feelings? It's something like the whole world's kinda like against you or down on you. I walked along with a sad feeling and cried to myself. I have. I've had a sad feeling, just walking on, cry to myself, tears run out of my eyes. But I go ahead on and sing the blues 'til I kinda get eased. When I get eased, well, it look like things kinda lighten up off of me."[12]

Beginning in the mid-1950s and continuing for nearly a full decade, Williams definitely needed his music to help lighten his heavy burden. On Saturday night, December 17, 1955, Williams went to a bar named Bradley's Club in Scotlandville, a little town just outside of Baton Rouge. According to the musician, "a great big guy" started bothering him, trying

---

[10] Al Wilson, "Robert Pete Williams: His Life and Music," *Little Sandy Review*, 2/1 (July 1966): 20.

[11] Guralnick, *Feel Like Going Home*, 141.

[12] Welding, "Haunted by the Blues," 17.

to provoke Williams to fight, but he just walked away. Not out of fear, for "The man didn't know how hard I was up under here, you know, with that gun I had.... He didn't know that. I had a .45." After talking with friends for a short while, Williams decided to avoid trouble by leaving. But "when [the big man] seen I was fixing to getting out of there, he broke for me. And he come out with one of them old knives that look like a hawk bill." With a crowd blocking the only exit, hoping to see a fight, Williams pulled his gun and fired at his attacker. He confessed, "I shot him below his navel...I knew that wouldn't kill him." But the man was too strong to be stopped by one shot. "He was too big to fall," said Williams. When the man straightened up to come at him again, Williams shot him once more and pierced his heart. The man slumped to the floor and later died.[13]

In a 1970 interview with music writer Pete Welding, Williams lamented his actions and wondered about the motivation behind them: "If I hadn't had anything that night, I maybe wouldn't have got in trouble—if I hadn't been carrying that gun. Why was I carrying it? Well, it was the devil; I'm just showing you how it is with the devil. I was carrying a gun, and I guess it was about the biggest piece they make; it was a .45. I was carrying a .45, and if I hadn't of [sic] had that .45, I tell you, I could have been in the ground too. But after it was over with, I was sorry I had that .45—after it was over with."[14] During the course of his trial, Williams took the stand and told this story again, emphasizing that it was him or the other man, that self-defense had been the true motive.

Unfortunately for the bluesman, this tale did not convince the jury. No knife was found at the crime scene, and most witnesses testified to only to seeing Williams shooting the other man. Even with this damning evidence, he did avoid the ultimate punishment. According to Williams, "they was trying me for the hot cap, that's the electric chair."[15] On March 23, 1956, the 19th Judicial District Court judge sentenced Williams to a life term, and two weeks later, he entered Louisiana's prison farm, Angola.

---

[13] Robert Pete Williams, "Monologue," *When a Man Takes the Blues*. Arhoolie 395, 1994.

[14] Welding, "Haunted by the Blues," 17.

[15] Williams, "Monologue."

Originally, Angola had been a cotton plantation, located next to the Mississippi River in West Feliciana Parish, and that land had been worked by slaves in the hot Louisiana sun. In 1901, this former plantation became the central facility of Louisiana's prisons when authorities ended the convict lease system and the state became responsible for the containment and control of its convicted felons. Throughout the first half of the twentieth century, little changed at Angola—whites remained in control of a largely black population. Whippings and beatings were often used to keep prison laborers in line. In fact, by the beginning of the 1950s, this prison was considered one of the worst in America. In particular, a scandal broke out about the conditions at Angola in 1951 after thirty-seven inmates slashed their own heel tendons, a permanent disability, as a protest against abusive conditions. Soon thereafter, Louisiana's governor Earl Long appointed a thirty-four-member Citizens Committee to look into the prisoners' allegations. One of the main witnesses in the investigation, prison nurse Mary Daughtry, called then-warden Rudolph Eastley "an arrogant, uncouth, narrow-minded, unprincipled bigot." Soon after giving her testimony, she quit her post, saying, "I have no desire to stay at Angola to witness the carnage in human lives and taxpayers' property that can be wrought by petty despots and rotten politicians."[16] Under pressure from the resulting scandal, Warden Eastley finally resigned in November 1951. By the time that Williams entered Angola in spring 1956, the prison had improved somewhat due to the efforts of reformist Governor Robert Kennon—but Angola must still have seemed like a dark and foreboding place to this forty-two-year-old man who had never before had trouble with the law.

After Williams came to Angola, officials encouraged him, just as they had other prisoners, to ease the burden of their sentences by playing music. At the time, the prison boasted several jazz, hillbilly, and early rock bands. But Williams's ability to play blues, especially songs of his own composi-

---

[16] "Angola Nurse Resigns Post," *State-Times* (Baton Rogue LA), April 3, 1951, 1.

tion, set him apart. He believed that he became a favorite of the guards through his music:

> My folks sent me a guitar, and I started to playing that guitar, and the captain heard me, and they tell me, say, "Come in here." So I went into the office. They said, "Play that thing." I played for them. They said, "Gee, you're good. Like you play that thing, you don't have no business here." Then they dialed the telephone, said hush a minute, get their wives on the phone, and then they'd tell me start to playing. Then I'd start to playing, and they'd let their wives listen at it as long as they'd want to, on the telephone. And when they'd hang up, they'd say, "You know, my wife wants to know if we having a party down here. Those blues sound good."[17]

Hence, when Oster visited the prison in to collect various folksongs, warden Sigler singled out Williams to perform for the folklorist.

As noted earlier, Williams composed "Prisoner's Talking Blues" on the spot for Oster, who commented about this song, "the despair of the prisoner who is in for life has never been better captured."[18] In the song "Up an' Down Blues," Williams again addressed the theme of despondency that a long-term prisoner feels—but in this instance, unlike in "Prisoner's Talking Blues," the reason for his woes was his desertion by his family. In "Up an' Down Blues," the narrator laments, "You know when a man is down, it ain't long 'fo'e his folks forget all about where his is," then adds, "it don't be long fo'e the folk get him off their mind." In particular, the narrator addresses his woman, complaining, "Sometime that I sit down, baby, …I have to write my own self sometime. / I have to fool these other inmate like I'm receiving mail from home."[19] Although some might dismiss these

---

[17] Welding, "Haunted by the Blues," 34.

[18] Harry Oster, liner notes, *Angola Prisoners' Blues*. Folk-Lyric Recording Company LFS A-3, 1959.

[19] Oster, *Living Country Blues*, 334.

lines as exaggeration, Oster noted that the song "expresses a frequent complaint of prisoners."[20]

In other songs recorded by Oster, Williams put aside his self-destructive musings and his feelings of abandonment to comment directly on Louisiana's legal and pardon systems. As blues scholar Samuel Charters commented, "The legacy of the blues of Robert Pete Williams has been their direct responsiveness to what he's thinking, what he's feeling."[21] During the late 1950s, the bluesman definitely thought and felt that the court had dealt him a great wrong. In the song "Some Got Six Months," Williams confronted the injustice he saw in his sentencing. As Oster pointed out, this song employed some verses that appear in other recorded blues pieces, such as Gus Cannon's "Viola Lee Blues."[22] But even in the standard verses, the situation fit Williams's circumstances, for the song opens, "Some got six months, some got a solid year / But me and my buddy, we got lifetime here." However, Williams's version contained a few specifics from the singer's own situation. The last verse contains the line, "First time in trouble, I done get no fair trial at all," reflecting his disappointed reaction to his life sentence despite his previously clean record and his plea of self-defense. Earlier, in verse four, Williams mused, "Yeah, that old judge must have been mad, darling / When he gave me my sentence, he throwed the book."[23] This song emphasized what Williams perceived as a disparity in the law, as Guralnick noted: "[T]hough [Williams] conducted himself in exemplary fashion[,] by the curious terms of a white South he was sent up to prison for three and a half years and ended up serving nearly ten for an act which could at most be called a minor infraction of Southern justice."[24] Another of Williams's songs reflected upon the singer's experiences with the parole board. In the years prior to his discovery by Oster, Williams had requested parole three times, only to be denied in each instance. These

---

[20] Ibid., 335.

[21] Samuel Charters, *The Legacy of the Blues: Art and Lives of Twelve Great Bluesman* (New York: Da Capo Press, 1977) 56.

[22] Ibid., 309.

[23] Williams, "Some Got Six Months," *Angola Prisoners' Blues.*

[24] Guralnick, *Feel Like Going Home*, 148.

experiences led the singer to document his frustration in the song "Pardon Denied Again," in which the narrator lamented his rejection: "I know my case ain't too bad. I just can't see, just can't see why they do me this way."[25]

Williams's creative abilities led to an effort to have him released from prison. Led by Oster, a letter-writing program aimed at Governor Earl Long pushed for the singer's parole or pardon. Also, a recording of Williams' work, made by Oster, was sent to the governor's office. As a result of this advocacy, Williams even made up a song, entitled "Freeman Blues," in tribute to Oster:

> I met a friend of mine,
> He came to see me today.
> How glad I was to see him,
> I shook his hand.
> He did a whole lot for me,
> Helped get me outta prison.[26]

Williams did owe Oster some gratitude, for in December 1959, through the efforts of the folklorist and others, Governor Long paroled the singer. Williams was free—well, almost free.

Unfortunately, he did not receive a full pardon but a so-called "servitude parole." In fact, Williams was basically leased labor to a Denham Springs farmer named Rudolph Eastley—the very man who had been Angola's warden at the time of the prisoner protest. Through a program set up by Governor Long, early releases were rendered possible by having parolees work off their debt to the state through outside employment. As a result, Williams remained a virtual prisoner of Eastley for almost five years, working eighty hours a week in Eastley's fields for only $75 a month, plus room and board. The hard work and the denial of true freedom often got Williams so depressed that he expressed his frustration in the song "Death

---

[25] Robert Pete Williams, "Pardon Denied Again," *I'm Blue As a Man Can Be*. Arhoolie 394, 1994.
[26] Oster, *Living Country Blues*, 340.

Blues." Here, he sang the lines, "you know the way I work out here, baby, / I have some min' to go back to Angola."[27]

Finally, in 1964, Williams won a full release, becoming his own man for the first time since the mid-1950s. In subsequent years, he toured America and Europe, playing his music for appreciative audiences. He also recorded over a dozen albums and appeared in a number of documentary films on the blues. But his eclectic style never made him a star on the level of John Lee Hooker or B. B. King. Small offers came to him, but no big break. Then, beginning in the early 1970s, his health began to suffer, further limiting his ability to perform. Williams died on December 31, 1980, at the age of sixty-six, and he was buried in Baton Rouge.

Perhaps Williams meant for his blues to be his alone, his means of testifying to others of the misery he felt, a chance to cleanse his soul. But in several of his songs, chronicling the details of his experiences in jail and the repercussions of his incarceration, Williams touched on a greater history. The stories he told in his blues reflected the experience of many other black prisoners—men who likewise contemplated committing suicide, who felt as if their wives, friends, and family had forgotten them, men who had also tried for parole or pardon and had failed. Guralnick speculated, "It may perhaps be necessary…to look on [Williams's] prison blues as the product of a unique combination of genius and circumstances."[28] Yet Williams also shared the fate of other black men who were separated by prison walls from their communities, from their families, and often from even the hope of freedom. Unlike many other prisoners, though, Robert Pete Williams had a unique ability to document his life in prison, leaving behind a recorded legacy of memorable music.

---

[27] Ibid., 342.

[28] Guralnick, *Feel Like Going Home*, 144.

RANDALL HORTON AND HIS SISTER LESLIE HORTON, MAY 1972. Photo courtesy of Eunice Horton.

Working Overtime at Bryant Chapel AME

BY RANDALL HORTON

At 1:00 P.M. before church lets out,
Reverend Jamar bellows a deep groan,
folds over, raises his large frame
with baritone belts of "Amazing Grace."

There is a certain verbosity
in how a blind man's words hold us;
it is like he can peep through mud,
and visualize dry land.

In the second pew, my sister and I
watch him sway a stoic congregation
of old fruit hats holding brown hymnals,
their arms stretched to a plastic Jesus.

Elderly men in the steward's corner
provide *yes suh's!* and *preach it Rev!*

Guiding a sea of fanatics to that crescendo
where people gotta believe in something.

The sunlight from stained windows
blinds our eyes with flashes of revelation
until Sister Ola's body jerks down the aisle
like a macramé doll on an elastic tether.

Tears rain from mascara-smeared eyes.
She grits, pulls God's breath,
knocks over the attendance banner—
Ms. Julia commences to hum *miry clay.*

Smith and Gaston fans windmill nonstop,
sweat trickles down faces full of brimstone;
somebody faints, scripture grows longer
against a chorus of low tenor nightingales.

In-between moans, collection plates circulate
in Usher Board #3 third Sunday's name.
Everybody digs deep for the new building fund
and soon-to-be Headstart program.

At precisely 1:45 P.M., my sister and I
surrender any chance of heathenism
as pastor discovers the hedge of his pulpit,
reaches out—extends an invitation to Christ.

Involuntarily, our legs stand up straight,
do a tuxedo shuffle to the organ's timbre.
In this out-of-body experience, we become
filled with the Holy Ghost, ready for baptism.

Jim Crow Ordained: White and Black Christianity in the Civil Rights South

BY THOMAS AIELLO

"God wanted white people to live alone," urged the official newspaper of the White Citizens' Councils of America, instructing children of the late-1950s South. "And He wanted colored people to live alone.... The white men built America for you," the newspaper continued. "White men built the United States so they could make their rules.... God has made us different. And God knows best."[1] Religion held a dual role in Southern society. While churches maintained a vested interest in the status quo and traditional values, Christians in the South generally believed in divine justice, and the fundamental goodness of man carried influence among social reformers and activists. Religion remained the most significant organizing principle of the Civil Rights Movement, and Southern civil rights leaders constantly cited biblical mandates for equality to justify their cause and to convince their oppressors of wrongdoing. The oppressors, however, steeped their segregationist message and policy with quotes from the very same Bible.[2]

Morality could be used as a rationalization for discrimination, but also as a motivating force for organizing action. Robert N. Bellah argued that

---

[1] Anonymous, "A Manual for Southerners," *The Citizens' Council*, February 1957, 1, 4; James Silver, "Mississippi: The Closed Society," *Journal of Southern History* 30/1 (February 1964): 12.

[2] The true role of religion in activist politics has been widely debated, with social theorists such as Gunnar Myrdal arguing that religion pacified black protest and focused black attention on otherworldly rather than immediate issues, while scholars such as Daniel Thompson emphasize the use of the black church as a vehicle of organization and social protest. Gary T. Marx, "Religion: Opiate or Inspiration of Civil Rights Militancy Among Negroes?" *American Sociological Review* 32/1 (February 1967): 64–65; Jane Cassels Record and Wilson Record, "Ideological Forces and the Negro Protest," *Annals of the American Academy of Political and Social Science* 357/1 (January 1965): 92; Frank S. Loescher, *The Protestant Church and the Negro: A Pattern of Segregation* (1948; reprint, Westport CT: Negro Universities Press, 1971) 50; Rodney Stark, "Class, Radicalism, and Religious Involvement," *American Sociological Review* 29/5 (October 1964): 698; Richard Rose, "On the Priorities of Citizenship in the Deep South and Northern Ireland," *Journal of Politics* 38/2 (May 1976): 258–59; Christopher Beckham, "The Paradox of Religious Segregation: White and Black Baptists in Western Kentucky, 1855–1900," *Register of the Kentucky Historical Society* 97/3 (Summer 1999): 322.

social tradition and practice created a de facto American civil religion that existed concurrently with, but apart from, actual religious communities. This civil religion set societal mores and gave Americans an idea of correct behavior. While the white and black religious communities diverged at the issue of race equality, for instance, both communities could acknowledge a correlation between church membership and community standing, or that general adherence to biblical principles generally kept a proponent in line with American legal principles.[3]

The religious and social beliefs of US churchgoers, however, were not uniform. A 1963 survey conducted by the National Opinion Research Center demonstrated that white integrationist attitudes were most prominent in the moderate religionists, while opposition to the integration manifested itself most plainly in the polar extremes of religious dedication.[4] There has never been a consistent American ethic. Civil rights activists and members of the White Citizens' Councils, for instance, certainly had different "American Dreams," and both groups extracted vindication from similar faiths, causing each other to fully perceive the "dark side" of its belief system.[5] Any vindication of one position was necessarily a denunciation of the other. In such instances, the Bible was essentially battling itself. Religion was a multipurpose weapon in those ideological struggles and lent legiti-

[3] Record, "Ideological Forces and the Negro Protest," 90; and Robert N. Bellah, "Civil Religion in America," *Daedalus* 96/1 (Winter 1967): 5. In this atmosphere, the church became the original and primary societal stratifier in post-bellum America. Beckham, "The Paradox of Religious Segregation," 321–22.

[4] In 1964, approximately 90 percent of African Americans and 65 percent of whites were Protestant. Paul B. Sheatsley, "White Attitudes Toward the Negro," *Daedalus* 95/1 (Winter 1966): 228–29. Also see the chart on p. 226; Norval Glenn, "Negro Religion and Negro Status in the United States," in *Religion, Culture and Society*, ed. Louis Schneider (New York: John Wiley & Sons, Inc., 1964) 623. Also see the table on p. 624. Also see, http://norc.uchicago.edu.

macy to a pervasive Protestant Americanism. The ability of the Bible to justify Jim Crow as well as to encourage full equality demonstrated the problem of using such a malleable and cryptic document as a foundation for argument, but the collective faith of both races was not radically erased when shown through the looking glass.

Inherently, religious groups participating in the American civil rights debate clung to their Bibles as written documentation that God was on their side. The most common biblical defense used by segregationists involved the story of Ham, cursed son of Noah, whose descendants settled in modern-day Ethiopia. Segregationists argued that since God cursed Ham, and Ham's descendants were black, then that curse became generationally and biologically adaptable to all proceeding manifestations of the black bloodline. Southern preachers such as Carey Daniel, of the First Baptist Church of West Dallas, Texas, proclaimed from the pulpit that the "nations" formed from these different tribes were actually "races" to be kept separate and distinct. Anti-segregationists argued that biblical mandates for the restoration of world unity mitigated any claims to the story of Ham. Leviticus 19:18 required biblical adherents to "Love your neighbor as yourself," and integrationist thinkers such as Daisuke Kitagawa, executive secretary of the Protestant Episcopal Church's Domestic Mission, argued that this mandate included both strangers and acquaintances.[6]

Segregationists also posed arguments based on the idea that God deemed the Hebrews his "chosen people," emphasizing the demonstration

---

[5] The Citizens' Councils, though statistical minorities throughout the South, served as both mainstream symbols of white resistance and active defenders of the anti-integration ideology. Neil R. McMillen, *The Citizens' Council: Organized Resistance to the Second Reconstruction, 1954–64* (Urbana: University of Illinois Press, 1971) 159; Record, "Ideological Forces and the Negro Protest," 90–91.

[6] In actuality the original story of Canaan did not even include a father named Ham. Ham's presence was a later editorial addition, which gave the false impression that the sons of Ham were born to be slaves. Andrew M. Manis, "'Dying From the Neck Up': Southern Baptist Resistance to the Civil Rights Movement," *Baptist History and Heritage* 34/1 (Winter 1999) Infotrac pdf file. Article A94160905, 1–10, http://web2.infotrac-custom.com/pdfserve/get_item/1/S1d1829w6_1/SB729_01.pdf, accessed 24 March 2003: 3 [page numbers refer to pdf pages, rather than original bound journal pages.]; anonymous, "Pastor Says 'Bible Orders Color Line,'" *The Citizens' Council*, May 1956, 4; R. Tandy McConnell, "Religion, Segregation, and the Ideology of Cooperation: A Southern Baptist Church Responds to the *Brown* Decision," *Southern Studies* 4/1 (Spring 1993): 22; I. A. Newby, "Epilogue: A Rebuttal to Segregationists," in *The Development of Segregationist Thought* (Homewood IL: The Dorsey Press, 1968) 171; David L. Chappell, "Religious Ideas of the Segregationists," *Journal of American Studies* 32/1 (April 1998): 241, 244–45; Mother Kathryn Sullivan, "Sacred Scripture and Race," *Religious Education* 59/1 (January–February 1964): 11; Daisuke Kitagawa, "The Church and Race Relations in Biblical Perspective," *Religious Education* 59/1 (January–February 1964): 7, 8–9.

of a creational favoritism. The Apostle Paul, however, refuted any calls to Hebrew superiority or divine partisanship by claiming that his God was the God of everyone. "He made from one the whole human race to dwell on the entire surface of the earth," wrote Paul. Liberal integrationists understandably stressed this passage. The Bible's dual mandates allowed each group to ground its case in scripture and emphasized the inability of the book to support reasoned arguments for or against segregation. Paul's work often became the backbone of segregationist versus integrationist argument. In his letter to the Galatians, Paul stated that all were God's children, but in his letter to the Ephesians, he encouraged slaves to serve their human masters as if they were serving Christ. Statements such as "watch out for those who create dissensions and obstacles, in opposition to the teaching that you learned" offered fodder for segregationists in the White Citizens' Council journal *The Citizen*, but could also theoretically represent the other side. God "is not the author of disorder, but of peace" offered additional, seemingly innocuous advice that both groups, particularly the segregationists, recruited for their cause. These arguments and others stemmed from the same book, which ostensibly stemmed from the same author, but were inconsistent in their respective uses and reuses for various ends. When God asked, "Are ye not like the Ethiopians to me, O people of Israel?" America awkwardly answered with contradictory responses.[7]

Sociological studies conducted in the 1940s and 1950s generally described church-attending communities more opposed to integration than their non-church-attending counterparts. Thomas F. Pettigrew's 1959 analysis demonstrated a proportional relationship between church attendance and racial intolerance, but most sociologists concluded that the greatest level of tolerance existed at polar extremes—avid church attenders as well as non-attenders formed a faction of racial acceptance, while the

[7] Deuteronomy 7:7, 10:14–15; Ezekiel 16:3–14; Acts 17:26–27; Galatians 3:26–28; Amos 9:7; Ephesians 6:5 NAB; Romans 16:17 NIV; Medford Evans, "A Methodist Declaration of Conscience on Racial Segregation," *The Citizen* 7/4 (January 1963): 12–13; Albert S. Thomas, "A Defense of the Christian South," in *Essays on Segregation*, ed. T. Robert Ingram (Houston: St. Thomas Press, 1960) 70–71; Henry T. Egger, "What Meaneth This: There Is No Difference," in *Essays on Segregation*, 27-29; John H. Knight, "The NCC's Delta Project—An Experiment in Revolution," *The Citizen* 8/9 (June 1964): 9; anonymous, "Pastor Says 'Bible Orders Color Line,'" 4.

majority of churchgoers tended toward segregationist attitudes.[8] The church developed an ideology based around the desires and feelings of the people committed to membership. The white Southern Protestant church was an agent of Southern society at large, tied as much to community fellowship and social stability as it was to spiritual endeavor. That church's rejection of integration was not simple hypocrisy, but a conscious choice of the civil religion.[9]

Religion was both a reason for and product of the prevailing culture. "Despite assertions in favor of compulsory integration," stated William Workman in his 1960 defense of segregated society, *The Case for the South*, "a massive wall of resistance has arisen within the framework of many of the churches themselves." Historian David L. Chappell has demonstrated in the book *A Stone of Hope* that Workman's claim was largely bluster, but the Southern Baptist majority did prefer and work for segregation. A 1964 study demonstrated that a minister's social activism, or lack thereof, remained fundamentally proportional to the activity of his college-aged congregants. The biblical literalism of conservative Protestantism promoted obedience and submission to religious as well as to secular authority figures, thereby placing any thought of rejecting the established societal norms out of the realm of possibility. Therefore, among Protestant Christians, belief in the Bible as the final word of the Lord had an inversely proportional relationship with the likelihood of their becoming involved in any form of social protest. Southern Baptist Pastor Wallie Amos Criswell, at a 1956 South Carolina Baptist Convention, referred to integrationist reformers as "infidels," and this conservatism in local church life trumped any progressive liberal leanings within groups such as the Southern Baptist

[8] Elizabeth M. Eddy, "Student Perspectives on the Southern Church," *Phylon* 25/4 (Fourth Quarter 1964): 369. For examples of various American sociological studies, see Thomas F. Pettigrew, "Regional Differences in Anti-Negro Prejudice," *Journal of Abnormal and Social Psychology* 59/1 (July 1959): 28–36; Bruno Bettelheim and Morris Janowitz, "Ethnic Tolerance: A Function of Social and Personal Control," *American Journal of Sociology* 55/2 (September 1949): 137–45; Robert W. Friedrichs, "Christians and Residential Exclusion: An Empirical Study of a Northern Dilemma," *Journal of Social Issues* 15/4 (1959): 14–23.

[9] Samuel S. Hill, "Southern Protestantism and Racial Integration," *Religion in Life* 33/2 (Summer 1964): 426–27; David Edwin Harrell, *White Sects and Black Men in the Recent South* (Nashville: Vanderbilt University Press, 1971) ix–x, 3–4, 18, 47; Manis, "Dying From the Neck Up," 2, 7; Kenneth K. Bailey, *Southern White Protestantism in the Twentieth Century* (New York: Harper & Row, 1964) 162, 164–65.

Convention. As the Civil Rights Movement grew, white Southern churches at national conferences replaced rigid demands for strict segregation with vague references to abstract concepts of an integrated society.[10]

D. M. Nelson, president of the Southern Baptist-affiliated Mississippi College, argued in 1955 for segregation's Christian foundation against integration's communistic tendencies, declaring the latter position "is untenable and cannot be sustained either by the Word or the works of God." Eight years later, delegates to the 1963 Mississippi Baptist Convention refused to ratify a statement favoring universal good will. In response, a Nigerian missionary living in Mississippi, frustrated by domestic action, wrote the Convention a letter arguing that, "Communists do not need to work against the preaching of the Gospel here; you are doing it quite adequately."[11]

The religious activism moving through American society in the late 1950s and early 1960s was not the religion familiar to conservative critics. Swedish sociologist Gunnar Myrdal argued that there existed a significant "American Dilemma," in which the practice of democracy did not match the commonly assumed ethic of equality and justice—the "ever-raging conflict" between the traditionally understood "American Creed, where the American thinks, talks, and acts under the influence of high national and Christian precepts," and the reality of "personal and local interests," "group prejudice against particular persons or types of people," and "all sorts of

[10] Joseph H. Fichter, "American Religion and the Negro," *Daedalus* 94/4 (Fall 1965): 1094; William D. Workman, Jr., *The Case for the South* (New York: The Devin-Adair Company, 1960) 101; David L. Chappell, *A Stone of Hope: Prophetic Liberalism and the Death of Jim Crow* (Chapel Hill: University of North Carolina Press, 2004); James F. Findlay, "Religion and Politics in the Sixties: The Churches and the Civil Rights Act of 1964," *The Journal of American History* 77/1 (June 1990): 66; Senate, "Civil Rights Act of 1964," Richard Russell, 88th Cong., 2nd sess., *Congressional Record*, 110, pt. 11 (18 June 1964): 14300; Gordon F. DeJong and Joseph E. Faulkner, "The Church, Individual Religiosity, and Social Justice," *Sociological Analysis* 28/1 (Spring 1967): 35–36. Also see the charts on pp. 40 and 41; Darren E. Sherkat and T. Jean Blocker, "The Political Development of Sixties' Activists: Identifying the Influence of Class, Gender and Socialization on Protest Participation," *Social Forces* 72/3 (March 1994): 823, 833; Nancy Tatom Ammerman, *Bible Believers: Fundamentalists in the Modern World* (New Brunswick NJ: Rutgers University Press, 1987) 188; David Stricklin, *A Genealogy of Dissent: Southern Baptist Protest in the Twentieth Century* (Lexington: The University Press of Kentucky, 1999) 164–65, 168–69; Charles W. Eagles, "The Closing of Mississippi Society: Will Campbell, *The $64,000 Question*, and Religious Emphasis Week at the University of Mississippi," *Journal of Southern History* 67/2 (May 2001): 335.

[11] Anonymous, "Conflicting Views On Segregation," *The Citizens' Council*, October 1955, 4; Silver, "Mississippi: The Closed Society," 9; anonymous, "Christian Love and Segregation," *The Citizens' Council*, August 1956, 1–2; anonymous, "Pinkos in the Pulpit," *The Citizens' Council*, December 1956, 2; anonymous, "Methodist Patriots Expose Pinks," *The Citizens' Council*, August 1957, 1; Thomas R. Waring, "Aroused Churchmen Are Studying Leftist Trends," *The Citizen* 6/7 (April 1962): 11.

miscellaneous wants, impulses, and habits." White religious communities that failed to respond to civil rights imperatives could deflect guilt and take solace in the shared ideals of fellow congregants and the relative inaction of the ministerial community. "The moral struggle," wrote Myrdal, "goes on within people and not only between them." Meanwhile, segregationists went relatively unchecked, arguing that the North had more racial problems than the South, and warning against "pseudo-Christian panaceas which produce only trouble." "Our neighbor's sin always looks larger than ours," declared Alabama Presbyterian minister John H. Knight in 1964, "especially if our neighbor lives in the South."[12]

White ministerial trepidation empowered black ministers to increased militancy, a point made plainly clear in Martin Luther King, Jr.'s, "Letter from Birmingham Jail": "In the midst of blatant injustices inflicted upon the Negro," wrote King, "I have watched white churches stand on the sideline and merely mouth pious irrelevancies and sanctimonious trivialities." Civil rights leaders and segregation defenders shared the common belief that God supported them and fully backed and encompassed their worldview, but the groups held differing conceptions of the religious endgame. Civil rights leaders saw a pluralistic society of communal equality as a viable Christian desire, while the religion of segregation defenders dictated the desirability of individual liberty and traditional values. Integration, then, became friend or foe dependent on the offering plate into which one dropped his or her donations.[13]

The leaders of the Civil Rights Movement did not emerge unanimously, and being a black minister did not automatically qualify one as a civil rights leader. Many preachers, such as Reverend W. J. Winston of

---

[12] Homer H. Hyde, "By Their Fruits Ye Shall Know Them," *American Mercury* 94/459–461 (Summer 1962): 35–36; Homer H. Hyde, "By Their Fruits Ye Shall Know Them," *American Mercury* 94/462 (August 1962): 22; David L. Chappell, "The Divided Mind of the Southern Segregationists," *Georgia Historical Quarterly* 82/1 (Spring 1998): 50; Henry Clark, "Churchmen and Residential Desegregation," *Review of Religious Research* 5/3 (Spring 1964): 158, 161–62; Gunnar Myrdal, *An American Dilemma: The Negro Problem and Modern Democracy*, twentieth anniversary ed. (New York: Harper & Row, 1962) lxxii; Ernest Q. Campbell, "Moral Discomfort and Racial Segregation—An Example of the Myrdal Hypothesis," *Social Forces* 39/3 (March 1961): 228–29; Knight, "The NCC's Delta Project," 8.

[13] Chappell, "Religious Ideas of the Segregationists," 240, 251; S. Jonathan Bass, ed., "A Documentary Edition of the 'Letter from Birmingham Jail'," in *Blessed Are the Peacemakers: Martin Luther King Jr., Eight White Religious Leaders, and the "Letter from Birmingham Jail"* (Baton Rouge: Louisiana State University Press, 2001) 251; Andrew Michael Manis, *Black and White Baptists and Civil Rights, 1947–1957* (Athens: The University of Georgia Press, 1987) 106.

Baltimore's New Metropolitan Baptist Church, continued to support doctrines of patience, focusing their calls on heavenly equality and divine justice. Activist black theology, however, argued that equality could probably be attained on Earth and that the unequal sector of society had a duty to fight for that equality. More reticent ministers responded by claiming that activist preachers in protests and jails did more harm to religious institutions than good. Martin Luther King, Jr., however, proved that ministers could make a successful transition into political activism, and that political issues could be cast in a moral and religious light. "First and foremost we are American citizens, and we are determined to apply our citizenship to the fullness of its means," said King in his first major civil rights address, delivered in December 1955, at Montgomery's Holt Street Baptist Church. As the oratory evolved and the speech progressed, King's message began to shift. "I want it to be known throughout Montgomery and throughout this nation that we are a Christian people," said King. "We believe in the teachings of Jesus. The only weapon we have in our hands this evening is the weapon of protest." King moved focus from legality to conscience. Of course, a declaration of principles by a minister did not necessarily come with a requirement that his congregation agree with him. African-American churchgoers responded by making decisions influenced by the clergy, but not solely with their mandate.[14]

"Any religion," argued King in 1958, "that professes to be concerned with the souls of men and is not concerned with the slums that damn them, the economic conditions that strangle them, and the social conditions that cripple them is a dry-as-dust religion." Liberation, in King's view, could only be achieved through suffering. "Unmerited suffering," wrote King in 1958, "is redemptive." Suffering would not only lead to black equality, subsequently erasing the inherent inferiority complex present in a dispossessed

---

[14] David Milobsky, "Power from the Pulpit: Baltimore's African-American Clergy, 1950–1970," *Maryland Historical Magazine* 89/3 (Fall 1994): 279–81; Joseph L. Scott, "Social Class Factors Underlying the Civil Rights Movement," *Phylon* 27/2 (second quarter 1966): 140. Also see the chart on page 140; Martin Luther King, Jr., "Speech by Martin Luther King, Jr., at Holt Street Baptist Church," in *The Eyes on the Prize Civil Rights Reader: Documents, Speeches, and Firsthand Accounts from the Black Freedom Struggle, 1954–1990*, ed. Clayborne Carson, David J. Garrow, Gerald Hill, Vincent Harding, and Darlene Clark Hine (New York: Penguin Books, 1991) 48–49.

people, but it would attack the conscience of the white populace. King understood the necessity of self-respect often promoted by the black power movement, but maintained that bitterness only begat bitterness and would lead to unnecessary confrontation rather than to beneficial negotiation.[15]

The 1956 Religious Emphasis Week, an annual University of Mississippi event that featured speakers on religious topics from throughout the nation, uninvited Alvin Kershaw after the preacher at a separate function noted his support for the NAACP and for the principle of desegregation. The lack of pluralism in Mississippi created a closed society that required religious organizations and representatives to accept, if not openly endorse, segregation. The crisis generated many editorials from local newspapers, reprinted in the Jackson *Clarion-Ledger*, arguing that only truly Christian ministers merited a place on the dais at Religious Emphasis Week and that such ministers understood segregation was the product of biblical mandate. One such editorial urged that only ministers "who know that segregation is of God" should be invited to the annual program, while another editorial compared inviting NAACP supporters to Ole Miss to "coddling a viper in your own bosom." Morton King, Jr., chair of the Ole Miss Sociology and Anthropology Department, resigned in protest, and Duncan Gray, Jr., an Episcopal reverend in Oxford, acknowledged that silent religious communities were playing a role in propagating segregationist policy. Interpreting a direct threat, Ole Miss never held Religious Emphasis Week again.[16]

Two years prior, in 1954, the Supreme Court desegregated America's schools with its *Brown vs. Board of Education* decision, and the Southern Baptist Convention responded with a recognition of the "Christian principles of equal justice and love for all men," along with a declaration of tacit support. Vigorous debate and much opposition ensued, and the majority of

---

[15] Martin Luther King, Jr., *Stride Toward Freedom: The Montgomery Story* (New York: Harper & Row, 1958) 28; William Augustus Banner, "An Ethical Basis for Racial Understanding," *Religious Education* 59/1 (January–February 1964): 18; Marc H. Tanenbaum, "The American Negro: Myths and Realities," *Religious Education* 59/1 (January–February 1964): 34.

[16] Eagles, "The Closing of Mississippi Society," 348; Ernest M. Limbo, "Religion and the Closed Society: Religious Emphasis Week, 1956, at the University of Mississippi," *Journal of Mississippi History* 64/1 (Spring 2002): 2, 10, 15; Silver, "Mississippi: The Closed Society," 3, 7, 32.

letters-to-the-editor in the various state Baptist newspapers, such as the *Alabama Baptist* and the *Mississippi Baptist,* clearly described a local Christianity that did not recognize that legal decision as legitimate. The 1954 Georgia Baptist Convention adopted a resolution endorsing the necessity of peace and a generic form of justice, but only after an extended floor fight. The year of the *Brown* decision also witnessed the Southern branch of the Presbyterian Church and its Northern counterpart fail in an attempted merger. Racial politics hovered over the stalled negotiations. The debates over segregation never congealed into one unified defense or damnation of the practice. In the face of an active black religious community arguing desperately that the Bible mandated equality, white Southern denominations reacted with either combative hyperbole or deafening silence.[17]

The white Southern churches, as institutions, attempted to balance a devotion to principles and a budget that required local contributions. In the end, the financial perpetuation of the physical organization won the day. Of course, formal segregation of Southern Protestant churches was never enacted because there was no need for it. Each congregation was unrecognizable to the other. Segregation in housing only exacerbated the segregation in churches, because church attendance normally revolved around neighborhoods and social circles. Residential patterns formed not only along color lines, but, as a 1961 Canadian study demonstrated, along religious lines within that broader color category. Churches formed in neighborhoods, from groups of like-minded believers who sustained the church's existence through attendance and financial support. White Southern ministers often turned from civil rights activism due to job security concerns, or they abandoned their pulpits in the face of a congregation hostile to integration. White civil rights activist Will Campbell quit his job

[17] Manis, "Dying From the Neck Up," 2; David M. Reimers, "The Race Problem and Presbyterian Union," *Church History* 31/2 (June 1962): 203; Benton Johnson, "Do Holiness Sects Socialize in Dominant Values?" *Social Forces* 39/4 (May 1961): 309–10; Joseph A. Tomberlin, "Florida Whites and the *Brown* Decision of 1954," *Florida Historical Quarterly* 51/1 (July 1972): 31; Chappell, "The Divided Mind of Southern Segregationists," 47–48.

as pastor of the Taylor Baptist Church in Taylor, Louisiana, in 1954, when faced with a congregation vehemently opposed to integration.[18]

During the 1957 crisis over the desegregation of Central High School in Little Rock, Arkansas, local Protestant preachers acknowledged the right of Christians to disagree over the policy of integration, and those ministers also made public pleas for prayer. "Good Christians can honestly disagree on the question of segregation and integration," said one participant in a community-wide prayer service held in response to the Little Rock crisis. "But we can all join together in prayers for guidance, that peace may return to our city." In April 1961, the Southern Baptist Theological Seminary in Louisville, Kentucky, invited Martin Luther King, Jr., to speak. Many churches throughout the South publicly disagreed with the seminary's actions, the loudest denunciations emanating from Alabama. Later, following the bombing of the Sixteenth Street Baptist Church in Birmingham, Alabama, on September 15, 1963, the Southern Baptist Convention's Executive Committee proposed a sympathy resolution encouraging Christian unity, but the Convention's participants soundly defeated the measure. The politics of endorsing such a proposal were simply untenable. Each convention member represented a white congregation, most in the South, and for many of those congregants back home, an activist black

[18] The historical social situation of Southern whites and blacks necessarily influenced the tendency of social reticence from white congregations and social activism from their black counterparts. Church segregation originally manifested itself through social mores, but as the twentieth century progressed, both white and black congregants began to recognize value in the operation of an independent religious body that offered the opportunity for free expression and a "home base" for organization and community activities. Glenn, "Negro Religion and Negro Status in the United States," 630; Hill, "Southern Protestantism and Racial Integration," 423; Ernest Q. Campbell and Thomas Pettigrew, "Racial and Moral Crisis: The Role of Little Rock Ministers," *American Journal of Sociology* 64/5 (March 1959): 509; David M. Reimers, *White Protestantism and the Negro* (New York: Oxford University Press, 1965) 158; James Reston, "The Churches, the Synagogues, and the March on Washington," *Religious Education* 59/1 (January–February 1964): 5; Fichter, "American Religion and the Negro," 1087, 1089; Thomas F. Pettigrew, "Wherein the Church Has Failed in Race," *Religious Education* 59/1 (January–February 1964): 64, 72–73; Liston Pope, "The Negro and Religion in America," *Review of Religious Research* 5/3 (Spring 1964): 148, 149; Peter Smith, "Anglo-American Religion and Hegemonic Change in the World System, c. 1870–1980," *The British Journal of Sociology* 37/1 (March 1986): 99; Roland Gammon, "Why Are We Changing Our Churches?" *American Mercury* 86/412 (May 1958): 66; Gordon Darrock and Wilfred Marston, "Ethnic Differentiation: Ecological Aspects of a Multidimensional Concept," *International Migration Review* 4/1 (Autumn 1969): 79, 80, 90; Mark Newman, "Southern Baptists and Desegregation, 1945–1980," in *Southern Landscapes*, ed. Tony Badger, Walter Edgar, and Jan Nordby Gretlund (Tübingen: Stauffenburg-Verlag, 1996) 186, 188–89.

church like Sixteenth Street was practicing something that they could no longer recognize as viable religion.[19]

After the 1968 assassination of Martin Luther King, Jr., the Southern Baptist Convention's Executive Committee drafted a "Statement Concerning the National Crisis," which, in part, acknowledged "our share of the responsibility" for the creation of the hostile environment that fostered the murder. No states in the Deep South reaffirmed the "Statement." Black churches were able to use the incident to draw the black community in and mitigate prior differences among factions and groups, whereas white church membership fluctuated throughout the period as the different sects continued to waffle on support or denial of segregation. This phenomenon led to a fundamental inability among white churches to muster support equal to their black counterparts, sustaining the devotional divide between the competing versions of religion and religious purpose.[20]

A study by the National Opinion Research Center published in 1954 indicated that white support for integration generally hovered between 40 and 50 percent, with younger adults (aged 21 to 24) revealing the greatest acceptance of the practice and the elderly (age 65 and older) exhibiting the least. When support for integration was divided regionally, however, the results indicated no white Southern response rate above 20 percent. New findings by the National Opinion Research Center ten years later demonstrated an increase in both Northern and Southern support for integration, with Southern numbers reaching as high as 35 percent approval in the 25 to 45-year age range.[21] Progress, it seemed, was slow but evident. An analysis of the findings of that organization and of a series of corresponding Gallup Polls by sociologist Paul Sheatsley demonstrated that, as of 1963, a younger generation of whites, whose formative years had witnessed *Brown*

---

[19] Campbell and Pettigrew, "Racial and Moral Crisis," 510–11; Mark Newman, "The Arkansas Baptist State Convention and Desegregation, 1954–1968," *Arkansas Historical Quarterly* 56/3 (Autumn 1997): 300–301; Bill J. Leonard, "A Theology for Racism: Southern Fundamentalists and the Civil Rights Movement," in *Southern Landscapes* (Tübingen: Stauffenburg-Verlag, 1996) 168; Fichter, "American Religion and the Negro," 1089; Manis, "Dying From the Neck Up," 5.

[20] Manis, "Dying From the Neck Up," 5–6; Milbosky, "Power from the Pulpit," 285; Chappell, "Religious Ideas of the Segregationists," 259.

[21] Herbert Hyman and Paul Sheatsley, "Attitudes Toward Desegregation," *Scientific American* 195/6 (December 1956): 38; Herbert Hyman and Paul Sheatsley, "Attitudes Toward Desegregation," *Scientific American* 211/1 (July 1964): 23.

and its aftermath, comprised the majority of white civil rights proponents in the South. A growing media in the 1950s and 1960s ensured that civil rights gains and losses would reach a wide scope of the population, offering each American the opportunity to evaluate the merits of segregation and integration arguments on his/her own. In essence, the white newspapers accomplished what the white churches could not—or would not.[22]

Nancy Tatom Ammerman noted that many church membership lists dropped significantly during the Civil Rights Movement because of dissension among congregants and clergy. Some church members accepted that the movement as a viable religious action, while others saw traditional Southern religion as clear in advancing integration. White Southerners tried to squeeze everything possible from the old Southern civil religion, while black Southerners attempted to create a new civil religion within the black community to rally and organize adherents. Accordingly, both religions dictated acceptable feelings and behavior to congregants increasingly wary of the religion being practiced on the other side of the railroad tracks.[23] When one group did not recognize the values infusing an otherwise familiar biblical source as used by another group, the exchange was not unlike a believer's encounter with a non-believer. Each value system was unrecognizable to the other, yet the coexistence of the two groups in the South posed a fundamental threat to the existence of both. No biblical analysis would ever allow the activist, equalitarian relativism of, say, Martin Luther King, Jr., to accept that, "God wanted white people to live alone."

[22] Sheatsley, "White Attitudes Toward the Negro," 223. Also see the tables on pages 222 and 224; Ammerman, "The Civil Rights Movement and the Clergy in a Southern Community," 339.

[23] Ammerman, "The Civil Rights Movement and the Clergy in a Southern Community," 339–40; Fichter, "American Religion and the Negro," 1086.

Emmitt Till (after all these years)

BY JAMES E. CHERRY

After fifty years, Bobo,* you aint dead yet. You'd be mid
sixties by now gone through that mid-life thang, receding
hairline or any hair at all, prosperous paunch from ex-
cessive pounds or the saccharin of success and kids, maybe
even grandkids bouncing upon your knee by now.

Can you believe it? After all these years ever since being
dragged from Uncle Mose's place before daybreak, beaten,
shot, tied to a gin fan and buried in the muddy bosom of
the Tallahatchie, you won't leave these white folk alone, a
ghost hovering over the consciousness of America.

Now, they want to re-open a case with lukewarm leads looking
for accomplices of Bryant and Milam, hoping they'll be black
and that they'll be able to bury you once and for all. You should've
kept your ass on that train, enjoyed the lushness of crops ready
for harvest or cotton fields like small clouds coming out
of the earth, or read your favorite book until you fell asleep between
its pages; the Pullman porters would have had your back. Or
better yet, played stickball in the streets of Chicago where fire
hydrants are used to cool the swelter of summer days and it
is no crime to whistle at pretty brown-skinned girls or play a
game of hide-and-go-get-it when sunset covers everything in shadow.

But hey, a Northern lynching is the same as a Mississippi one: robes and hoods exchanged for suits and ties behind institutional walls. So there's not much difference between 1955 and 2005,
a short journey between pain and remembrance.

I guess it really would not have mattered at all.
Eventually, they would have got you.
It just happened sooner than later.

*Till's nickname

Cultural Conservation: The Influence of the Irish Literary Revival on the Harlem Renaissance

BY MAUREEN E. TORPEY

As Tracy Mishkin claims in her book *The Irish and Harlem Renaissances*, art is "created often at the intersection of two or more cultures."[1] The preservation, or perhaps the recreation, of cultural identity was a primary theme of both the Irish Literary Revival and the Harlem Renaissance. Although critics cite different dates for the beginning and end of each of these literary movements, they are roughly, the 1880s to the 1920s for the Irish Literary Revival and the 1910s to 1930 for the Harlem Renaissance. Both literary movements arose from cultures in crisis, from cultures in danger of decline or disappearance. In Ireland around the turn of the twentieth century, the Irish culture was in danger of being lost completely after so many years of repression by the ruling English. Even the Irish language had slipped into obscurity and was coming close to being forgotten entirely. In the United States, by the 1920s, the New Negro Movement was in full swing, especially in the Northern cities. Many African Americans were caught up in the fervor of migrations to the North, forgetting or neglecting their Southern and African roots. Several writers in both Harlem and Ireland saw the need to reclaim their respective cultures. Zora Neale

---

[1] Tracy Miskin, *The Harlem and Irish Renaissances: Language, Identity and Representation* (Gainesville: University Press of Florida, 1998) ix.

Hurston, following the path laid by Lady Augusta Gregory and the writers of the Irish Literary Revival, sought to revive her Southern roots by engaging the mythology and language of her culture in her writing.

In *Fables of Identity*, literary critic Northrop Frye asks, "Why did the term [myth] ever get into literary criticism? There can only be one answer to such a question: because myth is and always has been an integral element of literature, the interest of poets in myth and mythology having been remarkable since Homer's time."[2] Frye argues that every civilization has a stockpile of folklore, including myths that are considered "more serious, more authoritative, more educational, and closer to fact and truth than the rest."[3] These myths become the canon of that civilization, and are used by parents as well as by the ruling classes to teach the morals, lessons, and values of the culture. Within the given cultural context, all of the surface aspects of the myth immediately gain a deeper meaning. Myths become central to the conservation of that culture, since, from childhood, group members are taught the myths as a means of learning the culture's fundamental values. For authors, these myths become the simplest form of literary creation, a framework upon which to build their writings. Frye claims that "Writers are interested in folk tales for the same reason that painters are interested in still-life arrangements: because they illustrate essential principles of storytelling."[4] Thus, the preservation of myth in a given culture's literature is critical to the preservation of that culture itself.

At the time of the Harlem Renaissance, many black traditions in the rural South were disappearing. Reconstruction had not greatly improved life for Southern blacks, who had begun moving to Northern urban centers in large numbers. Fueling that migration was the New Negro Movement (even the title of which implies that there was something wrong with the "old Negro"), which offered encouragement to blacks to leave the South. Another motivation was the stigma attached to Southern rural culture.

[2] Northrop Frye, *Fables of Identity* (New York: Harcourt, Brace and World, 1963) 21.

[3] Northrop Frye, *Anatomy of Criticism* (New York: Antheneum, 1969) 54.

[4] Ibid., 27.

Scholar Theresa R. Love recreates the setting of that era in her essay "Zora Neale Hurston's America," observing that "many blacks denied anything pertaining to blackness. They rejected their dark coloring and kinky hair. They endeavored to make the old Negro spirituals sound like European anthems. They said that black writers should not write about 'low types'...; they warned that Paul Laurence Dunbar's use of black dialect did more harm than good, since it did not present blacks in a 'proper light.'"[5] Dialect, skin color, everything pertaining to Southern black culture had become a source of shame for the new, urban Negro.

The writers of the Harlem Renaissance attempted to alleviate such a sense of shame in different ways. They made an effort to reclaim a usable black culture to shape their cultural identity. Most writers were not wholly prepared to go back to Africa to recover their roots, and, indeed, some writers were too many generations removed to relate to that historical journey; so, as J. Martin Favor claimed, "'Go south, young intellectual; and discover the true meaning of blackness' be[came] a motto of the day."[6] By 1925, a New Negro Theatre was being born, and Zora Neale Hurston saw herself in the position of "chief mid-wife"[7] alongside W. E. B. DuBois and Langston Hughes. The perimeters of that theatre were set by DuBois who said, "It must be: (1) about us, (2) by us, (3) for us, and (4) near us."[8] He also demanded that there be a propagandist theme in every play. Other writers thought DuBois had become snobbish, and, in response, Hughes wrote, "The Negro Artist and the Racial Mountain" for the periodical *The Nation*, the crux of whose argument was:

> We younger skinned Negro artists who create now intend to express our individual dark-skinned selves without fear or shame. If white people are pleased we are glad. If they are not, it doesn't matter. We know we are beautiful. And ugly too. The tom-tom

[5] Theresa R. Love , "Zora Neale Hurston's America," in *Zora Neale Hurston: Modern Critical Views*, ed. Harold Bloom (New York: Chelsea House Publishers, 1986) 48.

[6] J. Martin Favor, *Authentic Blackness: The Folk in the New Negro Renaissance* (Durham: Duke University Press, 1999) 15.

[7] Valerie Boyd, *Wrapped in Rainbows: The Life of Zora Neale Hurston* (New York: Scribner, 2003) 117.

[8] Ibid., 118.

cries and the tom-tom laughs. If colored people are pleased we are glad. If they are not, their displeasure doesn't matter either. We build our temples for tomorrow, strong as we know how, and we stand on top of the mountain, free within ourselves.[9]

Zora Neale Hurston was the embodiment of the ideal Hughes established in this essay. Together and separately, she and Hughes set out on a path to restore respect to the Southern black culture.

In his preface to Hughes's and Hurston's play *Mule Bone: A Comedy of Negro Life*, Henry Louis Gates, Jr., included part of a letter written by Hurston to Hughes in April 1928 concerning her plans for "a culturally authentic African-American theatre"[10] that would be based upon the Southern rural black dialect. In the letter, Hurston asked, "Did I tell you before I left about the new, the *real* Negro theatre I plan? Well, I shall, or rather we shall act out the folk tales, however short, with the abrupt angularity and naivete of the primitive 'bama Nigger. Quote that with native settings. What do you think?"[11] Although it would eventually cause the end of their friendship and was never performed in either of their lifetimes, *Mule Bone* was the result of Hurston's desire for an authentic Negro theatre. That play incorporated Southern black vernacular speech and also featured verbal word play and traditional verbal contests. At the end of the play, Jim and Dave take the courting ritual to a whole new level, and their "one-upping" of each other is reminiscent of the "lying contests" that Hurston encouraged in order to gather material in the South. When Daisy accuses them of being interested in other girls, Jim replies, "Cross my feet and hope to die! I'd ruther see all de other wimmen folks in de worl' dead than for you to have de toothache." Not to be outdone, Dave adds, "If I was dead and any other woman come near my coffin de undertaker would have to do his job all over... 'cause I'd git right up and walk off."[12] In *Mule Bone*,

[9] Langston Hughes, "The Negro Artist and the Racial Mountain," quoted in Boyd, *Wrapped in Rainbows*, 119.

[10] Henry Louis Gates, Jr., "A Tragedy of Negro Life" (preface), Langston Hughes and Zora Neale Hurston, *Mule Bone: A Comedy of Negro Life* (New York: Harper Collins, 1991) 9.

[11] Ibid.

[12] Hughes and Hurston, *Mule Bone*, 146.

Hurston and Hughes captured not only the dialect, but also a strong sense of the richness and value of black culture. As Tracy Mishkin claims, "[Hurston] believed that presenting the intricate verbal play of rural African Americans to white and urban African American audiences would demonstrate that material poverty did not entail a similar cultural state."[13] Furthermore, when Hurston was criticized for her use of dialect in this play as well as in her fiction and folklore collections, her reply was, "I was a Southerner and had the map of Dixie on my tongue."[14] Hurston made the black dialect of her native South an acceptable and necessary voice in literature.

ZORA NEALE HURSTON. Library of Congress, Prints & Photographs Division, Carl Van Vechten Collection, reproduction number, e.g., LC-USZ62-54231.

The play *Mule Bone* was based upon one of the folktales that Hurston collected near her hometown of Eatonville, Florida. Trained in anthropology after winning a scholarship to Barnard College, Hurston had an extensive background in collecting folklore, having studied under leading anthropologist Franz Boas, whose teaching had a lasting effect on Hurston. Trained in the scientific methods of collecting data, Hurston immediately after graduation set off for her home region in Florida, where she was eager to apply her new fieldwork techniques. She stated, "It was only when I was off in college, away from my native surrounding that I could see myself like someone else and stand off and look at my garment. Then I had the spy-glass of Anthropology to look through at that."[15] Hurston was not initially successful in gathering oral lore—partly because her newly acquired Barnard accent alienated her contacts in the field. She returned to the South a few years later, this time under the patronage of Charlotte Mason, the white "Godmother" of many creative artists associ-

[13] Mishkin, *Harlem and Irish Renaissances*, 62.

[14] Boyd, *Wrapped in Rainbows*, 71.

[15] Ibid., 115.

ated with the Harlem Renaissance. Hurston was ecstatic that she was not restricted during this collecting trip by the rules of anthropological collection; she declared, "I want to collect like a new broom."[16] Hurston gathered folk tales from across the South and in Haiti, though she could not publish them under her name until she broke free of Mason's hold.

Hurston finally published some of these stories in 1935, in her first collection of folk tales, *Mules and Men*. In 1934, she wrote to Boas to ask him to write the introduction, fearing he would refuse. In the letter, Hurston explained, "I have inserted the between-story conversation and business because when I offered it without it every publisher said it was too monotonous. Now three houses want to publish it. So I hope that the unscientific matter that must be there for the sake of the average reader will not keep you from writing the introduction."[17] Although *Mules and Men* contained valuable reference material, the "unscientific matter" was what made the folklore accessible to the average reader. In "Hoodoo: Chapter IV," for example, Hurston describes Father Watson, or "Frizzly Rooster," in analogies that most people of her day would understand: "He had the physique of Paul Robeson with the sex appeal and hypnotic what-ever-you-might-call-it of Rasputin. I could see that women would rise to flee from him but in mid-flight would whirl and end shivering at his feet."[18] The folkloric materials were written in a language and style familiar to Hurston's readers. In response to her request, Boas did agree to write the introduction, and even praised Hurston's material and style, thus justifying her "unscientific" technique. As scholar Valerie Boyd writes in her biography *Wrapped in Rainbows*, "Hurston wrote about black folk life from the inside out—as a person who'd been born 'in the crib of negroism.'"[19] By writing as someone who had lived within that traditional culture rather than as a detached observer, Hurston was not aiming to capture an audience of scholars and social scientists, but rather an audience of non-specialists.

---

[16] Ibid., 162.

[17] Carla Kaplan, ed., *Zora Neale Hurston: A Life in Letters* (New York: Doubleday Books, 2002) 308.

[18] Zora Neale Hurston, "Mules and Men," in *Hurston: Folklore, Memoirs, and Other Writings* (New York: Literary Classics, 1995) 202.

[19] Boyd, *Wrapped in Rainbows*, 253.

The idea of gathering myths for a diverse audience and of writing in dialect was not entirely new. That same feat had been attempted in Ireland at the end of the nineteenth century, by Lady Augusta Gregory and the other writers of the Irish Literary Revival. Although no evidence exists to prove that Hurston was influenced directly by Lady Gregory, the Irish National Theatre in fact traveled to New York City as part of a North American tour in the late 1800s. As early as 1852, the black abolitionist Martin R. Delany noted the similarities between Ireland and black America, commenting on their positions as "a nation within a nation."[20] Black Americans could relate to the struggle of the Irish to achieve and maintain a degree of national identity. At the time of the Irish Literary Revival, traditional Irish culture was as endangered as was rural, black culture prior to the Harlem Renaissance. Having been under English rule for centuries, the Irish endured the Great Famine of 1845 to 1848, during which period about one million people died through starvation and disease, and, according to R. F. Foster, editor of *The Oxford History of Ireland*, many Irish emigrated: "[B]y 1847, nearly a quarter of a million were emigrating annually, often comprising the most potentially fertile sector of the population."[21] The population of Ireland was plummeting, and those Irish who remained in Ireland were living under English law. After the many years of repressive English rule and England's suppression of Irish culture, the Irish people began to push for control of their nation. In the political arena, Irish politicians proposed several Home Rule Bills, few of which gathered any support in the British parliament. Despite political suppression of the Irish by the British, a longing for political and cultural autonomy was taking hold in the minds of many Irish citizens (creative artists as well as politicians), and Irish nationalism began to permeate their culture.

[20] Mishkin, *Harlem and Irish Renaissances*, 11.

[21] R. F. Foster, ed., *The Oxford History of Ireland* (Oxford: Oxford University Press, 1989) 167.

Moved by this spirit of nationalism, Lady Gregory and William Butler Yeats applied this nationalist sentiment to theatre and literature. In *Our Irish Theatre*, her recollections of the Irish National Theatre as well as of the Irish Literary Revival, Gregory declares the main purpose of the Irish cultural renaissance: "We will show that Ireland is not the home of buffoonery and of easy sentiment, as it has been represented, but the home of an ancient idealism. We are confident of the support of all Irish people, who are weary of misrepresentation, in carrying out a work that is outside all the political questions that divide us."[22]

LADY AUGUSTA GREGORY.

As Gregory was part of the Anglo-Irish Protestant ruling class, returning to the ancient Irish myths served the purpose of encouraging her contemporaries to embrace the national identity of a pre-sectarian time, thereby unifying the Irish regardless of class and religion. Indeed, myth was the focus of the Irish Literary Revival. It would be treated in such a way as to restore it to a position of significance and dignity, just as Hurston strove to do in her folklore, literature, and drama. DuBois's command that the New Negro Theatre in Harlem be "about us, by us, for us, and near us" echoed the guidelines established by Gregory and Yeats. In order to make myth accessible to the Irish people, Gregory and Yeats proposed "to have performed in Dublin, in the spring of every year certain Celtic and Irish plays which whatever be their degree of excellence will be written with a high ambition, and so to build up a Celtic and Irish school of dramatic literature."[23] Indeed, the many plays based on the history and folklore of Ireland became the driving force of the Irish Literary Revival.

[22] Lady Augusta Gregory, *Our Irish Theatre*, (New York: The Knickerbocker Press, 1914) 9.
[23] Ibid., 8–9.

At the time of the Revival, however, no main text of the myths of Ireland existed. Irish folklore had been relegated to the scholars at Trinity College who were not ready to relinquish their iron grip on that cultural material. Lady Gregory took it upon herself to break open the field. After collecting folklore from the peasants of Sligo, Gregory published two very readable volumes, *Cuchulain of Muirthemne* in 1902 and *Gods and Fighting Men* in 1904. Similar to the letter that Hurston wrote to Boaz in anticipation of criticism for her piecing together of the myths she had gathered in the South, Gregory attempted to rationalize her interpretation of her nation's myths. In *Cuchulain of Muirthemne*, Gregory included a dedication to the people of Kiltartan, from whom she gathered her stories, in which she stated her intentions:

> It is what I have tried to do, to take the best of the stories, or whatever parts of each will fit best to one another, and in that way to give a fair account of Cuchulain's life and death. I have left out a good deal I thought you would not care about for one reason or another, but I put in nothing of my own that could be helped, only a sentence or so now and again to link the different parts together.... And indeed if there was more respect for Irish things among the learned men that live in the college at Dublin, where so many of these old writings are stored, this work would not have been left to a woman of the house.[24]

Despite her preemptive attempts to avoid it, Gregory did suffer much criticism, both for her renditions of the myths and for the fact that she was viewed as unqualified to collect the folklore. Since Gregory was a member of the Protestant ruling class, the peasants from whom she collected stories would not likely have shared the sometimes crude versions of the myths. Thus, unlike Hurston, Gregory did not have the advantage of writing from

---

[24] Lady Augusta Gregory, "Cuchulain of Muirthemne," in *A Treasury of Irish Myth, Legend, and Folklore*, ed. Claire Booss (New York: Grammercy Books, 1986) 332.

an insider's point of view. Also, Gregory had no official training as an anthropologist. Nevertheless, in the absence of writings compiled by those who did have training in folklore studies, Gregory saw a need to put the myths she collected into accessible, non-scholarly volumes.

The results of Lady Gregory's endeavors were the first truly readable English-language translations of Irish myths (those myths were originally told in Gaelic), including the stories of Cuchulain and the warriors of the Red Branch and of Finn MacCool and the Fenians. Upon its publication, *Cuchulain of Muirthemne* was immediately praised by the Anglo-Irish writers involved in the Irish Literary Revival. In his preface to the collection, Yeats said, "I think this book is the best that has ever come out of Ireland; for the stories which it tells are a chief part of Ireland's gift to the imagination of the world—and it tells them perfectly for the first time."[25] John Millington Synge called the book "part of my daily bread."[26] Both Yeats and Synge used *Cuchulain* as the source for their own folk-history plays, which were later performed at the Abbey Theatre.

There were many critics of Lady Gregory's efforts, though Elizabeth Coxhead asserts in her book *Lady Gregory: A Literary Portrait* that Lady Gregory's "aim [was] popularization, not scholarship."[27] More importantly, as Robert Kee notes, "[Gregory's] popularizations of the legends of Cuchulain and other heroes, though they met with the disapproval of some scholars, did much to make available to anyone who might want to adopt it a new Gaelic warrior pride."[28] At a time when the Irish were searching for symbols behind which to unite in their fight for independence, Lady Gregory published a popular version of pre-sectarian, wholly Irish myths told in the Irish dialect of English.

This dialect represented in *Cuchulain of Muirthemne* was another aspect of the book that was both praised and criticized. In the 1700s, the British enforced the Penal Laws under which Catholics were forbidden to buy or

---

[25] Ibid., 333.

[26] Elizabeth Coxhead, *Lady Gregory: A Literary Portrait* (London: Secker and Warburg, 1966) 111.

[27] Ibid., 58.

[28] Robert Kee, *The Green Flag: A History of Irish Nationalism* (London: Penguin Books, 2000) 434.

lease land, to obtain any Catholic education, or to make any written mention of Ireland. As a result, "Catholicism and all the older traditions of Ireland, including the Gaelic language, now coloured poverty with a special identity."[29] The social and economic limitations created an inferior "nation within a nation." Although the various Penal Laws were repealed in 1778 and 1782, the stigma on the Irish language remained, which was passed on to the Irish dialect. Those who spoke in dialect were considered to be "low types," as with rural African Americans in the South. The dialect was part of the caricatured image of the Irishman to whom Lady Gregory and the other writers of the Irish Literary Revival were attempting to restore dignity. By utilizing dialect in her literary retellings of the Irish myths, Lady Gregory sought to reclaim the Irish dialect and to infuse it with the same level of respect with which she was infusing the old myths.

Lady Gregory's use of dialect is most prominent in the final story of *Cuchulain of Muirthemne*, "The Death of Emer." After Cuchulain dies, his wife Emer discovers him, and she pleads with Conall Cearnach to make a grave for the two of them. In syntax that reflects the speech of the native Irish speaker, Lady Gregory wrote,

> she laid herself down beside her gentle comrade, and she put her mouth to his mouth and she said: "Love of my life, my friend, my sweetheart, my one choice of men on earth, many is the woman, wed or unwed, envied me till today: and now I will not stay living after you."
>
> And her life went out from her, and she herself and Cuchulain were lain in one grave by Conall. And he raised one stone over them, and he wrote their names in Ogham, and he himself and all the men of Ulster keened them.[30]

[29] Ibid., 20.

[30] Gregory, "Cuchulain of Muirthemne," in *A Treasury of Irish Myth, Legend, and Folklore*, 693–94.

Lady Gregory received more criticism than praise for her efforts, often being accused of using dialect to make fun of the rural Irish, which was the exact opposite of her original intentions. Needless to say, Lady Gregory had a keen sense of language, though she was not the most qualified folklorist. Sometimes, others accomplished her goals better than she had. Her friend and peer, John Millington Synge, was (and still is) praised for his use of dialect in his play *Playboy of the Western World*, though he himself claimed that his dialect was based upon that of Gregory. Lady Gregory's most important role, therefore, and one not even her staunchest critics can begrudge her, is that she opened the door. She took Irish myths off the academic pedestal and brought them to the people. She made dialect acceptable in literature and in drama. Her work set the stage for writers in both Ireland and in Harlem.

In *The Book of American Negro Poetry* in 1922, James Weldon Johnson made an appeal to African-American writers. He proposed, "What the colored poet in the United States needs to do is something like what Synge did for the Irish; he needs to find a form that will express racial spirit by symbols from within rather than by symbols from without, such as the mere mutilation of English spelling and pronunciation. He needs a form that is freer and larger than dialect, but which will still hold the racial flavor."[31] Hurston rose to this challenge in her literary works. She sought to alleviate the perceived shame of a Southern, rural, African-American background by treating respectfully in her writings Southern dialect and word play. In her folklore collections and fiction, Hurston replaced the stereotypes with a more accurate, and often more entertaining, portrayal of the South. Despite her involvement in the Harlem Renaissance and her numerous publications, Hurston's contributions to her culture were nearly forgotten. Her legacy was revived by Alice Walker. Needing a book on voodoo, Walker had only found books by white writers who dismissed it as silly and superstitious, until she discovered *Mules and Men* and immediately recognized

[31] James Weldon Johnson, *The Book of American Negro Poetry*, quoted in Mishkin, *The Harlem and Irish Renaissances*, 17.

Hurston as a writer who treated the subject with respect. In her essay "Zora Neale Hurston: A Cautionary Tale of a Partisan View," Walker describes introducing *Mules and Men* to her family, who were, as she writes, "Very regular people from the South, rapidly forgetting their southern cultural inheritance in the suburbs and ghettos of Boston and New York, they sat around reading the book themselves, listening to me read the book, listening to each other read the book, and a kind of paradise was regained. For Zora's book gave them back all the stories they had forgotten or of which they had grown ashamed…and showed them how marvelous, and, indeed, priceless they are."[32] Walker's description of the effect of *Mules and Men* on her family is exactly the effect Hurston sought to achieve. Through the use of folklore and dialect, her book restored dignity to the culture and the past of Southern African Americans and returned the stories to the people.

The efforts of Lady Augusta Gregory and Zora Neale Hurston in their respective literary movements have been criticized over the years, and have only recently begun to be widely appreciated. Despite all criticism, these two women served as conservers for their respective cultures. Both recognized the importance of preserving the myth and dialect of their people in order to help reestablish their cultural identity. Northrop Frye envisioned myth as the core of all great literature and culture. Hurston saw that the myths of her culture were being forgotten and, following in the footsteps of Gregory, gathered those myths into collections for the average reader. These collections then served as sources for works in all genres by herself and by other writers. The trend of using folklore—of examining that space where cultures collide and intersect—has continued to this day in both African-American and Irish literature. By using "literature as a means of social change,"[33] by treating the myth and dialect of each of their cultures with respect, Lady Gregory and Hurston removed the stigma from rural Irish and Southern culture and thus regained "a kind of paradise" for their people.

---

[32]Alice Walker, *In Search of Our Mothers' Gardens* (Orlando: Harvest, 1983) 84–85.
[33]Mishkin, *Harlem and Irish Renaissances*, 46.

Celticity in the Old South

BY MICHAEL NEWTON

Thistle & Shamrock is one of the best-loved syndicated radio programs in the US. Having expanded from its original base in Charlotte, North Carolina, to over 350 radio stations all over the United States, *Thistle & Shamrock* broadcasts weekly music popularly understood to be "Celtic," from Irish fiddle tunes, to Scottish bagpipe music, to traditional ballads. That program's appealing vision of Celticity is both traditional and contemporary, rooted in old Europe but extending into North America and beyond. This unifying musical theme of Celticity, with many regional variations, plays very well with an audience that is searching for "authentic" folk culture, both exotic and familiar.

The rise of interest in "Celtic music" parallels a recent trend among many white Americans who identify themselves as Celtic. Today, Celtic festivals and "Highland Games" are held across the nation on nearly every weekend of the year, with local Irish pubs and Celtic heritage organizations scattered widely in major cities. Perhaps nowhere else in the United States is the allure of Celtic heritage more tempting, and more potentially dangerous, than in the South.

Upon its publication in 1988, the flawed but influential book *Cracker Culture* by Grady McWhiney called for the reclamation of the lost Celtic heritage of the American South: "What is most remarkable about the Old South's predominant culture, which I call Cracker culture, is how closely it resembled traditional Celtic culture," wrote McWhiney.[1] Although the

[1] Grady McWhiney, *Cracker Culture: Celtic Ways in the Old South* (Tuscaloosa: The University of Alabama Press, 1988) xiv.

unsound premises of the "Celtic South" hypothesis have been exposed in academic journals,[2] echoes of its assertions of Southern Celticity, sometimes amplified and accentuated, have since made their way into popular rhetoric. James Webb's popular 2004 book *Born Fighting* claims of Appalachia, "Mountain culture was Celtic culture."[3]

Most of this ethnic reinvention is relatively harmless, but some of those grasping at the Celtic label clearly have a racist agenda: by making an erroneous equation between Celticity and whiteness, such people are attempting to root their ethnic origin myth in a culture that has recently seen a boom of public approval. The website of the League of the South, for example, alleges that the Anglo-Celtic foundations of the South have come under pressure from less deserving ethnic rivals:

> The League of the South champions without apology the traditional core Southern culture that has defined the national character of Dixie for generations. That dominant culture was historically handed down to us by the Anglo-Celtic peoples of the British Isles who settled the South and formed its original political community. Over the centuries, our culture has been enriched in subtle ways by the influences of other non-dominant, cultural groups, particularly by black Southerners and the French-speaking Cajuns of Louisiana, but at its essense [sic], the South has always remained a predominantly Anglo-Celtic civilisation.
>
> Unfortunately, in these politically-correct times, open season has been declared on Anglo-Celtic Southern culture while, iron-

[2] Particularly Rowland Berthoff, "Celtic Mist over the South," *The Journal of Southern History* 52/4 (November 1986): 523–50.

[3] James Webb, *Born Fighting: How the Scots-Irish Shaped America* (New York: Broadway Books, 2004) 168.

ically, other minority ethnic subcultures of the South are universally celebrated and advanced as a matter of public policy. The League stands at odds with an elitist zeitgeist that coldly seeks to condemn the traditional South to a sentence of cultural genocide.[4]

The term "Celtic" is useful to modern scholars in identifying a language family and a broad set of shared cultural features traceable in the literature and law of Celtic-speaking peoples, but the term "Anglo-Celtic" is an oxymoron. Any trained researcher would no doubt be baffled as to the definition of a supposed "Anglo-Celtic civilization." Researchers might also wonder why African contributions to the South—such as the banjo or gumbo—do not qualify as elements of the "traditional core Southern culture."

It is not surprising that, in recent years, scholars have reappraised the term "Celtic." Until very recently, it was a label applied by outsiders (Greeks, Romans, Classicists, English, etc.) in reference to various peoples who did not necessarily think that they had anything particularly significant in common with one another. There is no evidence that the early Celtic-speaking immigrant communities in America identified themselves collectively as Celts. The uses and misuses of this ethnonym at present are so vexing that Celto-skeptics have suggested banning the term altogether.[5]

Granted the numerous problems of definition and continuity within the modern reinterpretations of Celticity in the US, the Old South (along with the rest of mainstream America) adamantly rejected any identification with the Celts. During the nineteenth and early twentieth centuries, there was little dispute that race was a biological reality that historically formed the basis of a wide range of personal experience, including politics, art, and personal character. What was open for debate was exactly how to define and

[4] http://www.leagueofthesouth.org, accessed June 2005. The website has since been revised, however, and this text is no longer available.

[5] Ruth and Vincent Megaw, "Celtic Connections Past and Present: Celtic Ethnicity Ancient and Modern," in *Celtic Connections: Proceedings of the Tenth International Congress of Celtic Studies*, ed. Ronald Black, William Gillies, and Roibeard Ó Maolalaigh (East Linton: Tuckwell Press, 1999).

identify specific races and how to employ race in the interpretation of history. Regardless of specific classification schemes or historiographic renderings, in American discourse the apex of the grand "race" narrative was reserved for the Anglo-Saxon.

Exactly how the Celt fit into these narratives of race was less clear: social and political contexts certainly influenced the depiction of Irish, Scottish, Welsh, Breton, Manx, and Cornish peoples (when American writers bothered to mention them at all). Whether texts silently elided the presence of Celts in the New World or allowed for their assimilation into the variously named British, European, Caucasian, or white race, there is ample evidence for continued prejudice against Celtic peoples. White Southerners, no less than other white Americans, preferred to think of themselves as Anglo-Saxons and Southern texts continued to reflect the anti-Celtic biases across the United States through at least the mid-twentieth centrury.

If history offered any lesson to Americans about race, it was that civilization required constant vigilance among elite groups lest the general population bring about their downfall. Narratives centered on the Roman Empire or the Anglo-Saxons became popular parables about progress, and in many such narratives it was the Celt who played the adversary. According to such a notion, the Celt had to be repressed, just as the African and Native American had to be repressed, for the good of civilization. America's shining beacon of Anglo-Saxon liberty could fulfill its racial responsibility by repeating the historical patterns of conquest and colonization. In an 1855 history text, for instance, Thomas Thorpe wrote:

> The heading of this chapter intimates that the Anglo-Saxon is the only race capable of sustaining freedom. We base that opinion on the facts we have adduced, and on the additional one, that America is the only country in the world that has sustained institutions perfectly free.
>
> The history of the Anglo-Saxon race affords abundant material for the reflective mind. It exhibits in an unusual degree the

HARPER'S WEEKLY.
A JOURNAL OF CIVILIZATION
SOUTH
NORTH
BLACK
WHITE

The Iberians are believed to have been originally an African race, who thousands of years ago spread themselves through Spain over Western Europe. Their remains are found in the barrows, or burying places, in sundry parts of these countries. The skulls are of low, prognathous type. They came to Ireland, and mixed with the natives of the South and West, who themselves are supposed to have been of low type and descendants of savages of the Stone Age, who, in consequence of isolation from the rest of the world, had never been out-competed in the healthy struggle of life, and thus made way, according to the laws of nature, for superior races.

> fact that the national characteristics of a race do not change. [...] But the truth is, the Anglo-Saxons never settled among the Celtæ—as the Franks among the Gauls—but drove them out, and receiving continued accessions of their countrymen from the shores of the Baltic and adjacent islands, repeopled the conquered territory.[6]

Such a position held that the rationality and masculinity of Anglo-Saxons made them fit for governance, while the Celts were marginalized due to their supposed emotionality and femininity. The entry about the Celts in the *Cyclopædia of Political Science, Political Economy, and the Political History of the United States* (1899) reflects a belief in the irrational Celt:

> The Celtic race, which formerly occupied all of Gaul and Great Britain, and a great part of the territories of Belgium and Helvetia, can not now be found anywhere in a pure state except in Armorica, or French Brittany, in Wales, in Scotland, particularly in the Highlands, in the Shetland and Hebrides islands, and finally, in Ireland. The domain of this valiant, imaginative, sensitive and adventurous race, once so extensive, is now reduced to this mere remnant of territory. The Celts are the most interesting and unfortunate of all the barbaric races. Their conquerors, exasperated by their stubborn resistance, never spared them, but always pitilessly tracked them, and exterminated them without mercy. This race owes its cruel destiny in part to its very qualities: its extreme sensitiveness often turned into harmful rage, imprudent, hasty hatred, and capricious sallies of contempt, while it on the other hand, easily engendered despair, discouragement and silent melancholy. This sensibility explains why the

[6] Thomas Thorpe, *A voice to America; or, The model republic, its glory, or its fall* (New York: Edward Walker, 1855) 89–90.

Celts have never been able, despite their valor, to preserve their independence, and why, after having lost it, they have never been able to cause their masters to bid them welcome, or to make their subjection the starting point of a new destiny. Conquered races have been known to govern their conquerors, like the Greeks, or to use the masters which fate had given them, like the Italians generally; but the Celts have never been capable of such miracles. The Celt does not know how to control his emotions.[7]

That such an interpretation of history was also incorporated into the debates about the extent to which African Americans should be granted political and social concessions is clear in various nineteenth- and early twentieth-century texts, such as the 1901 book *The American Negro: What He Was, What He Is, and What He May Become: A Critical and Practical Discussion,* which makes an explicit parallel between Africans and Celts: "What are the negro's qualifications for such leadership as a movement of this sort implies? It is an observed fact that negro and Celtic leadership is susceptible to the weakness of ungovernable desire; that both acknowledge but slight amenability to wholesome restraint; and that, in the case of each, inconsiderate zeal has wrought irreparable injury to the race which it represents."[8]

The alleged similarities between the two races in terms of mental propensities reflected that era's positioning of races on the evolutionary ladder. For some scholars, such as Samuel George Morton in an 1854 article, the distance between Anglo-Saxon and Celt was greater than that between Celt and African: "This affinity, however, is not so close between all races—the blacks and whites, for example—as to enable them to amalgamate perfectly. Dr. Nott maintains that mulattoes partake, to some extent, of the nature of hybrids, especially when one of the parents is an Anglo-Saxon, that race being further removed in its affinities from the negro, than the Celtic or Iberian stock."[9]

---

[7] John Lalor, ed., *Cyclopædia of Political Science, Political Economy, and the Political History of the United States by the Best American and European Writers* (New York: Maynard, Merrill, and Co., 1899) section 3.116.18.

[8] William Hannibal Thomas, *The American Negro: What He Was, What He Is, and What He May Become: A Critical and Practical Discussion* (New York: The Macmillan Company, 1901) 336.

Political and social privilege was seen as the natural result of inherent racial qualifications. The dominance of the Anglo-Saxon within the American social hierarchy was the result of a "natural selection" of nations that endowed him with superior faculties. This is evident, for example, in the 1905 booklet *Natural Selection and the Race Problem*, which was reprinted from the *Charlotte Medical Journal* of Charlotte, North Carolina:

> With the many barriers to development which nature had placed in the way the Anglo-Saxons contended successfully. Of their struggles with other races I will quote from Major Robert Bingham:
>
> > "They touched the Celt, and in a hundred years there were no Celts except in the mountains of Wales and in the mountains of Scotland. The Norman touched them, and the Norman was absorbed and his identity disappeared. They came in contact with the Red man in America; and, as the Celt vanished away at the touch of the barbarian Angles and Saxons, so the Red man vanished away at the touch of their descendants, the civilized Anglo-Americans. This same man touched the Frenchman from the mouth of the St. Lawrence to the mouth of the Mississippi, and the Frenchman's power in that vast region is with last year's snow, and what was once French America is now the heart of Anglo-American civilization and power. The yellow man touched the Anglo-American and has been excluded more by the unwritten written law of race hostility and race antagonism than by any formal acts of Congress. And the Anglo-American has just touched

[9] Samuel George Morton, "On the Unity of the Human Race," *The Southern Quarterly Review* 10/20 (October 1854) 292.

> the Spaniard and the Spaniard has vanished from this hemisphere."[10]

White privilege in America was secured with hard-line racial solidarity in the name of, and under the auspices of, the Anglo-Saxon, despite the plurality of ethnic origins behind the biological facade. Neglect toward the other cultural influences upon American culture can be seen, for example, in the Cape Fear Valley of North Carolina, which in the eighteenth century was the largest settlement of Scottish Gaels outside of Scotland. Pockets of Gaelic survived in the Cape Fear Valley into the late nineteenth century, and descendents of these Gaelic-speaking immigrants came to hold prominent positions in state government and social life. Nonetheless, the 1898 manifesto of the People's Party of North Carolina declared: "Neither this State nor any other State will ever be governed and controlled by any but the Anglo-Saxon race as long as that race shall dwell in it. Powers, both moral and physical, sustain the statement. The moral power is the innate consciousness of superiority on the part of the Anglo-Saxon, which will forever keep him in the ascendancy and a recognition by all other races of that superiority."[11]

The Scotch-Irish, the subject of much ethnic hagiography in the nineteenth century, were of greater numerical significance in the United States than the Scottish Highlanders. The manner in which texts about the Scotch-Irish deal with the relationships between Celtic peoples and Anglophones is an indication of racial stereotypes and attitudes. Most nineteenth- and early twentieth-century writers dealing with Scotch-Irish settlement in America went to great lengths to disclaim any taint of Celtic blood in that population:

> Now, who were, and who are the Scotch-Irish? The common notion is that they are a mongrel breed, partly Scotch and partly Irish; that is, the progeny of a cross between the ancient Scot and

---

[10] Benjamin K. Hays, *Natural Selection and the Race Problem* (Charlotte: The Charlotte Medical Journal, 1905) 6–7.

[11] *People's Party Hand-Book of Facts. Campaign of 1898. State Executive Committee of the People's Party of North Carolina* (Raleigh: Capital Printing Company, Printers and Binders, 1898) 10.

> the ancient Celt or Kelt. This is an entire mistake. Whatever blood may be in the veins of the genuine Scotch-Irishman, one thing is certain, and that is that there is not mingled with it one drop of the blood of the old Irish or Kelt. From time immemorial these two races have been hostile, and much of the time bitterly so.[12]

Such unambiguous hostility to Celtic identity in the past is ironic given the lengths to which many current authors (such as James Webb) go in order to bring the Scotch-Irish into the "Celtic" fold.

Various changes in popular perceptions during the final decades of the twentieth century have caused "Anglo-Saxon" to be displaced by "Celtic" as the ethnonym of choice among many white Americans. Contributing factors include the Nazi tarnishing of the "Germanic idea" and the consolidation of the Celts into the Caucasian category in American society. Before such shifts occurred, however, old England was the primary target of Americans' atavistic yearnings.

European emigrants brought their vibrant folk cultures to America before industrialization and the homogenizing effects of the nation-state caused the virtual extinction of those folk cultures in the Old World. By the early twentieth century, folklorists became aware that rural America, and the South in particular, retained what had long since withered in Western Europe, but in no respect was this inheritance seen as something particularly "Celtic." Indeed, Cecil Sharp—an English folklorist who was also an early collector of Old World ballads in the New World—wrote in his diary of August 13, 1916, while collecting material in the mountains around Asheville, North Carolina, of how very English his subjects were:

> My experiences have been very wonderful so far as the people and their music is concerned. The people are just English of the late eighteenth or early nineteenth century. They speak English,

---

[12] John Dinsmore, *The Scotch-Irish in America* (Chicago: Winona Publishing Company, 1906) 7–8.

> look English, and their manners are old-fashioned English. Heaps of words and expressions they use habitually in ordinary conversation are obsolete, and have been in England a long time. [...] They own their own land, and have done so for three or four generations, so that there is none of the servility which, unhappily, is one of the characteristics of the English peasant. With that praise, I should say that they are just exactly what the English peasant was one hundred or more years ago. They have been so isolated and protected from outside influence that their own music and song have not only been uncorrupted, but also uninfluenced by art music in any way.[13]

While English researchers looked to backwoods sections of the United States for the survival of their vanished traditions, Americans saw themselves as equal partners in Anglo-Saxon self-realization. Throughout the nineteenth and early twentieth centuries, Manifest Destiny supposedly demonstrated the inherent superiority of the Anglo-Saxon on American soil, while the British Empire claimed possession of vast territories upon which the sun never set. It is little wonder, then, that many Americans would want to identify with the racial classification so clearly on the ascendancy. Indeed, as *Cracker Culture* suggests, "Standard histories of the South give no indication that Celts were important in the region."[14]

The American identification with Anglo-Saxon civilization must have discouraged the survival of linguistic and cultural features within immigrant communities that were recognizably Celtic. Native Scots traveling in the US remarked that the immigrant community of the Cape Fear became effectively assimilated by their Anglophone neighbors. Rev. David Macrae visited that area just after the American Civil War and recorded with surprise that "Highland songs and dances were once common; but 'Dixie's Land' is better known now than the pibroch."[15] The Reverend John C.

---

[13] Quoted in Michael Yates, "Cecil Sharp in America: Collecting in the Appalachians," *Musical Traditions* http://www.mustrad.org.uk/articles/sharp.htm, accessed July 2005.

[14] McWhiney, *Cracker Culture*, 3.

[15] David MacRae, *The Americans at Home* (New York: Dutton, 1952) 254.

Sinclair, a Gaelic-speaking minister in the Cape Fear, announced as early as 1872: "The old race is gone and their descendents have given up, in a great degree, the customs and manners of the old Gaels. The ancient Celtic language is nearly dead, except with the few families who arrived within the last thirty years."[16]

Identity is a dynamic phenomenon that often has more to do with perception than with the actual constituent cultural elements. A culture might mask or deny influences from outside sources, an attitude that mainstream American society has long taken regarding African- and Native-American cultural influences. It is an uncontestable fact that settlements of Celtic-speakers did exist in the South, even if they were minorities. Still, persistent Celtic elements in Southern culture cannot be taken for granted or assumed to be self-evident. Making any realistic appraisal will require a much more concerted and critical approach than has been attempted to date, requiring the efforts of scholars specializing in the distinctive cultures of the several Celtic groups that settled in the South.

Despite numerous calls for its development, the field of Celtic Studies has been largely neglected in American academia, especially in the analysis of American culture and history. Some critics of such an endeavor might think that that field would only extend white privilege in higher education, but that would be to misunderstand the critical tools that academia could provide in breaking down racial myths being exploited by racist groups. In the vacuum of intellectual leadership and the lack of an educated public, Celtic identity has been appropriated for purposes that contradict the facts of history. Most people of color in America, in fact, have as much right to claim and celebrate Celtic heritage as "white" people do. The longer that misrepresentations of Celticity are ignored and unchallenged by those best equipped to deconstruct them, the more entrenched those misrepresentations may become in the rhetoric of racial polarization and hatred.

[16] Rev. John C. Sinclair, letter to the editor, *An Gàidheal* 1 (June 1872): 97.

Rebels and Kin: Modern Nationalism in Scotland and the American South

BY ANDREW J. WALTERS

Nationalism is both a cohesive and a divisive force among men and women. When nationalist movements succeed, the victors are hailed as patriots and heroes. However, when such insurrections fail, the losing side is often branded as a band of rebels and traitors. In Scotland as well as in the American South, nationalist movements have emerged and failed, and dire ramifications have resulted in each case from the failure. Nonetheless, in both regions the impetus for nationalism has remained in place, if altered significantly from the initial nature of the movement.

Similar conditions and circumstances characterize nationalist aspirations in Scotland and the South historically as well as today, even though those regions were separated by a great distance. Shared failure and a "lost cause" mentality engendered in both Scotland and the South resulted in an effort to connect the two cultures and to find common cause for their predicaments. Nationalist movements in Scotland and the South have been expressed in similar ways and have shared many commonalities due to the connections held and forged between the two lands.

The failure of the Jacobite Rebellion in 1745 marks the beginning of the modern Scottish nationalist movement. No open warfare or violent rebellion would spring up after 1745 on the scale that would pose a threat to destabilizing the hold of England over Scotland. No great figure such as William Wallace or Robert Bruce would emerge to stir a violent rebellion. After the fall of the Jacobites, Scotland was firmly in the grip of the United Kingdom, which in the wake of the rebellion began a campaign of suppression to eliminate any further organization of nationalist ventures among the Scots. Although defeated militarily, Scotland maintained its distinctive culture and way of life within the greater United Kingdom. Great Britain may have governed Scotland, but London could not control the tenacity and resolve of the Scottish people in refusing to be assimilated.

The denationalization of Scotland that began with the suppression of Scottish ways and symbols during the mid-eighteenth century only expanded by the final decades of that century. The Disarming Acts of 1746 ordered that all weapons throughout Scotland be surrendered. Included in this order was the fact that all bagpipes were proclaimed "weapons of war" by London. The display of clan tartans and the wearing of kilts or "any part whatever of what peculiarly belongs to the Highland garb" was also outlawed. Gaelic was forbidden to be spoken throughout the realm.[1] Beyond the suppression of traditional ways and implements, Scotland suddenly found itself part of a rapidly industrializing state, and the changes brought to England would not remain confined to itself. Traditional Scottish society, particularly the established clan structure, was transformed in order to create a new social system that would be more economically viable and not as easily swayed to revolt.[2] From the Highlands to the Lowlands, Scottish society was fundamentally altered to make Scotland politically and economically suitable for inclusion in Great Britain.

The denationalization that was instituted in Scotland following the failure of the Jacobites can be seen in modern times. Hugh MacDiarmid, the noted twentieth century Scottish poet, related the situation in Scotland to the Soviet Union and the People's Republic of China. He wrote that the Scottish people today know little of their native history and literature.

---

[1] Magnus Magnusson, *Scotland: The Story of a Nation* (New York: Grove Press, 2000) 622–24.

[2] T. M. Devine, *The Scottish Nation: A History*, 1700–2000 (New York: Viking, 1999) 172.

Schools and universities fail to offer studies in native Scottish literature, either historic or modern, and they pay little accord to the native languages, Scots and Gaelic. These cultural elements are usurped by English subjects and only mention Scottish affairs when related to the greater United Kingdom. Further, most of the primary media outlets in Scotland are headquartered in London, including the major newspapers, radio, and television stations.[3] As a result, the elements of a society that help create nationalist sentiment are suppressed and replaced with those of greater British interest. In his writings, MacDiarmid decried the emphasis in Scotland on non-native culture as not only a cultural travesty but also a violation of the stipulations regarding the preservation of native Scottish society in the Treaty of Union of 1707.[4]

Granted the greater importance placed on British culture over native Scottish customs, the Scots have attempted to see past this encroachment on their traditional ways and maintain a cultural identity to perpetuate nationalism within the land. It is often argued that Scotland today, due to a lack of sufficient internal political organization, seeks to find its national identity through the propagation of myths and legends. Scots romanticize figures and events from their past to foster a renewed sense of identity. The struggles of William Wallace and Robert Bruce are embellished to promote the Scots' continued resistance of English encroachment into Scottish society, as are the Jacobite uprisings and the Highland Clearances of the eighteenth century. St. Andrew is elevated as the national saint and is employed to extol the Christian history and virtues of Scotland as being a much older society than that of England.[5] Each of these events and persons are inflated beyond the historical record to produce a mythology by which the people of Scotland can derive a shared history and can foster nationalist spirit.

Perhaps the most exploited myth of Scotland in modern times is the elevation of Highland culture to represent the common way of life across

---

[3] Owen Dudley Edwards, Gwynfor Evans et al., *Celtic Nationalism* (New York: Barnes & Noble, 1968) 343–44.

[4] Edwards, Evans et al., *Celtic Nationalism*, 344.

[5] David McCrone, *Understanding Scotland: The Sociology of a Stateless Nation* (New York: Routledge, 1992) 17–18.

the entire country. The division between the Highlands and Lowlands of Scotland is readily apparent when examined over the course of Scottish history. The Lowlands were located closer to England and thus fell more under the influence of European development, while the Highlands were a region that developed independently from mainstream Scottish culture. In the seventeenth century, the Highlands were seen as a dangerous part of Scotland due to what was perceived as the unstable and uncontrollable nature of its inhabitants, a view that was no doubt reinforced by the rampant participation of Highlanders in the 1715 and 1745 Jacobite uprisings. The subsequent suppression meant that all vestiges of Highland culture were outlawed within Scotland, which ironically meant that the Highland way of life was later adopted to promote a common Scottish identity.[6] Today, when people around the world mention Scotland, immediately conjured are images of bagpipes, kilts, and tartans—cultural components that each find their origins in the Highlands.[7] The most rural and underdeveloped part of Scotland over the course of history, the Highlanders and their culture have often been reviled by Lowlanders as "barbarian, backward, and savage." This historically ridiculed part of Scottish society is now clung to as the "real" Scotland, one untouched by the effects of British hegemony.[8]

The twentieth century brought great change across the globe. One of the most marked transformations was the decline and ultimate loss of the mighty British Empire that had endured for centuries. The spread of national independence movements within that empire did not go unnoticed by the Scots, especially among those who have actively sought to reclaim Scottish nationhood.[9] The years following the Second World War saw a resurgence in nationalist sentiment in Scotland. As after World War I, Scotsmen who had fought for Great Britain, returning home with a new objectivity, questioned what they had fought for and developed a greater

---

[6] Celeste Ray, *Highland Heritage: Scottish Americans in the American South* (Chapel Hill: University of North Carolina Press, 2001) 24.

[7] Devine, *The Scottish Nation*, 231–32.

[8] McCrone, *Understanding Scotland*, 17.

[9] J. M. Reid, *Scotland's Progress: The Survival of a Nation* (London: Eyre & Spottiswoode, 1971) 184–85.

realization of the suppression of native Scottish heritage, which brought about a renewed spirit of nationalism.[10]

In the latter half of the twentieth century, Scotland increasingly diverged politically from Great Britain. The economic turmoil generated after World War II led the Scottish Office, the governing body established by Parliament in 1885 to oversee domestic matters in Scotland, to take a leading role in restructuring the Scottish economy.[11] By the 1980s, the Office had in effect become a "Scottish semi-state" with a bureaucratic apparatus pursuing a Scottish rather than a British agenda. The Scottish Office restored a level of political self-governance in Scotland not known since the Treaty of Union in 1707, and that development served as a rallying cry for Scottish nationalists in taking back political control of their country.[12]

A number of political organizations emerging in Scotland during the twentieth century have been intent upon making independence a reality once again. The most noted and recognized of these organizations, the Scottish National Party (SNP), experienced dramatic growth as a political party over the second half of the twentieth century. Winning its first Parliament seat in 1945, the party exploded to a membership of over 60,000 by the mid-1960s.[13] The SNP succeeded in turning the "cultural meaning" of Scotland into a political issue.[14] By the 1970s, the party became a viable force in competing with the Conservative and Labour parties for Scottish seats.[15] The SNP remains a power in Scottish politics, actively working to secure independence and "bring greater freedom for individuals, families and communities, within a society built on common interests" as outlined in their "Manifesto for Independence."[16]

Other smaller and more radical nationalist groups also exist in Scotland. The 1320 Club, named after the signing-date of the Declaration

---

[10] Edwards, Evans et al., *Celtic Nationalism*, 349.
[11] McCrone, *Understanding Scotland*, 163.
[12] Ibid., 22–23.
[13] Edwards, Evans et al., *Celtic Nationalism*, 355.
[14] McCrone, *Understanding Scotland*, 31.
[15] Ibid., 151.
[16] "Our Manifesto—SNP—Scottish National Party," http://members.snp.org/elections/manifesto/, accessed April 3, 2005).

of Arbroath, is viewed as a potentially militant nationalist group along the lines of those found in Ireland.[17] Hugh MacDiarmid expressed his belief that the movement for Scottish nationalism would take on a more extreme nature in the coming years than that promoted by the SNP.[18] His prediction has proven correct—today, the Free Scotland Party ardently seeks to achieve "a government in Scotland elected by and answerable ONLY to voters in Scotland." The Free Scotland Party vehemently opposes British membership in the European Union, viewing incorporation as yet another step in the wrong direction for Scotland.[19]

In July 1999, for the first time since 1707, a Scottish Parliament convened in Scotland (in Edinburgh). After a heated campaign by both SNP and Labour representatives, the British Parliament voted, with a margin of nearly three-quarters in favor, to return to Scotland much of the power that that nation lost to England after the Treaty of Union.[20] The convening of a new Scottish Parliament marked a prominent victory in the struggle of Scottish nationalists and the promise of a new level of home rule not known for centuries. Despite this victory, Scotland is not totally free from the control of Great Britain. Until complete autonomy and independence is achieved, nationalists will continue to work toward the creation of an independent Scottish nation.

The failure of the Confederate States of America to win its independence during the American Civil War marks the beginning of the modern era of Southern nationalism in the United States. As in Scotland upon the final defeat of the Jacobites, the South after Appomattox was a land physically broken. Nevertheless, the will and resolve of the Southern people was not broken despite the Confederacy's unsuccessful effort to achieve nationhood. Southern nationalism endured after the Civil War and became a powerful societal factor in the creation of the New South. Although the Old South saw its demise as a result of the war and the Southern way of life would

---

[17] Edwards, Evans et al., *Celtic Nationalism*, 304.

[18] Ibid., 357.

[19] "Free Scotland Party," http://www.freescotlandparty.org/, accessed April 3, 2005.

[20] Devine, *The Scottish Nation*, 617.

never be the same as it was, Southerners retained pride in the culture and lifestyle of the South.

Reconstruction was a process by which the South was to be rehabilitated and brought back into the United States. It was meant to ensure that the South would conform to the expectations of the federal government and that sectional tensions would no longer give rise to political or military turmoil. The United States essentially attempted to denationalize the South just as Britain sought to achieve in Scotland. With the death of Abraham Lincoln, however, the task of reconstructing the South fell to weak leadership and political turmoil in Congress that would result in the nation's ultimate failure to eliminate sectional tensions and nationalist outcries.[21] The North prevented the South from militarily exerting self-governance and independence. When Reconstruction was abandoned in 1877, the antagonism between the North and South—because of political, economical, and cultural differences—continued, with Southerners remaining convinced that their way of life was superior.[22] The enmity that Southerners felt for the North demonstrated the supreme failure of Reconstruction—just as the subjugation of Scottish culture in Britain failed.

Perhaps the role in which Reconstruction failed the most dramatically was in dealing with the issue of race in the post-war South. Southerners were forced to confront the fact that those they once held in bondage were now "Southerners" themselves. Although African Americans living in the South were no longer held in chattel slavery, they were subjugated through segregation. The failure of the federal government to prevent such actions further demonstrates the breakdown of Reconstruction and the continuation of race conflicts across the nation.[23]

Southern nationalism in the post-war South was embodied in what would become known as the Myth of the Lost Cause. "The Lost Cause" was first used in reference to Southern history by Edward Pollard, who bor-

---

[21] Francis Butler Simkins, *The South, Old and New* (New York: Alfred A. Knopf, 1948) 175–77.

[22] Dewey W. Grantham, *The South in Modern America: A Region at Odds* (New York: HarperCollins, 1994) 1.

[23] Simkins, *The South, Old and New*, 225–27.

rowed the term from Sir Walter Scott; the latter author had explored in his writings the Lost Cause of Scotland and had echoed the romantic interpretation of history and events employed by the Scots.[24] Put simply, the Myth of the Lost Cause is a memory of the Civil War that is substituted for the factual history of the conflict.[25] The myth is an intricate web of misstatements and misconceptions woven to make the South's defeat in the war an easier reality to accept for the men and women of the vanquished Confederacy. This definition does not do justice to the immense effect of the Lost Cause on postwar Southern society. The myth in fact undergirded Southern nationalist sentiment, serving as a rallying cry for those who have sought to restore Southern independence.

Lost Cause doctrine echoes many of the beliefs held during the antebellum era in the South, though modified and expanded upon to justify the Civil War and to defend the defeat of the Confederacy. At the heart of the myth was the contention that slavery was not the critical issue of the war. Rather, that myth asserted that defense of the Southern way of life was the main motivation for Southern independence. The Lost Cause doctrine also contended that the South would have given up slavery on its own if the region had been given time to internally eliminate the institution rather than being forced to do so by an outside power. Central to the myth was the view that secession was a legal right ensured by the Founding Fathers of the United States and that the federal government usurped this right by forcefully imposing its will over the South.[26] The Lost Cause idealized the South as a superior society and, consequently, the Confederate soldier was presented as a heroic patriot for the cause in contrast to the myth's representation of the Union soldier as a barbarian. The Myth of the Lost Cause elevated Robert E. Lee to near sainthood, just as Wallace and Bruce were venerated in Scotland. The myth held that Lee and the Army of Northern Virginia were overwhelmed rather than defeated by Union forces. Lee is

---

[24] Thomas L. Connelly and Barbara L. Bellows, *God and General Longstreet: The Lost Cause and the Southern Mind* (Baton Rouge: Louisiana State University Press, 1982) 2.

[25] Alan T. Nolan, "Anatomy of the Myth" in *The Myth of the Lost Cause and Civil War History*, ed. Gary W. Gallagher and Alan T. Nolan (Bloomington: Indiana University Press, 2000) 12.

[26] Nolan, "Anatomy of the Myth," 14–19.

presented as the epitome of gallantry and moral righteousness, the perfect man who emulated Christ in his efforts to preserve the Confederacy and Southern independence. [27]

With a mythology in place to preserve the Old South, the New South developed significantly influenced by traditional Southern values and way of life, even as plantations and widespread agriculture were supplanted. White men of the South maintained paramount control of society through Jim Crow laws.[28] Indeed, inspired by the Myth of the Lost Cause, the New South remained firmly rooted in the religious and cultural values that were such a strong part of Southern society before the war.[29]

Yet, over the passage of time, the South could no longer resist the influx of commercial and industrial forces into the region—forces that had been abhorred and labeled as evil traits of Northern society during the antebellum years.[30] Hence, like Scotland, the South was brought into the Industrial Era. The contrast between the value systems of the Old and the New Souths caused considerable conflict in the region, leading to the emergence of a distinctive kind of nationalism that differentiates it from Scottish nationalism.

"Most people live in a state of tension between what they are and what they want to be."[31] This quote by Emory Thomas embodies Southern nationalist thought and practice in modern times. Modern Scottish nationalism elevates and romanticizes suppressed and eliminated elements of culture and society. In the similar manner, Southern nationalists today look to the past—to the glory days of the Confederacy—as the model for what they wish to be. Many Southerners live in limbo between the two aspirations—they are ready to stand for Southern rights and values whenever threatened by an outside force, yet they are aware of where they stand in the modern political situation, making the realization of a renewed Southern republic unlikely. The stereotypical view of a modern Southern nationalist

---

[27] Connelly and Bellows, *God and General Longstreet*, 26–29.

[28] Edward L. Ayers, *The Promise of the New South: Life After Reconstruction* (New York: Oxford University Press, 1992) vi–vii.

[29] Simkins, *The South, Old and New*, 312.

[30] Simkins, *The South, Old and New*, 283–85.

[31] Emory M. Thomas, *The Confederate Nation, 1865–1865* (New York: Harper & Row, 1979) 21.

is one of the "redneck" proclaiming in a drunken stupor, "The South will rise again!" Closer inspection, however, reveals much sophistication in modern efforts to realize the Southern nationalist goal of preserving and promoting the values of the South in hope of one day resurrecting independence for the region.

To understand the sophisticated views of many Southern nationalists and their desire to perpetuate and spread their views, one may examine a few published nationalist works. *Southern by the Grace of God*, published by the Rebel Press in 1988 and authored by Michael Andrew Grissom, is meant to be a type of "handbook," whose intent is to "provide the Southerner with a general overview of his heritage, instill in him a greater pride in being Southern, point him in the direction for further pursuit of the separate elements of his heritage, and alert him to the fact that the distinguishing marks of our culture are fading away in the hope that a conscious effort will be made to maintain our heritage for posterity."[32] In that book, Grissom offers an analysis of the war and Reconstruction (he terms the latter the "nightmare of the South"). Grissom also speculates what it means to be "Southern," and he describes the character of Southern society. Grissom ends the book with a guide to researching Confederate ancestry, which the author believes may serve as a means for intensifying Southern pride among the book's readers through deepening their Southern identification.

In a more vehement work *The South Was Right!*, James Ronald Kennedy and Walter Donald Kennedy seek to inspire Southern nationalism through exposing the "Yankee Myth of History." In that book, now in its eleventh printing, the Kennedys contend that the South held legitimate aims during the war, and they respond to the North's criticism of the South on such issues as slavery and secession. The authors intend their book to serve as "a call to action to all people who love liberty and truth," calling on Southerners to "climb down from the 'stools of everlasting repentance' and

[32] Michael Andrew Grissom, *Southern by the Grace of God* (Nashville: The Rebel Press, 1988) vi.

to take pride in their Southern heritage." They hope to convince "every Southerner" to awaken to the "fact that no force on Earth can prevent us from reclaiming our lost estate if and when we decide to free ourselves."[33] *The South Was Right!* demonstrates the militancy some Southern nationalists feel toward their cause, and the book underscores that some Southerners, despite the unlikelihood of success, would rally to the cause and resurrect the Confederacy, through violence if necessary. These are but two of many works that not only promote pride in Southern heritage but also call for a defense of Southern rights and traditions in modern times.

The creation of the Lost Cause myth was facilitated by the rise of several organizations that served as remembrance and celebratory institutions of the Confederacy, such as the Association of the Army of Northern Virginia and the United Confederate Veterans.[34] Such organizations have continued into recent times. The Sons of Confederate Veterans, successor to the United Confederate Veterans, seeks to preserve "the history and legacy of these heroes, so future generations can understand the motives that animated the Southern Cause." That organization also identifies its mission as being to "serve as a historical, patriotic, and non-political organization dedicated to insuring that a true history of the 1861–1865 period is preserved."[35] While the SCV is focused on the past, the League of the South is an organization that seeks to facilitate present-day action in the South along the lines of what the Kennedys promoted in *The South Was Right!* The mission statement of the League of the South is to "advance the cultural, social, economic, and political well-being and independence of the Southern people by all honourable means." In order to achieve its goal of resurrecting an independent Southern nation, the League seeks to ally with "all peoples and groups in America and the world who share our general outlook, values, and principles and who wish to defend the remnant of Western civilization."[36]

[33] James Ronald and Walter Donald Kennedy, *The South Was Right!* (1991; reprint, Gretna LA: Pelican Publishing Company, 2003) 8–9.

[34] Gaines M. Foster, *Ghosts of the Confederacy* (1985; reprint, New York: Oxford University Press, 1987).

[35] "Sons of Confederate Veterans," http://www.scv.org/, accessed April 2, 2005.

[36] "League of the South Homepage," http://www.dixienet.org/, accessed April 2, 2005.

The survival of Southern nationalism into modern times was the topic of *Confederates in the Attic,* a popular 1998 book by Tony Horwitz. Attempting to understand "the places and people who keep the memory of the [South's] conflict [with the North] alive in the present day,"[37] Horwitz describes the extreme degree to which Confederate re-enactors strive to be absolutely correct in their tactical recreation of Civil War battles. That author in his trek across the South chronicles the pro-antebellum groups he encountered, including the Children of the Confederacy, an organization that seeks to revive and perpetuate the culture and traditions of the Old South. Addressing the lingering issue of race, Horowitz visits Alabama, where he witnesses Confederate memorial sites more prominent than Civil Rights memorials, and he visits Kentucky, where he finds the site of a racially charged murder. Concerning the controversial issue of the public display of the Confederate flag, Horwitz describes a protest he attended in Columbia, South Carolina, during the debate over whether or not to remove the flag from the capitol dome. What many people promoted as a politically motivated demonstration in defense of Southern heritage degenerated into a racial protest, with white men claiming to oppose an "ethnic cleansing" of the South and carrying banners stating "I have a dream, too!" embellished with the rebel flag. *Confederates in the Attic* reveals some modern manifestations of nationalist tendencies preserved and perpetuated in Southern society since 1865.

Thomas Connelly writes that "no Americanization of the South could erase totally" the evidence of a distinct regional culture within the South. The Southern culture that exists today, "heavily endowed with memory and legend" rooted in the Myth of the Lost Cause, is deeply ingrained in the mindset of many Southerners. Southern nationalists call to mind these factors and point to the glory days of history in their espousing of Southern rights and in their efforts to defend Southern values. Today, Southern nationalism is not dependent upon "a precise knowledge of the

---

[37] Tony Horwitz, *Confederates in the Attic: Dispatches from the Unfinished Civil War* (1998; reprint, New York: Vintage Books, 1999) 18.

Confederacy or a particular interest in the exploits of the Rebel army."[38] Southern nationalists simply believe that, in comparison with the remainder of the United States, the South is superior because of its heritage and is therefore worth fighting for so that "the South will rise again!"

The basic definition of nationalism holds that every movement is differentiated from others and is unique to each society in which it emerges.[39] Indeed, by examining the historical backgrounds and modern evidences of the two nationalist movements, one may identify obvious differences between the nationalisms in Scotland and the South. Scotland began as a sovereign nation which was conquered by a neighboring nation; whereas the South began as a full partner in a union, then unsuccessfully attempted to break from that union, leading to a voluntary rejoining of that union with their rights of membership fully returned to some of its citizens (Southern whites). In both Scotland and the South, the struggle for nationalism concerns independence and self-governance, but the issues of slavery and race mark the fight for Southern nationalism with a depth of controversy unassociated with Scottish nationalism.

Despite many differences, the development and expression of nationalism in Scotland and the South hold many similarities. For instance, the fundamental ideologies of the Scottish and Southern nationalist movements are essentially the same. The outpouring of nationalism in each nation erupted over perceived attempts that another political entity was encroaching upon its lands. In the centuries leading up to the Act of Union in 1707, Scotland was increasingly influenced by England despite the Scots having achieved independence from the English in the early fourteenth century under Robert Bruce. The South experienced a similar political encroachment from the US government beginning with ratification of the Constitution. The Southern states viewed the federal government as unwilling to recognize their distinctively regional needs and aspirations. After protests that fueled the two nationalist movements—the Jacobite rebellions

---

[38] Connelly and Bellows, *God and General Longstreet*, 137.

[39] Louis L. Snyder, *The Meaning of Nationalism* (1954; reprint, New York: Greenwood Press, 1968) xi.

in Scotland and the American Civil War—were in essence failed movements for independence, both Scotland and the South regained a level of self-rule, though they were both ultimately controlled by a governmental seat located outside their territory.

Scotland and the South each saw the outbreak of full-scale wars in seeking to achieve independence. In Scotland, the Jacobite Rebellion of 1745 led by Bonnie Prince Charlie is equivalent to the Civil War in the South. Militarily, the 1745 rebellion began with success, but was ultimately doomed to failure once the English forces amassed and launched a successful invasion of Scotland, much as the Union forces achieved during the Civil War with a successful invasion of the South. In both cases, an outside military occupation attempted to crush the populace from attempting to break away again. Attempts to reconstruct each land by the occupying outside army after the rebellion was quelled ultimately failed, as Scotland and the South both retained a strong sense of nationalism, actively seeking to reclaim what was lost by way of political and ideological warfare over the centuries that followed. Thus, the military failures, whether led by Bonnie Prince Charlie or by Robert E. Lee, were not enough to break the will of the Scottish or Southern people in promoting nationalism.

Political matters played paramount roles in the outcome of the two nationalist movements. Internal division in Scotland prevented political organization among those who opposed the Act of Union in 1707, resulting in passage of the act and incorporation of Scotland into Great Britain.[40] The Scots' failure to effectively organize marked the downfall of home rule in Scotland, just as the Southerners' failure to organize a sufficient Confederate government helped bring about the fall of the South during the Civil War. During its brief existence, the Confederate States of America was marred with internal division as to the role of the new nation and its relationship with the individual states, seriously handicapping the ability of the government to prosecute the war.[41] In both Scotland and the South,

---

[40] Reid, *Scotland's Progress*, 119.

[41] Thomas, *The Confederate Nation*, 58.

failure to adequately organize politically helped bring about the downfall of nationhood.

The common failure to achieve nationhood in the two lands resulted in similar responses involving the creation of a doctrine by which to perpetuate nationalism, and both doctrines were related. As mentioned previously, the term "lost cause" in the South's doctrine "the Myth of the Lost Cause" was derived from Sir Walter Scott's writings about the Scottish doctrine known as "the Lost Cause of Scotland."[42] In each case, a romanticizing of history occurred in order to intensify nationalist feelings. Scottish nationalists embellish the actions of William Wallace and Robert Bruce and hail the efforts of the Jacobites and Bonnie Prince Charlie, proclaiming all of them as heroes and patriots. Scotland looks to the glorious victory at Bannockburn and the crushing defeat at Culloden as inspirations for what was and for what they wish to see reborn again. In the South, the story is similar. Southerners romanticize such figures as George Washington and Thomas Jefferson in their founding of the US but vilify the actions of those Northerners who attempted to "undermine" what the Founding Fathers had established. Southern nationalists glorify the gallant victories of Lee and the Army of Northern Virginia, and nationalists see that army's defeat by the Union as inspiration for the cause of nationalism.

The same vestiges of nationalist expression in Scotland and in the South exist in modern times. Authors such as Hugh MacDiarmid and the Kennedys interpret the past and analyze modern political situations to envision ways by which Scotland and the South can once again achieve independence. Radical political extremists—left-wing liberals in Scotland and right-wing conservatives in the South—actively seek to bring about autonomy in each land. Organizations such as the Scottish National Party and the Sons of Confederate Veterans work to promote nationalism, while more radical groups (including the 1320 Club and the League of the South) take a more militant and potentially violent stance. Men and women in

---

[42] Connelly and Bellows, *God and General Longstreet*, 2.

Scotland and the South continue to believe in the mythologies of Scottish and Southern independence.

What has resulted in both Scotland and the South are complex mythologies, each different but derived through similar efforts to promote modern nationalism. In these mythologies, William Wallace and Robert E. Lee are heroes, and the governments of the United Kingdom and United States are portrayed as the villains. The Highlander is viewed as the idyllic figure symbolizing what has been lost, just as the Southern plantation aristocracy embodies the lost society in the South. An independent Scotland and the Confederate States of America are viewed as the lost homelands to which nationalists in each land seek to return in their odyssey to reclaim the past. In any culture, a myth can have a powerful effect on the people who believe its tenets. Clearly, the myths of a Scotland and an American South free of outside control inspire many men and women in each part of the world, and those myths provide a powerful influence on how these individuals define their views of both the past and present.

A further parallel between the two nationalist movements is developing in recent years. In the American South, men and women who seek to reclaim their independence from the United States are looking more and more to Scotland for inspiration and a model for their own struggle. Southerners observe the parallels between their nationalist movement and that of Scotland, and they see a much more successful effort than their own. As a result, Southerners are looking increasingly to Scotland for inspiration in the effort to achieve nationhood and in the preservation of a unique culture.

Southerners draw their modern-day connections to Scotland by looking back to the peopling of America through immigration in the eighteenth century. The Scots-Irish (or Scotch-Irish)—Lowland Scots who were resettled in Ulster in Northern Ireland—migrated in droves to America during the 1700s. James G. Leyburn asserts that as many as 250,000 Scots-Irish may have migrated to America, though this figure is considered to be a bit high by others.[43] A large number of these men and women moved south and west upon migrating to America, through the Appalachians and into the South.[44] Highland Scots also migrated to the future United States, establishing a settlement on Cape Fear in North Carolina in 1732; their numbers, however, would pale in comparison to those of the Scots-Irish.[45] All told, the Scottish influence on the South was significant. Grady McWhiney asserted that the "fundamental and lasting differences between Southerners and Northerners began in colonial America when migrants from the Celtic regions of the British Isles…and from the English uplands managed to implant their traditional customs in the Old South."[46] Many Southerners today look back to that initial colonization as a tie that binds the South to Scotland and to their Celtic kin across the Atlantic.

Inherent in Southern culture is an obsession with roots in the Old World. Southerners increasingly look to Scotland to find cultural identity and cohesion with others. The revival of this ethnic identity among Southerners, whether based in fact or imagined, has as its intention the creation of a more powerful union among the people of the South. As an outlet for this expression of common ethnicity, heritage celebrations "remind people to consciously stand together as a group apart" from the remainder of society, just as Southerners have attempted to do since the founding of the United States.[47] Essentially, the emphasis on Scottish ancestry and culture has a twofold objective: to increase Scottish identification with the South and to promote Southern ideology and nationalism.

In the latter half of the twentieth century, Scottish heritage festivals have expanded across the South, particularly in the form of Highland Games. Highland Games held at Grandfather Mountain, North Carolina, and Stone Mountain, Georgia, routinely attract over 100,000 visitors annually. Scottish people often comment that they view this Southern obsession as quaint.[48] These Southerners, however, take their actions very seriously, emulating events that they believe would take place in the mother country.

---

[43] James G. Leyburn, *The Scotch Irish: A History* (Chapel Hill: The University of North Carolina Press, 1962) 157.

[44] James Webb, *Born Fighting: How The Scots-Irish Shaped America* (New York: Broadway Books, 2004) 149.

[45] Ray, *Highland Heritage*, 3.

[46] Grady McWhiney, *Cracker Culture: Celtic Ways in the Old South* (Tuscaloosa: The University of Alabama Press, 1988) xii.

[47] Ray, *Highland Heritage*, 1–2.

[48] Barry Vann, *Rediscovering the South's Celtic Heritage* (Johnson City TN: The Overmountain Press, 2004) 168–69.

Each festival offers not only games for both participants and spectators, but also clan tents, with each Highland Clan presenting Clan-related wares and attempting to enhance Southerners' awareness of their cultural ancestry. Tartan parades are also common at festivals, with each clan parading its symbols to promote Scottish identity in the South.[49] The goal of all these events is to increase awareness of a "reclaimed" Scottish affiliation among Southerners and to foster a greater sense of belonging to the South and to the Scottish heritage that underlies Southern tradition. Each of these festivals has its own distinctly Southern twist, and one is likely to see men in Scottish kilts and Confederate kepies eating barbecue rather than haggis.[50] The distinctive Southern manipulation of these festivals demonstrates a conscious effort to blend Scottish and Southern heritage.

During Reconstruction, writers who interpreted the Myth of the Lost Cause took great pains to equate the ancestry of Robert E. Lee with Robert Bruce, as they elevated Lee to mythic hero status. This romanticized genealogy represented the beginning of a trend toward relating the dual lost causes of Scotland and the South.[51] The parallel mythologies that underlie Scottish and Southern nationalism allow a "harmonious blend" of Scottish identity with folk memories of the Old South. In effect, Scottish heritage is incorporated into the Myth of the Lost Cause as a further legitimization for the cause of Southern nationalism, both past and present.[52] It is even contended that the sectional differences that emerged in the United States resulted directly from a carrying-over of sectional animosity in Britain.[53] Southerners view Scotland as "a nation of romantic outlaws and do-it-yourself spirituality, a place where men are men, women are ladies, and nature is always photogenic…[,] where slavery…[is] dissipated into benign paternalism, where feminism is unheard of, Christianity unchallenged, multiculturalism a bad dream."[54] Scotland is used to embody the culture

[49] Ray, *Highland Heritage*, 115–20.

[50] Diane Roberts, "Your Clan or Ours?" *Oxford American* 29 (September–October 1999): 24–30.

[51] Connelly and Bellows, *God and General Longstreet*, 2.

[52] Ray, *Highland Heritage*, 182–84.

[53] Vann, *Rediscovering the South's Celtic Heritage*, 7–8.

[54] Roberts, "Your Clan or Ours?" 24–30.

and society that Southern nationalists wish to revive in modern times. Such Southerners look to the cause for Scottish nationalism as a direct inspiration for their own struggle, romanticizing Scotland as a haven for the sort of white Protestant "purity" that they are hoping to restore in the South.

The above quote introduces a dangerous and controversial facet of the heritage movement in the South. Imagining a South where "slavery…[is] dissipated into benign paternalism" and where "multiculturalism" is a "bad dream" brings to the forefront the lingering racial issues and tensions that continue to plague the South to this day. There are Southerners who think of Scotland as a "metaphor for the Old South" romanticized by the Lost Cause, as a land of white purity, which clearly reflects a strain of racism.[55] Even more disturbing, the League of the South celebrates the perceived racial whiteness of Scotland and seeks a return to the purity of an "Anglo-Celtic" Confederacy.[56] Scholar Thomas Brown argues that the celebration of Scottish heritage in the South is inextricably combined with white supremacy.[57] The addition of racial prejudice to the Scottish heritage movement in the South calls into question the motives of some celebrants of Scottish ancestry and culture.

Today, the League of the South website displays a Confederate tartan and offers links to the Scottish National Party, proclaiming SNP members as "our Celtic cousins."[58] The League of the South's attempt to ally with the SNP represents a new facet to the history of the two nationalist movements. Although the SNP disavows any connection, party literature increasingly crops up at Highland Games and heritage festivals across the South, and the organization has been publicly chastised for encouraging the actions of radical Southerners. The connection between the two organizations may not portend a political alliance between Scotland and the South to achieve inde-

---

[55] Ibid.

[56] Euan Hague, Benito Giordano, and Edward H. Sebesta, "Whiteness, Multiculturalism and Nationalist Appropriation of Celtic Culture: The Case of the League of the South and the Lega Nord," *Cultural Geographies* 12/2 (April 2005): 151–73.

[57] Thomas Brown, "H-South Review: Brown Responds to Ray's Comments on Southern Heritage on Display," 8 June 2005 http://h-net.msu.edu/cgi-bin/logbrowse.pl?trx=vx&list=h-south&month=0506&week=b&msg=pM2jjtUj0N8bLr1K8TtgJA&user=&pw=, accessed November 12, 2005.

[58] "League of the South Homepage," accessed April 2, 2005.

pendence for the two lands, but the connection does present a startling development in the parallel evolution of Scottish and Southern nationalism.

With modern movements continuing, the furtherance of Scottish and Southern nationalism will continue to pose a cultural and societal issue in both Great Britain and the United States. Only the future will tell if either Scotland or the South will once again achieve independence. Nevertheless, the tenacity and endurance of each movement over time assures that nationalism in Scotland and the South will remain a powerful force in the two lands.

Up & Down in America, October 1969

BY DAVID HUDDLE

He'd flown two tours,
I'd done one on the ground,
both of us visiting home,

my brother and I drove
to the football game
at Fort Chiswell High School.

Fall night in the Blue Ridge,
the stars just coming out,
the air cool and sweet,

I got a little teary
when we stood for the Star
Spangled Banner, our hands

over our hearts, good country
boys who'd served honorably
in a dishonorable war. Then

they played Dixie,
which kept him standing
after I sat down.

Flag on the Barn

BY ROBERT MORGAN

The old barn in the valley may
be weathered almost silver but
a pole thrust from its ridge displays
the stars and stripes aflutter at
the tip. Such patriotic zeal
refreshes the lone traveler:
Old Glory quickened by the wind
and shivery as a trout, stirs pulse,
stops breath, with streaming colors high
above the yard and cow stalls, pens
for chickens, hogs and nursing calves,
above the heap of gold manure
that steams on winter mornings, smokes
a crown of flies at summer noon.
It thrills to think that loyalty
and dedication can extend
to hayloft, feed room, sty, and trough,
out this far in a distant cove.
As wind shifts, suddenly the limbs
of poplars pledge allegiance.
And when the wind goes still the flag
hangs brighter than a blood-stained rag.

Spirit of the Mountains in Rhyme: The Life and the Poetry of J. D. Meade

BY JOHN SPARKS

One of the earliest memories I harbor comes from my days as a toddler when I saw my very first pack of cards. I picked them up, wondering what on earth the pretty things with the horse pictures on the back were, and my father gently but immediately and firmly took them away from me with the admonition, "Don't bother those, honey. They're your uncle Joe's cards." Dad's deep voice must have done the trick: from then on, I accorded that pack of cards with every bit of the respect I gave to my grandfather's "church hat," which was considerable. I don't really know why I've retained that memory as I have, but I definitely do remember the cards, the dice that went with them (which, up until recently at least, my father still owned along with the pack of cards as an heirloom), and, most importantly, I remember the only one whom my mother ever would have allowed to bring such "idle pastimes" into our house: Joseph Davis Meade, my great-uncle and, in his day, one of the better-known minor poets of Eastern Kentucky and the Appalachian mountains.

I can't really say that Uncle Joe brought anything novel or distinctive to the discipline of poetry as such. A William Carlos Williams or an Ezra Pound he was definitely not. His imagery was mostly homely, simplistic, and often coarse, and the structure of many of his published works (all in traditional metrical verse, because he shunned other poetic forms) was derivative, with a heavy display of influence from the poets he himself liked best: Burns, Byron, Kipling, A. E. Housman, and Robert Service, with just a dash of Jack London and Francois Villon thrown in for good measure. But he lived and wrote in the day before the craft of serious poetry (and, alas, the literary short story as well) became the exclusive purview of the academic world, when Jesse Stuart and James Still were mere children and some of Uncle Joe's own heroes as well as his deservedly better-known national contemporaries such as Edna St. Vincent Millay made a good living or at least supplemented their incomes composing poetry for popular periodicals. Thus, for many years, his poems found a ready audience with newspaper readers all up and down the Big Sandy valley of Eastern Kentucky, who could easily identify with and be alternately inspired and scandalized by both his down-to-earth, frequently salty themes and the vigor of his rhetoric—blazing, ironically, right alongside the insipid paeans to God, flag, and mother that made up so much of the content of the "Poetry Corners" of rural newspapers years ago.

Uncle Joe's only verse collection—*Spirit of the Mountains in Rhyme,* self-published in 1964 with the aid of Catlettsburg writer Billy C. Clark and others—was compiled many years after he wrote most of the poems contained therein, and over the next few years that book sold perhaps well enough locally to pay for the cost of its printing. By that time the Prohibition era that had given Uncle Joe his main inspiration to write was long gone, and a new crop of agents of change urged on by presidents Kennedy and Johnson had already supplanted the old-style Temperance crusaders and revenue men. But in the volume's introduction, his nephew by marriage, the late Dr. P. J. Evans of Ashland, Kentucky, recalled that in the early 1920s J. D. Meade had been hailed briefly as both "poet laureate of Appalachia" and "the Robert Burns of the mountains."

Admittedly, both tributes were perhaps a bit overstated even at the time they were first proclaimed, but, still, Burns was Uncle Joe's favorite poet, and there were in fact some distinctive parallels between the lives of the two men and their respective muses, far apart historically and geographically though they were. Uncle Joe had a healthy ego and a good many strong and

DR. J. D. MEADE, "POET LAUREATE OF APPALACHIA" AND "THE ROBERT BURNS OF THE MOUNTAINS."

often contradictory passions—at least one of these that, to put it delicately, he shared with Lord Byron as well as Burns, and which had perhaps best not be discussed in depth here, though Uncle Joe himself sometimes wrote about it with more frankness, honesty, and dry wit than my grandmother and his other sisters would have liked. But conventionally-structured and derivative or not, his poems always reflected the same tension as those penned by Burns: that of a sharp, searching, analytical intellect juxtaposed with a basically rural and rustic outlook on life, trying to come to terms with his own personal advancement in a world both familiar and somewhat unfamiliar, wherein culture had begun to change and evolve at a rapid, and sometimes frightening, pace. In other words, what Edinburgh in the latter days of the Enlightenment was to the young and ambitious plowman-turned-literary-celebrity Robert Burns, the new industrial cities and coal camps of the Big Sandy and upper Kentucky River valleys in the last days of the Gilded Age and the outset of the Roaring Twenties were to Joe Meade. His poetry always reflected the alternating and sometimes simultaneous love and hate he embraced for his own life and for his world. Even today, much Appalachian literature always seems to reflect something of that same tension, so much so that we might well wonder if it will always be a cultural dynamic in this area.

Uncle Joe was born on November 9, 1874, in Greasy Creek, Johnson County, Kentucky, the second of thirteen children of Henry and Zina (Davis) Meade. Although Henry Meade was remembered by all his children as "a very good farm manager, but never so work-brittle as he insisted that his sons be," he had been a schoolmaster in Virginia before and immediately after the War Between the States and was ambitious for his offspring.

Henry Meade sent his daughters as well as his sons to school and continually urged them all to excel. Between his prodding and his children's own ambitions, nearly all of them became country schoolteachers, one became a successful merchant, and three older sons managed, with much supplemental manual labor, and a good many "subscription" schools conducted in off-seasons between academic terms, to put themselves through professional schools in Louisville. Paris became a physician, and Joe and Lloyd both became dentists. And for all this, theirs were no Horatio Alger success stories, for their lives all showed some of the negative effects of having been worked so hard when they were young. Paris died at age fifty-six of the long-term effects of hypertension, and Lloyd's health was compromised to an extent as well, though he survived into his sixties. Uncle Joe lived until the tender age of ninety-five, but then again, he had his own distinctive coping mechanisms.

Perhaps Uncle Joe's first impression that he was going to be compelled to figure life out on his own terms came to him in summer 1884, when he was not quite ten years old. His little sister Florence, age four, fell sick with diphtheria or, as it was known at the time, membranous croup. His great-uncle by marriage, a Methodist preacher named Zephaniah Meek, exhorted the entire family to pray for her, quoting the fifteenth chapter of the Gospel of John to assure them that, if they truly asked God to heal Florence in Jesus' name, their prayers would surely be granted. Late in life, Uncle Joe was wont to remark that no one could have prayed harder or more earnestly or faithfully in Jesus' name for Florence than he himself did. And yet his prayers seemingly had no avail whatsoever: Florence slowly and painfully smothered to death on the sweltering afternoon of August 8, 1884, her mother Zina, herself almost ready to bear yet one more child, rocking and embracing the little girl tightly in her lap as life left her. Four days afterward, that next baby, Elizabeth (whom I knew as "Maw"), was born, and for a while the entire family was terrified that she wouldn't survive either. In the guarded language employed in that era, she "couldn't make water" for a day or two after her birth, and the newborn infant's medical problem was rectified only when an old neighbor well versed in "herb doctoring" made a tea from boiled watermelon seeds and administered it to her by squeezing it drop by drop from a clean cloth into her mouth.

But the joy of the new arrival could not take away the pain of the cruel death either for Henry Meade or his older sons. That death, and Elizabeth's "cure" with watermelon-seed tea, may have been the impetus for eleven-year-old Paris's first resolve to become a physician, and after Florence's demise and three other infant deaths that followed it over the years, when Henry happened to hear somebody rationalize a baby's death with the cliché that "God had taken" the infant, he would stamp his foot, swear, and exclaim, "Well, I say *damn* a God that'd take a child!" On one occasion Henry was even run out of another home for so saying, the terrified owner being convinced that lightning would strike the house if such a blasphemer was allowed to stay there. For his part, nine-year-old Joe was simply convinced that one couldn't place very much trust either in preachers or in pat, simplistic answers, but for all his grief and bitterness over Florence's suffering and death he never became an atheist. Once, when a more pious acquaintance of his accused him of being an "infidel," Uncle Joe retorted, with all the considerable temper that he had inherited from his father, that "I can see more of God in a single blade of grass than you've ever seen out of anything in your life!"

Other aspects of his youth were less than positive. The Meade boys inherited much of their intellect and their personalities from their father, but Henry's tendency to issue orders, rather than to demonstrate by example, often threw father and sons into sharp collision. Walter, Joe's younger brother by two years, used to describe the first time in his life that he ever uttered swear words: the Meade farm, like many in Eastern Kentucky of that day and time, was nestled in a fairly steep hollow, and one spring day teenaged Walter was hard at work trying to ready a hillside for corn planting with a horse and a double-shovel plow. Henry, sitting in the yard in a cane-bottomed chair, yelled up the hill at Walter to stop the horse and pull the plow's trace chain up another link. As he remembered it, Walter was so incensed at his father's obvious unwillingness to come up and assist him that he just stood back and let the curses roll out of his system. Whether because of this occurrence or another I can't say with certainty, but the tension between Henry and Walter did become so strong that the father actually "ran Walter off" for a time, literally banishing him from the house and farm until he became ready to modify his behavior to suit Henry. Such occurrences were not uncommon in late nineteenth- and early twentieth-century Eastern Kentucky, and though the mother Zina undoubtedly wanted to arbitrate the fight, there was very little she could do. A husband's word was law for a household. But it happened that, at the time of the fight, Uncle Joe was already a country teacher, and for the school off-season he was living some miles up the creek with his aunt and uncle by marriage, Alice and John Mollett, and was working as a clerk in their small general store. Not too many hours after Walter's unwilling departure, Henry, sitting on his porch, saw Joe walking back up the hollow to the house. Joe climbed the steps, looked his father in the eye, and growled, "Walt came to the store. He said you'd run him off, and he didn't have any place to go. I talked Uncle John and Aunt Alice into giving him my job and my bed. So now Walt's there, I'm back home, and by God, you won't run *me* off." He then simply walked on into the house, and Henry perhaps wisely chose not to pursue the matter any further. They all made up eventually anyway; that was usually the way it went, for better or worse, with Eastern Kentucky farm families. Walter, incidentally, was the son that became a merchant, and one might wonder if Uncle Joe got him started in life after that remarkable turn of events.

Uncle Joe listed his occupations as farmer and teacher when he married Jemima "Jege" Price of Oil Springs, Kentucky, in 1898. He got another temporary job as census taker for Johnson County, Kentucky, in 1900, where he listed himself as a teacher and as living with his wife and baby son in the same household on Two Mile Creek with his father, mother, and siblings. His older brother Paris had already worked his way through medical school by this time, and had begun a long and hard career as a country doctor for the farming community of Flat Gap in western Johnson County. It's interesting to note, though, that for the 1900 census, heads of households were required to state the number of months they had been unemployed during the previous year; while Uncle Joe listed virtually all the farmers on Greasy, Two Mile, Banjo, Lick, Chestnut, and Nat's Creeks as being unemployed for three months out of the year, one supposes during the winter season, he listed his father as having worked only five of the previous twelve months. Perhaps that notation was his own idea of a small revenge, and if so it was entirely in keeping with Uncle Joe's dry wit. However, the time of his marriage must have been around the time when he enrolled in Central University's Dental Department in Louisville, and his presence back home in spring 1900 was only temporary. He graduated from dental school, at the top of his class no less, in 1902. As he recalled it later in a poem dedicated to his brother Lloyd, who was by then ready to leave home for the big city himself:

I stayed four years in Louisville
And came whole-skinned away,
When Berod [du Pont] and Tom Johnson
Were princes in that day;
No one ever hinted
They would like to have my fleece;
Through every tribulation
I came out slick as grease.

One can now only wonder what some of his "tribulations" might have been, but if they held much in common with the content of some of his later autobiographical verses, those tribulations must have proven, to say the least, intriguing. At any rate, as a newly-graduated dentist, Uncle Joe undoubtedly would have been able to pick and choose between a wide variety of professional opportunities, the likes of which he couldn't even have dreamed as a farm boy, but the turn of events of this particular moment in history gave him considerable incentive to return to the mountains. Indeed, these were the earliest days of the Eastern Kentucky mining camps, the brainchildren of John C. C. Mayo and likeminded entrepreneurs who built the camps to house both native and immigrant miners employed in the digging of the coal they had cannily acquired from mountain landholders by their aggressive purchase of mineral rights through vaguely-worded "broad form" deeds. All of a sudden, mountain farmers were becoming mountain miners by the thousands, crowding into the "company houses" in the new coal towns and reveling in "luxuries" that they had never known before. And at the top social tier in each and every one of these "company towns" were the "bosses," the professional men that absentee owners needed to keep the places running smoothly: the mine and tipple supervisors, accountants and paymasters of the business office, the manager and senior clerks of the company store, the clergymen employed by the company "missionary" churches to shine the light upon the benighted heathen of the Appalachian mountains, the company doctor, and, in the case of the larger towns, the company undertaker and the company dentist. Uncle Joe thus left the hills as a callus-handed young farmer and teacher with a sizable chip on his shoulder; he returned from Louisville to find a brave new world of twentieth-century progress spearheading its way into his own homeland, and he landed right in a top niche. His most prosperous and successful dental practices were in Pikeville, Kentucky, which was surrounded by these new company towns, and in the mining community of Elkhorn City, and perhaps his best friend at the time was Pikeville attorney and United States congressman John Wesley Langley.

Undoubtedly, several new and ambitious mining families in each coal camp immersed themselves in the new "culture" brought to the hills, and those families no doubt acted as the owners and bosses expected that they should. The term "company suck" didn't materialize out of nothing. For the most part, though, the mountaineers that came to work in the coal camps brought their culture with them and kept it or modified aspects of it to fit into their new environment, and they stuck to themselves on weekdays and left the camps on Sundays to attend the churches up the hollows they had known before the advent of the coal industry. Inevitably and quickly, a nigh-unbreachable social chasm between labor and management in the mountain county seats and company towns became a fact of life. The miners were there to make money to support themselves and their families; by and large they had little or no impetus to change the internals of their culture, while at the same time the management cliques in both coal camps and county governmental seats often did their best to bring into the hills the values of business-minded, free-market America. Conformity to the norm was a social necessity for this urbane, elite class; any man with enough "get-up and go" would come to understand the validity of the system, and if an individual was so lazy that he remained within the laboring class all his life, that was his own business and his own hard luck. Perhaps nowadays we can best appreciate the ethics, or lack of ethics, involved—not so much within the serious histories written about the era, but rather in the satires penned by Sinclair Lewis. And so with his success in dental practice and in business, Uncle Joe found himself immersed in a world of conventional lip service to white Anglo-Saxon Protestantism and its social expectations: providing economically for one's wife and children; regular churchgoing on Sunday followed up the rest of the week by the curious ritualized thievery that was, and remains, the sum and substance of all too much "sound" business practice; Republican politics wherein ends justified all means as long as a thick-enough veneer of religion and patriotism was applied; a mistress on the sly if one was disposed to maintain her and could get either rich or lucky enough to acquire her, and trustworthy and discreet ladies of the evening on out-of-town trips if one was bitten by the urge; and an outright disdain for the sinfulness of the coal-camp whores and the saloons wherein the tougher and wilder laboring men more openly practiced their own version of the disports of their social betters.

The Volstead Act of 1919, ostensibly intended to clean up America by eliminating the making and sale of all alcoholic beverages, only made things worse in Appalachia, since that act created the institution known so well both within and outside the mountains as bootlegging. "Destroy the stills and save the boys!" became the war-cry of missionaries and "progressives" intent on bringing Appalachia up to the standards of mainstream America, yet both Appalachian and mainstream American upper classes believed the Volstead Act would benefit their perceived inferiors who were supposedly ignorantly and carelessly ruining their lives with alcohol. Many individuals in the upper crust evidently thought that they themselves were morally strong enough to handle the stuff if they could get a good product discreetly. Thus while moonshiners went to prison by the score, the richer and more urbane bootleggers underwriting their enterprises—individual cases were known of bootleggers having a dozen or more "stillers" working for them, besides smugglers importing liquor when and where they could—often got off scot-free. The more charitable and business-oriented of these bootleggers often as not would try, in many cases successfully, to jiggle the legal system to obtain lighter sentences for their craftsmen, but that didn't stop the moonshiners themselves from trying to find and kill men who they suspected had "turned them up" once they were released from confinement. And overlaying the whole situation was a provision of the law little known and discussed today, but nonetheless horribly cruel and which proved to affect Uncle Joe in a most personal way: all alcohol dispensed by drug companies for medical purposes had to be laced with poison to prevent people from drinking it, a legal twist that had fatal repercussions at a time of widespread illiteracy. Once at the outset of Prohibition, Uncle Joe ordered a quantity of medical alcohol for his dental practice, and one of the old friends of his youth from the lower Big Sandy River valley, a deckhand on the steamboat that brought the alcohol upriver, was poisoned to death because he couldn't read the cargo's warning label and tapped into the barrel to sample a drink.

This, then, was the hothouse in which Uncle Joe's poetry began to germinate. If he was no Pound or Williams, neither was he a George F. Babbitt. In fact, one might describe Uncle Joe best not only as a kind of Appalachian Robert Burns making his living from the Scottish and English gentry by chuckling at their pretenses, but also as something of a crusty, outspoken, aggressive version of Babbitt's counterpart Paul Riesling. Even as he succeeded in dental practice, politics, and business in the heyday of the mining towns, though he liked a good strong drink and made no bones about it for the benefit of either Church or State, and though no one acquainted with him could deny that he was an aficionado of feminine charm whenever, wherever, and in whomever he found it, he had very few illusions about himself, any of his *nouveau-riche* friends and associates, or about the new, progressive lifestyle in which all of them had staked their existence in the wake of the coal boom. Throughout a long life, Uncle Joe never acted the part of a snob either for his own benefit or that of his family or community—except to those, regardless of their social status, in whom he perceived some sort of fakery, pretense, or feigned wisdom, and to such people he usually responded with the most cutting sarcasm he could muster. As an example of his overall demeanor and attitude, he once drove his wife, whom he did in fact love dearly, literally to tears by stubbornly insisting that the country girl she had hired as a cook and housemaid sit at their table and share a meal with the family and several important invited guests at a formal dinner. The girl had worked just as hard in her own way as he and his colleagues had at their trades, he reasoned, and was equally entitled to partake of her own good cooking in recompense; but while he was forthright with his opinions, it is just as likely that he got an immense amount of wry-faced enjoyment watching his urbane, class-conscious guests, and especially their prim and proper spouses, squirm at the glaring social breach into which he forced them to step. Even so, Uncle Joe's education and social position in Pikeville rendered him eligible to apply and be accepted for part-time editorial work at the local newspaper, but once entrenched in that position he used his pen to skewer flatland Northern editors and politicians condemning the supposed barbarity of Eastern Kentucky's common people, as well as the region's own natives who had, in his eyes, gotten just a tad too high above their raising and who considered themselves superior to the common herd because of their newly-made riches. The work that established his name and fame as a poet perhaps more than any other was entitled "Elkhorn City," and he wrote that poem in response to a New York reporter who had gotten a piece published by the Associated Press about the supposedly intrepid revenue agents working hard to establish Prohibition in Eastern Kentucky, at the risk of their own lives and in the face of near-insurmountable odds. Formerly one of the most frequently-quoted poems of Kentucky, according to one expert, "Elkhorn City" reads in part:

Uncle Sam has spent his millions
Just to cure his children's ills,
Sent romancers to the mountains
While he footed all the bills.
There they drank, deceived and boasted
Without honor or regret,
But in spite of Prohibition
There's a drop of moonshine yet.

These artillery-covered minions
Tell of each bloodthirsty raid,
Boast of dangers not existing
Just to show they're unafraid.
How they swept a hostile country,
How the dry succeeds the wet,
But despite these bold Goliaths
There's a drop of moonshine yet....

Come, and let not previous gossip
Here retard your power to think,
For we brew a cup of kindness
While we brew the stronger drink.
Come, for both are freely offered,
Please remember, don't forget,
Where the Elkhorn meets Big Sandy
There's a drop of kindness yet....

Come, the one who bids you welcome,
Native-born, has paid the price,
Blessed with every native virtue,
Cursed with every native vice.
Favorite land of God, Kentucky,
There's one spot we can't forget:

Where the Elkhorn meets Big Sandy
There's a drop of moonshine yet.

One could draw parallels between the outside Prohibitionists of nearly a hundred years ago and later urbane "do-gooders," and find the actions of both groups, as well as Eastern Kentucky natives' response to either, to be nearly identical. But in his description of "these bold Goliaths," Uncle Joe employed one of his favorite sources of metaphor despite his freethinking attitude: the Bible, with which he knew his country readers would identify immediately. Uncle Joe used biblical imagery in his own distinctive way, such as in this confession about a "touch of life," as he put it, which he once experienced on an out-of-town trip:

And there sat Highland Mary,
Sweet and divinely fair,
Whose lips were often kissed by Burns
Upon the banks of Ayr.
And Cleopatra's noble face
Made Antony's to shine,
As she dissolved a costly pearl
And drank it in her wine.

The vision passed that had for me
So many charms to please,
And Samson's locks were spread upon
Deliliah's dimpled knees.
A fearful din rang in my head
As of some grand carouse—
And John the Baptist's head appeared
Served as a plate of souse.

Dizzy, with an aching head,
I woke up with the dawn,

I could see the birds a-hopping
About the grassy lawn.
My Beauty vanished with the night
That ushered in the day,
And with her went my pocketbook—
And both had gone to stay....

Through winter's cold and summer's heat
With dearth of many tears,
I've dodged the shoals and quicksands
For nearly fifty years.
And with opinion at the top
It makes me weary, sad,
To know some little flapper pulled
My leg for all I had....

In every place I went, I found
All civil, cool, and calm,
Black, and white, and rich, and poor
Ne'er seemed to care a damn.
The devil figured wisely,
He knew just what it took—
And so he hung a petticoat
For bait upon the hook.

One might wonder today how many upright coal-camp and county-seat citizens may have gasped at their reading of that particular poem and clucked aloud over the sinfulness of "that awful Dr. Meade"—and how many of them might have cut the same verses out of the newspaper and tucked them away somewhere, to read and smile at, again and again. He might well have outraged them more, though, when he took that same biblical imagery and turned it against their own illusions and pretensions:

A man will worry over debts,
His visage seared with pain;
Once he survives calamity,
Will plunge in debt again.
"Hitch your wagon to a star,"
Ambition dares to ride;
Saul hitched his wagon to a star
And died by suicide.

Christ sought to make a wicked world
A nobler, happier place;
The rabble nailed him to a cross
And spat into his face.
Old Socrates would show the world
The path of higher aims;
He wrought, and taught, and drank at last
The hemlock for his pains.

When success shall find you
Prey to a gang of snobs,
Or else misfortune thrusts you
Among the frantic mobs,
Or when you find your chief ideals
Thrown in life's seething vat,
'Tis then you'll know man's made of mud,
And damn poor mud at that.

Uncle Joe's most scathing attack against the "upper crust" of county seats and coal company towns came in "Uncle Silas' Vacation," a fictionalized critique of the old-fashioned party-line telephone system. In the plot, a married couple utterly hoodwinks their neighbors by making it appear the wife is having an out-of-town love affair, when in truth she has only gone on a vacation with her husband. It is a bizarre but extremely amusing cross between Edgar Guest, James Whitcomb Riley, and Francois Rabelais:

> Do you know a small town, brother? Then you are with wisdom ripe;
> There talking comes as easily as suction to a snipe.
> For the good Lord they sell sandwiches, ice cream and striped cake,
> And leave mangled reputations a-following in their wake.
>
> They parade for foreign missions, let their children go pell-mell,
> Just to save some lousy derelict who ought to be in hell.
> The man they took from bachelorhood in his sweet-scented prime
> Has got a grindstone to his nose that's turning all the time.
>
> Each day he gets a notice of a note that's overdue;
> Each night he gets a lashing from some lingualistic [sic] shrew,
> While the minister most popular within the rube-town's soul
> Is he who is quite long on speed and short on self control.
>
> In their gayest social circles gossip rages like a pest,
> For the ignorant scandalmongers rarely ever take a rest.
> They forever talk of people; shoot out torture from their stings;
> They gloat about their smutted sheaves, but never talk of *things.*
>
> Imbecility and malice are the children of their brain,
> And their speech is honeyed poison, caring not who feels the pain;
> They fret themselves into a lather, hoping to be deemed as wise,
> But whoever saw an eagle fan the ether, catching flies?
>
> Yet fate doesn't always hand them an overflowing cup;
> For water mostly freezes with the slippery side up.
> Sometimes they get mistaken in the caliber of their guns,
> And he who taps a barrel must take cider as it runs....

Reform them? Law and statute, to dull the tattlers' knife,
Are as powerless as a preacher leering at his brother's wife.
No, sir. The only Gospel that they'll ever understand
Is a hickory *shelaleigh* in some good old callused hand.

At the same time, Uncle Joe in his poetry could be touchingly honest and reflective when addressing individual friends with his own concerns. Note the juxtaposition of faith and skepticism in this excerpt, which he dedicated to his friend Robert Hill:

Have you heard vain, pompous preachers
Boast some brilliant God-sent light,
Boldly hinting Heavenly wisdom,
Else the world be left in night?
Have you heard them preach salvation
To a woman fair, who trusts
In the livery of Heaven
Playing pander to their lusts?

Have you sometimes yourself suspicioned [sic]
Wisdom has no close-set rule?
That the fool may be a wise man
And the wise man be a fool?
For in spite of sage and teacher
Despite adage, law, or rule,
Rich are always deemed the wisest,
And the poor man thought a fool.

Have you not seen washerwomen
Scorned, though pure as heaven's dew,
While some gold-bespangled harlot
Is caressed and toddied to?
Have you not seen small offenders

Trampled 'neath the social ban,
And some million-dollar robber
Deemed a meek, God-fearing man?

Have you chummed up with logicians,
Figured long of rest and strife,
Trying hard to solve a riddle
Of each phase of human life?
Have you thought, To hell with logic!
Burn the books upon the shelf!
For in spite of all their reasons
My worst enemy is *self*?...

Have you heard the skeptic in you
Argue—You are as the clod,
No man, either dead or living,
Ever yet has seen a God?
Have you known the peace that follows
On the notes of some sweet song,
Knew, though while you couldn't prove it,
He was absolutely wrong?

Often, often in my study,
When the house was still and dead,
I have heard my baby daughter
Stealing gently from her bed.
Frightened by the awful silence
She crept softly o'er the floor
Till she saw the light still burning
Through the transom o'er my door.

Quietly her steps retracing
She reposed in peaceful sleep,

Knowing that her God, and father
Did a watchful vigil keep.
Ah, my babe! The childish lesson
Shakes the skeptic from his berth,
Faith, faith—faith in *something*
Is the sublime part of earth.

And so, through the ups and downs of the Roosevelt, Taft, Wilson, Harding, and Coolidge administrations, Uncle Joe wrote prolifically, alternately scandalizing, insulting, amusing, and inspiring anyone who cared to pick up and read his verses in Eastern Kentucky newspapers, in Pike, Floyd, and, occasionally, Johnson, Lawrence, and Boyd counties. His first wife died in Pikeville in 1923, leaving Uncle Joe with three grown sons and three teenaged daughters. A few years later, remarrying (to Cora Wells, of upper Daniel's Creek in Johnson County), Uncle Joe established a small office practice in the town of Inez, the county seat of Martin County, Kentucky. But apparently he never tried to relive the heyday of his Pike County coal-boom days, except within his memory and his poetry:

I am tired of the show and the seeming,
Weary of sham and pretense,
Constantly watching and scheming,
Always on guard, in defense.
I'm going back home to the mountains
Where each is a man in the strife;
Good or bad, he unblushingly lives it—
To hell with a pretense in life.

In his latter years, Uncle Joe became more or less an old-style peripatetic philosopher, alternating between the outlooks of Socrates and Diogenes, and he was always as common as an old shoe. In fact, he probably made more house calls during the later years of his dental practice than he spent time in his Inez office. He had a small portable drill that worked with a foot pump, which he carried along with his bag of dental instruments, Novocaine, and syringes and needles, and when on house calls he would position two old-fashioned cane-bottom chairs back-to-back, put his foot up in one, and have his patients sit in the other chair and throw their heads back over his knee. One might have seen him arrive at a house as the passenger inside a Cadillac or in the back of a beaten-up farm or delivery truck, because he was unconcerned about modes of transportation as long as he could get to wherever he was going. My mother and grandmother sterilized his forceps and needles for him many a time simply in boiling water on the stove, when he'd come to see our family on Greasy Creek after a day of drilling and tooth pulling. As my father remembers with a touch of rue, sometimes what looked like a full inch of grease would detach from the instruments and rise to the top of the seething water, as Uncle Joe proudly displayed his day's cache of teeth—often as not, with more than a little gum tissue to go with them. Of course, the pack of cards and pair of dice I mentioned earlier were permanent fixtures about his person as well; one could never tell where one might run into a game somewhere along the road.

Uncle Joe remained a wanderer until he was past ninety, having survived his second wife as well. He died around Christmastime 1969, by then living in a nursing home in Elkhorn City near one of his daughters. He was buried just outside the small town he had tried to immortalize in verse so many years before. The days that produced both his mindset and his poetic articulation are long gone, and perhaps it is just as well. Yet many of the aspirations and frustrations that he felt so keenly in that past era are still our own; and for its time, Joe Meade's poetry did indeed reflect the spirit of the mountains in rhyme, and he was a genuine Appalachian original. In closing this short memoir of him and his life, I have the sneaking feeling he would have liked for me to use one or two of his own verses as his epitaph:

> Why, oh why, the brand and curse
> Of one who won't fit in!
> Resolve, resolve, and re-resolve,
> Leave off but to begin;

Ever onward is the trail
That man has never trod,
Again a wild lure clutches and
I'm off again, oh God!...

When life's forces are all broken,
When restless days are gone;
When, like waves of restless ocean
The throngs are passing on—
Look not for me where grassy plots
Are hiding forms of men,
But where some lone wolf fiendishly
Howls out a requiem.

WILLIAM FAULKNER, CA. LATE 1920s.
Cofield Collection, Southern Media Archive, Special Collections, University of Mississippi. Used by permission.

Time Sacred vs. Time Profane: Reading Memory and History in Faulkner's *The Sound and the Fury*

BY LUMINITA M. DRAGULESCU

"Memory believes before knowing remembers."

William Faulkner

William Faulkner's narratives in *The Sound and the Fury* assemble a geometric model that can be read both horizontally—or synchronically—in that the stories generally refer to the same events told with different voices, and vertically—or diachronically—in that they refer directly or indirectly to a history, which is not only the Compson family's, but also the South's. As Faulkner forsakes authorial indirection, the history unfolds in four narratives that are both contrastive and complementary. The four accounts from four different characters display prismatic views of the occurrences that are told and also of the significances that tacitly stem from them. The complications that Faulkner's reader has to construct and deconstruct in these narratives revolve essentially around the knotty aspects of time, memory, and history, and around the writer's juggling with these concepts. Individual memory, as employed by the narrators, displays the problematic reading of chronology, of linear, irreversible profane time; memory also permeates the territory of sacred time, a time that is reversible and recoverable. The latter employment of memory is equivalent to the raconteur's attempt to escape or reconstruct history—so obsessive an issue for the South—since, as Mircea Eliade, a prominent Romanian historian of religion, theorized, "the cyclical regeneration of time poses the problem of the abolition of 'history.'"[1]

Conceptualized by Eliade (1907-1986) in *The Sacred and the Profane*, "sacred time is indefinitely recoverable, indefinitely repeatable…it does not 'pass,' it does not constitute an irreversible duration. It is an ontological, Parmenidean time; it always remains equal to itself, it neither changes nor is exhausted."[2] Sacred time, according to Eliade, can be accessed by means of rites by religious minds (It might be argued, hermeneutically speaking, that there is more than one god and that there are sacraments which invoke those gods outside an established, organized religious ideology.). Profane time, to the contrary, is "ordinary temporal duration," which can be measured in seconds, hours, days, or centuries, and which is unidirectional, hence irreversible.[3] The difference between these two aspects of time, the theoretician evinces, "strikes us immediately: *by its very nature sacred time is reversible* in the sense that, properly speaking, *it is a primordial mythical time made present.*"[4]

In the four accounts that make up *The Sound and the Fury*, Faulkner experiments with narrative techniques that seek alternatives to linear time as a means to articulate his preoccupation with a difficult past and with unresolved conflicts that persistently irrupt in the present. All these narrative sequences alternate, creating bridges between at least two interwoven temporal planes: a frame tale set in the narrative present, together with an embedded story, or stories, narration(s) of the past, thereby situating teller and audience in relation to that past. The Faulknerian time employed in these narratives can not be measured in spatio-temporal terms, as the "objective" time is; it is rather a Bergsonian subjective time, perceived and measured in affect-laden, emotional terms, as it unfolds in Quentin's and

---

[1] Mircea Eliade, *The Myth of the Eternal Return*, trans. Willard R. Trask (Princeton: Princeton University Press, 1991) 36.

[2] Mircea Eliade, *The Sacred and the Profane*, trans. Willard R. Trask (New York: Harcourt, 1956) 69.

[3] Ibid., 69.

[4] Ibid., 68; emphasis original.

Jason's accounts. Time's flow, however, is completely disrupted, if not discontinued, in Benjy's abstruse puzzle of seemingly unrelated tableaux. Although more straightforward, the last narrative sequence, Dilsey's section, recounts some of the previously revealed events more chronologically, wiping away some of the imprecision in communication and offering more hints in decoding connotations. Nevertheless, this section, too, is a chronology caught in sacred time, one which eternally returns to the beginnings, *ab origine*, as it will be later demonstrated.

Eliade's concept of sacred time, as escape from "the terror of history,"[5] is consistent with Octavio Paz's definition of narrative time in South American literature and, by extension, it practically labels the southern (both Latin and American) storytelling as an amalgamation of past, present, and future into one continuum, where "time was not succession or transition, but the perpetual source of a fixed present in which all times, past and future, were contained."[6] The conceptualization of time employed by Faulkner is germane to the American South's coexistence of multiple temporal moments, referring to the region's obsession with the lost war, to the moral burden and guilt drawn from the institution of slavery, and to the frustration of poverty emerging in the present and threatening the future. Stemming from this, the Foucauldian urge and pleasure to confess is objectified in the Southern tradition of oral history, of storytelling, a performance that practices remembrance and that also reclaims history while, in the same time, deconstructs it by challenging the voice of hegemony. Nonetheless, the past, troubled as it may have been, is also idealized and worshiped in Faulkner's narratives and is, implicitly as well as explicitly, juxtaposed with the perceived sterility and decay of the present.

Faulkner's emphasis on memory—both individual and communal—in his entire opus stems from his "own theory of time" as a "fluid condition which has no existence except the momentary avatars of individual people."[7] Memory and fragmentation of linear time keep the past alive, yet

[5] Eliade, *The Myth of the Eternal Return,* 156.

[6] Octavio Paz, *The Labyrinth of Solitude*, trans. Lysander Kemp (London: A. Lane, 1969) 208.

[7] Frederick R. Karl, *William Faulkner: American Writer: A Biography* (New York: Ballantine, 1989) 930–31.

they also make the past rcsponsible for condemning the present to death. Repeatedly, the characters in *The Sound and the Fury* strive to oppose the effects of irreversible time by engaging in acts of remembering aimed at resurrecting a past of (idealized) plenitude, hence making time reversible. Memory is granted this power since by nature it subverts linear, profane time and transports the past to present, subsequently accessing sacred time. Conversely, it is this access to the archaic, mythical time that confers memory the transcendental knowledge, or awareness, that Faulkner refers to when he states that memory "[b]elieves longer than recollects, longer than knowing even wonders" and that fuses memory with lived experiences: "[k]nows remembers believes a corridor in a big long garbled cold echoing building of dark red brick …"[8] In addition, though memory rarely gives an objective reflection of events, it is more persistent, possibly because it is more primal than knowledge. Appealing to modern writing for this very undermining of irreversible chronology, the coexistence of multiple levels of consciousness in the characters' minds, in their memory, transcends and obviates the formal unity of time marked out by one calendar day, as it becomes visible in the narratives of *The Sound and the Fury*. Accordingly, in "Unquiet Ghosts: Memory and Determinism in Faulkner," Lee Ann Fennell observes that: "It is memory, with its disregard for chronological time and its idiosyncratic and highly personal chains of association, that pulls pieces of the past into the present, resurrects the dead, and remakes family history. And it is memory, the subjective and selective construction of a private past, that ultimately dooms Faulkner's characters to fates that in retrospect appear unavoidable."[9] Remembrance holds center stage in Faulkner's opus, whether it is individual or collective memory; and remembrance both constructs and deconstructs the rapport between personal history(-ies) and the official history of the South.

Benjy's section is, among the four sections that build *The Sound and the Fury*, the most inscrutable for the reader because, on the one hand, that

[8] William Faulkner, *Light in August* (New York: Vintage, 1990) 119.

[9] Lee Ann Fennel, "Unquiet Ghosts: Memory and Determinism in Faulkner." *Southern Literary Journal* 31/2 (Spring 1999): 35.

account escapes temporal and spatial framing, and on the other hand, by reason of Benjy's mental capacity, the account is solely perceptive, the only level at which the narrator's mind can operate, as a result depriving the audience of the most basic comparisons, generalizations, or abstractions that normal human consciousness usually employs. Eliade observed that, "the primitive [man] lives in a continual present."[10] By all evidence, Benjy is less than primitive and close to what Eliade called the "paradise of animality" that the primitive man sought when "desir[ing] to have no 'memory'"; Benjy, in fact, has no voluntary memory.[11] Eliade states in *Images and Symbols* that for the archaic man "Time itself is ontologized: Time is made to *be*, which means that it ceases to become, it transforms itself into eternity."[12] Since Benjy does not comprehend either past or future, he lives in a perpetual present, which he perceives through a kaleidoscope of involuntary memory triggered by and merged with present perceptions. Primarily simple and plain in his sensory version of the story, this narrator's exclusive use of fractured sensorial perceptions confuses the reader unfamiliar with such a basic level of mental employment. Benjy's testimonials become recondite metaphors for the reader; his statements—restricted to the senses' system of references—cryptic and, at times, paradoxically, even poetical: "Caddy held me. She smelled like trees. *She smelled like trees. In the corner it was dark, but I could see the window. I squatted there, holding the slipper. I couldn't see it, but my hands saw it, and I could hear it getting night, and my hands saw the slipper but I couldn't see myself.*"[13] Benjy acts like a specular account of the events: he reproduces in bits and pieces what happens around him. Moreover, according to Robert A. Martin, "mirror"[14] is a key word in the first narrative sequence because, "[t]he mirror is what Benjy can

---

[10] Eliade, *The Myth of the Eternal Return*, 86.

[11] Faulkner, *The Sound and the Fury* (New York, Vintage, 1990) 91.

[12] Eliade, *Images and Symbols*, trans. Philip Mairet (New York: Harper & Row, 1960) 168.

[13] Faulkner, *The Sound and the Fury*, 72.

[14] Furthermore, Martin observes that "[a]lways there is the image of glass somehow distorting and rearranging one's view of the Compsons. The entire novel is set up on mirror principles, certain characters serving as mirrors of others, fashioned by Faulkner to give the reader slightly different views by which to draw conclusions" (Robert A. Martin, "The Words of *The Sound and the Fury*," *Southern Literary Journal* 32/1 [Fall 1999]: 49). This, in fact, extrapolates the indirectness of the specular approach to the other three sections, too.

see at any given moment, his entire frame of reference ...it seems to tell the reader that anything man sees may be but a reflection of something else uncertain, not sharply defined, elusive."[15] Benjy accurately perceives and mechanically reproduces *what* happens (and this testifies for his reliable, honest voice), but he never understands *why* things happen, and as a result, he never casts judgments upon either events or people. In addition, his way of mixing the signals of his sensorial perceptions leads to a synaesthesia that is difficult to decipher. Consequently, it is the reader's task—or rather toil—to understand the semantic meaning with which the master ventriloquist behind Benjy's voice, Faulkner, charges Benjy's section of narrative. The episode in which Caddy is fighting Jason, because the latter cut up Benjy's toys, stands proof for this raconteur's baffling report: "Caddy and Jason were fighting in the mirror. [...] Jason was crying. He wasn't fighting anymore, but we could see Caddy fighting in the mirror and Father put me down and went into the mirror and fought too. He lifted Caddy up. She fought. Jason lay on the floor, crying. He had the scissors in his hand."[16]

Landmarks, be they temporal or spatial, are set in this narrative, mostly through names that delineate occurrences. While these landmarks are momentous for the reader, they are never important to the narrator, Benjy, who eludes both time and space (and who is forever dwelling in sacred time, in the kaleidoscope of the same events. For instance, readers can orient themselves by how Benjy is addressed, or by the people who populate his limited, yet complicated world: "*His name's Benjy now, Caddy said. How come it is, Dilsey said. He ain't wore out the name he was born with yet, is he.*"[17] In this context, the reader is informed that from this moment on (1900), the narrator will not be called Maury anymore, but Benjamin/Benjy. Helpful for the reader in this labyrinth of perception are the names of Benjy's caretakers, Versh, T. P., and Luster, who, in that order, attend to him throughout his life, and thus act like temporal milestones. Also, Faulkner's alternating paragraphs in either italics (mostly to indicate

---

[15] Martin, "The Words of *The Sound and the Fury*," 48.

[16] Faulkner, *The Sound and the Fury*, 65.

[17] Ibid., 58.

the narrator's thoughts) or standard lettering (to represent Benjy's efforts to reproduce events and dialogues around him, or to represent when people address him) operate as helpful devices for reading the section, at least in delineating one temporal frame from another. Even so, many of the tableaux addressed in Benjy's section can be deciphered and given meaning only in the novel's subsequent narratives, therefore forcing readers to read and re-read the accounts and to employ *their* memory in reconstructing the occurrences, and inviting *them* to evaluate their importance.

However, ambiguous repetitions of names and pronouns without referents enhance temporal confusion in both Benjy's and Quentin's narratives and occasionally even in Jason's. In Benjy's section, for example, there are two Jasons (his father and his older brother), two Maurys (his uncle and Benjy himself, initially), and two Quentins (his oldest brother and his niece, Caddy's daughter), and these names are rarely given a direct referent. The temporally disruptive narration, the juxtaposition of scenes with few temporal and spatial indicators, and the manipulation of the reader through confusing repetition of names with unspecified referents, all correspond to Faulkner's perception of a chaotic world where events do not unfold in a chronological, sequential manner, and in which there is no transcendental authority who may guide or make sense of the experience (other than, perhaps, the reader himself). Since multiple temporal planes and scenes are interwoven through conversations and recollections, the four narratives rely heavily on the reader's skill to suture these together.

If Benjy's inarticulate, innocent mind is not bound by the *a priori* categories of space and time, Quentin's mind has an even more problematic position in regards to spatial and temporal framing. The narrator of the second section is trapped in the continuum mentioned earlier, which hinders progress. Quentin is perpetually navigating among layers of memory, while dreamily registering the present—many times through hallucinations. All the while he is longing for his family's idealized history and haunted by his own tormented past. The unresolved conflicts of his younger years at home in the South, especially his romantic fixation with his sister, Caddy, and the instance of her marriage, overshadow and impinge upon the present.

Memory is the point at which notions of historical time and individual perspective intersect, and Quentin's memory makes no exception; his personal outlook is troubled by recollections of real incidents and also by imaginary scenarios that he persistently appears to construct, such as his "shooting" Dalton Ames for having seduced Caddy, and, later, Herbert Head, for having abandoned Caddy after their marriage. On a different plane, Quentin's explorations of historical consciousness come explicitly into view when he vividly revisits conversations with his father or with Caddy. In fact, Quentin is far more "alive" in his recollections than in his present (un)awareness of the world that surrounds him; in effect, his exacerbated sense of past proves a handicap for his fitting in the present. The narrator's remembrance transports past incidents to the present; it concentrates the past into a single moment, which is a dead end that impedes his moving forward and that eventually will push him to commit suicide.

Quentin's ultimate effort to obstruct the flow of time by taking his own life has a precedent in the recalled episode with Caddy, when the two (especially Quentin) consider their suicide, another attempt to elude time, or possibly to forcefully enter sacred time by performing the definitive ritual: death. The narrator is utterly angry with the present, which he continually tries to escape. The memory of the past haunts him; he is a Southerner who has an honor to protect and a sacrifice to complete in order to redeem the family of General Jason Lycurgus Compson II, who became his mythical ancestor, because, as Eliade remarks, "[t]he transformation of a dead person into an 'ancestor' corresponds to the fusion of the individual into an archetypal category."[18] Furthermore, Eliade observes that "the memory of historical events is modified, after two or three centuries, in such a way that it can enter into the mold of the archaic mentality, which cannot accept what is individual and preserves only what is exemplary," and from here, the "transformation of an event into myth."[19] Following Eliade's reasoning, the General ceases to be the grandfather and instead becomes *the* ancestor (in

[18] Eliade, *The Myth of the Eternal Return*, 46–47.
[19] Ibid., 44.

America's condensed history) for Quentin, in the same way that European aristocrats (primarily royalties) claimed godly lineage to justify their privileges. Correspondingly, Quentin is pressured by the *noblesse oblige* of his family's ancestry and of the Southern tradition of defending honor.

Quentin's desperate struggle with present time and with time past appears from the beginning of the second section, when his father passes on to him both an heirloom (a watch) and the bitter lesson about the eternal human struggle with time:

> [I]t was between seven and eight oclock and then I was in time again, hearing the watch.[20] It was Grandfather's and when Father gave it to me he said I give you the mausoleum of all hope and desire; it's rather excruciatingly apt that you will use it to gain the reducto absurdum of all human experience which can fit your individual needs no better than it fitted his or his father's. I give it to you not that you may remember time, but that you might forget it now and then for a moment and not spend all your breath trying to conquer it.[21]

Quentin's obsession with clocks, with watches, and, ultimately, with passing time, is omnipresent in his narrative, a direct indication of his rapport with time. The narrator recalls that, "Father said clocks slay time. He said time is dead as long as it is being clicked off by the little wheels; only when the clock stops does time come to life";[22] therefore, real time, sacred time, the only time which matters, cannot be accessed when subjected to measuring, which applies only to linear, flowing time.[23] As Octavio Paz stipulates, "[w]hen man was exiled from that eternity in which all times

---

[20] Due to his consideration of the measurable aspect of time, Quentin forcefully returns, I believe, in profane time, which is measurable and irreversible, unlike sacred time which is reversible, thus immeasurable.

[21] Eliade, *The Myth of the Eternal Return*, 76.

[22] Faulkner, *The Sound and the Fury*, 85.

[23] According to Eliade, "[t]he abolition of profane time and the individual's projection into mythical time do not occur, of course, except at essential periods—those, that is, when the individual is truly himself: on the occasion of rituals or of important acts (alimentation, generation, ceremonies, hunting, fishing, war, work). The rest of his life is passing in profane time, which is without meaning: in state of 'becoming'" (*The Myth of the Eternal Return*, 35). Quentin seems to force his projection into sacred time when he symbolically breaks his watch; it is the watch's tick that brings him back in the present.

were one, he entered chronometric time and became prisoner of the clock."[24]

The mythical past emerges to Quentin in more than one way. The sale of Benjy's pasture to pay for Quentin's Harvard education echoes the South's capitulation to and dependence on the North; it is a continuous remembrance of the region's decay and perpetual source of frustration. In his love/hate relationship with the past, Quentin recreates it in his memory, which encompasses events recalled (his conversations with his father or with Caddy) and events imagined (his revenging his sister's lost honor)—all enwrapped in his passionate feelings of regret (regarding the sale of Benjy's beloved pasture to pay for his own studies), longing (for his sister), jealousy and anger (for Caddy's immorality), etc. The narrator's act of recalling past occurrences and searching in them for meanings and solutions, transplants him into the midst of those events which he relives continually. According to Eliade, such acts, when observed as rituals, are conducive to escaping the flow of time and to permeating sacred time, and consequently cyclically reliving certain past experiences: "Insofar as an act (or an object) acquires a certain reality through the repetition of certain paradigmatic gestures, and acquires it through that alone, there is an implicit abolition of profane time, of duration, of "history"; and he who reproduces the exemplary gesture thus finds himself transported into the mythical epoch in which its revelation took place."[25]

Quentin's main fear is that the events that haunt him will be eventually forgotten, that he might even forget Caddy, as his father keenly observes: "you cannot bear to think that someday it will no longer hurt you like this."[26] The narrator's sole option to escape time's stream is to stop it, or to go outside it completely: "[a]nd then I'll not be. The peacefullest words. Peacefullest words. *Non fui. Sum. Fui. Non sum*,"[27] a testimonial that will echo in Faulkner's 1956 interview with Jean Stein vanden Heuvel, where the novelist affirmed that, "[t]here is no such thing as *was*—only *is*. If *was*

---

[24] Paz, *The Labyrinth of Solitude*, 208.

[25] Eliade, *The Myth of the Eternal Return*, 35.

[26] Faulkner, *The Sound and the Fury*, 129.

[27] Ibid., 174.

existed, there would be no grief or sorrow."[28] The Latin statement testifies for Quentin's negating his *being* in the present and his affirming a desire to attain *being* in the past by to reliving it.

The third narrative sequence is, in comparison with the previous sections, straightforward, coherent, and chronological. Jason's greed and cynicism characterize him as down-to-earth, living in the present, with both feet on the ground; the teller is not characterized by any trace of idealism, just utter mercantilism. Ironically, Jason, of all his siblings, carries a sum of the moral features of his Old South ancestors—he possesses a cupidity and ruthlessness characteristic of slave owners—and thus represents the Old South of unromantic plantations and black slaves. The ideological memory of the region transcends, "before knowing remembers," in Jason's mentality of slave master: "I feed a whole dam kitchen full of niggers to follow around him, but if I want an automobile tire changed, I have to do it myself."[29] Displaying nostalgia for *that* past, Jason confesses, "I says my people owned slaves here when you all were running little shirt tail country stores and farming land no nigger would look at on shares."[30] If Jason is not caught in the mythical time of the prosperous Compsons', conversely, that time claims and haunts him: he sees with powerless contempt how his once respected and affluent family has crumbled through alcoholism, madness, and depravity. Jason Compson IV is essentially a sadistic, petty thief who steals his niece's money, cynically deceiving his mother with an obscene ritual of burning the "dirty" checks that Caddy sends to her daughter. Being that he is denied access to the idealized past of the once wealthy and respected Compsons, Jason's ultimate goal is hoarding money, the sole similarity he may have in common with his family's time of glory. To Jason, though not to Quentin, moral issues and concern for the Compsons' good name have little, if any, importance; what *this* Compson seeks is profit. Although a survivor at any cost, Jason's miserly, Scrooge-like means prove ineffective, leaving him with the burden of incessantly and angrily contem-

---

[28] Karl, *William Faulkner*, 930–31.

[29] Ibid., 186.

[30] Ibid., 239.

plating his loss and forcing upon him the humiliation of being outwitted by his niece, a mere girl: a satirical version of a reversible time.

The fourth and last section of *The Sound and the Fury* disrupts the semantic code that characterizes the style of the previous narrative accounts: this sequence is not advanced through a first person narrative, but rather through a third person, objective perspective. Additionally, unlike any of the preceding sequences, the fourth section attempts to cast a cone of (Easter) light onto the events that occurred in those previous narratives. Dilsey's role in the narrative is merely that of a spectator, not that of an actor, who is employed by the previous narrators. Of all the characters who populate *The Sound and the Fury*, Dilsey is the personification of the archaic human, due to her lack of access to education and to her having been confined to the Compsons' household virtually all her life; hence, she is the person most expected to have access to sacred time and to live mainly in a continual present.[31] As a paradigm of the archaic, religious human—who has exclusive access to sacred time and the mythical instance of the cosmic beginning—Dilsey is engaged in ritualistic acts of repetition of the primordial state, ensuring the perpetuation of what Eliade calls *illo tempore* (that time), the time of origins, of the beginning.[32] Eliade's concept of the archaic ontology links the eternal return constituted by sacred time to repeated performance[33]: "[I]nsofar as an act (or an object) acquires a certain reality through the repetition of certain paradigmatic gestures, and acquires it through that alone, there is an implicit abolition of profane time, of duration, of "history"; and he who reproduces the exemplary gesture thus finds himself transported into the mythical epoch in which its revelation took place."[34] The archaic ritual act of Easter celebration constitutes the occasion that transports Dilsey within sacred time and generates her revelation. During the sermon, when the tiny guest priest, Reverend Mr. Shegog, performs the Eucharist, reopening the door to mythical time, he also bids

[31] "[A]ny repetition of an archetypal gesture," Eliade evinces, "suspends duration, abolishes profane time, and participates in mythical time… the man of archaic cultures tolerates 'history' with difficulty and attempts periodically to abolish it" (*The Myth of the Eternal Return*, 36).

[32] Eliade, *The Myth of the Eternal Return,* 76.

[33] I refer here to Butler's definition of performativity as "the reiterative and citational practice by which discourse produces the effects that it names" (*Bodies that Matter*, 2).

[34] Eliade, *The Myth of the Eternal Return,* 35.

the parishioners to transcend their time and space and to "see," to participate in *the* crucifixion and *the* resurrection: to see the very Alpha and Omega. The preacher's sublimely disembodied voice, representing the Word of God, empowers Dilsey to access sacred time, as she reveals in her emotional, dramatic statement. She actually *saw* both the beginning and the end (of the Risen Lord, of the world, of the Compsons) as she testifies: "I've seed de first en de last…I seed de beginnin, en now I sees de endin,"[35] which means that she, much like the preacher, has access to *illud tempus*.[36]

Dilsey's memory of the family's history is what gives her authority and respect in the household; she knows the Compson's grandeur in addition to their evident fall, symbolically pictured in "the square, paintless house with its rotten portico."[37] Therefore, Dilsey's presence in both sacred and profane time makes her a most valuable witness.

For all their intellectual, moral, or religious variety, the four characters in *The Sound and the Fury*, by whose names the narrative sequences are tied, possess a common contrivance that allows them to master time and access and rewrite history: their memory. Memory, be it voluntary or involuntary, is the one tool with which Benjy, Quentin, Jason, and Dilsey bring back people and events past, and memory also conjures incidents and figures preceding their human memory's span. On the other hand, memory, be it individual or transcendental, is the means to escape linear time and permeate sacred time.[38] As a result, memory permits the respective characters to relive the past over and over again. Thus and so, those characters of *The Sound and the Fury* find themselves at the confluence of history and present as employed by memory, which is empowered to transcend physical time and to dwell in a temporal space which has no beginning and no end, and which forever revolves around the same happenings, but can all the while change them.

[35] Faulkner, *The Sound and the Fury*, 297.

[36] *Illud tempus [that time] / Time of origins*, according to Eliade is that "in which the world had first come into existence" (*The Sacred and the Profane*, 80). It is the basis for all the religious rituals which are conducive to recreating and reliving the time when "reality began" (81) and, by extension, when certain occasions of paramount importance occurred, such as, in the Christian world, Jesus' Resurrection.

[37] Faulkner, *The Sound and the Fury*, 298.

[38] Faulkner, *Light in August*, 119.

IN THE EARLY 1930s, EUDORA WELTY STAGED PLAYFUL PHOTOGRAPHS WITH FRIENDS.
IN THIS ONE, SHE IS PRESUMABLY DISGUISED AS GROUCHO MARX.

Eudora Welty's Comic Vision

BY M. THOMAS INGE

Critical appreciation for the fiction of Eudora Welty has gradually increased over the past half-century until now most would agree that she was one of America's most distinguished writers. In a career that spanned five decades, she produced a body of fiction addressing topics of universal importance—the interrelatedness of human beings in their struggle for survival, the isolation and alienation of men and women in modern society, the need for family and community in a time of social disintegration, and the importance of persistence when dreaming of new possibilities in the face of defeat.

While these were among her major themes and preoccupations, Welty also reflected in her writing a belief in the dominance of comedy over tragedy in life. In this endeavor, she drew upon the major techniques and patterns of American humor. From the school of frontier humor, she adopted the oral traditions of folk comedy, the ironic narrator or tale teller, the incongruous juxtaposition of regional dialect and educated language, and the unsettling use of the grotesque—all characteristics of the humorists of the Old Southwest. She also moved easily in the more sophisticated world of Northeastern humor, where urbanity came into conflict with common sense, and she created characters who draw on such traditional American comic figures as the wise fool, the braggart, and the little man overcome by the complexities of the industrial society.

Commentators have frequently taken note of the presence in Welty's fiction of a comic sensibility, something she shared with many other Southern writers, especially Mark Twain, William Faulkner, and Flannery O'Connor. Welty often praised the presence of comedy in the work of Faulkner,[1] and in 1972 when an interviewer quoted to her a statement by O'Connor, who said, "Mine is a comic art, but that does not detract from its seriousness," Welty replied: "I think Flannery O'Connor was absolutely and literally right in what she says: that the fact that something is comic does not detract from its seriousness, because the comic and the serious are not opposites. You might as well say satire is not serious, and it's probably the most deadly serious of any form of writing, even though it makes you laugh. No, I think comedy is able to tackle the most serious matters that there are. I'm delighted that the [critics think] I have a good comic spirit."[2] Thus, as in so much great writing, be it Shakespeare, Cervantes, Swift, Twain, or Faulkner, beneath the serious surface of Welty's narrative there always lurked the spirit of comedy, ready to emerge to relieve the tedium of the most tragic circumstances. Indeed, Welty arguably may be counted among America's major literary humorists, alongside Twain and Faulkner.

It is significant that Twain, Faulkner, and Welty were all Southerners, perhaps not coincidently because Southern culture has always been enriched by the presence of a distinctive sense of humor. "We've always appreciated humor and humorous things" in the South,[3] said Welty, and this becomes especially evident in the love of conversation and tale telling across the region:

> I think you feel that in Faulkner a lot, you know, especially in the little hamlets where people sit on the store porch and talk in the evenings. All they have to talk about is each other, and what they've seen during the day, and what happens to so and so. It

---

[1] Peggy Whitman Prenshaw, ed., *Conversations with Eudora Welty* (Jackson: University Press of Mississippi, 1984) 303.
[2] Ibid., 54–55.
[3] Ibid., 330.

> also encourages our sense of exaggeration and the comic, I think, because tales get taller as they go along. But I think beneath all of that is a sense, really, of caring about one another. It is a pleasure and an entertainment, but it's also something of deep significance to people.... I think we have a native love of the tale.[4]

In mentioning the passion for conversation, the love of exaggeration, and the sense of community expressed in their tales, Welty identified the central characteristics of Southern humor, from the days of the humorists of the Old Southwest (as expressed in the writings of George Washington Harris, Augustus Baldwin Longstreet, and Johnson Jones Hooper, among others) to the present comic journalists (such as William Price Fox, Lewis Grizzard, and Roy Blount, Jr.). That Welty belongs to the tradition of Southern humor is evident from an examination of her fiction in general, but for the sake of space and time, this essay will focus on her first collection, *A Curtain of Green and Other Stories* (1941), and on the short novel *The Ponder Heart* (1954), both of which are closer to the folk and oral sources of Southern humor than her more mannered, stylistically self-conscious fiction.

In all seventeen of the stories in *A Curtain of Green*, which were originally published over a six-year period, conversation abounds. The language used in these stories is the vernacular of ordinary people who love to talk, gossip, and tell tales. Either the narrator or the characters are talking to the reader or to each other at full speed, unself-consciously, unaware that we are strangers overhearing them. Sometimes the narrator addresses the reader directly as if in the middle of a conversation: "I was getting along fine with Mama, Papa-Daddy and Uncle Rondo until my sister Stella-Rondo just separated from her husband and came back home again"[5] begins Sister breathlessly in "Why I Live at the P.O.," and she doesn't let up until she has

---

[4] Ibid., 164–65.

[5] Eudora Welty, *The Collected Stories* (San Diego: Harcourt Brace Jovanovich, 1980) 46.

thoroughly and hilariously justified her action of leaving home. At other times, readers, without warning, are permitted to witness a round of gossip, as in "Petrified Man": "'Reach in my purse and git me a cigarette without no powder on it if you kin, Mrs. Fletcher, honey,' said Leota to her ten o'clock shampoo-and-set customer. 'I don't like no perfumed cigarettes.'"[6] The Southern dialect, of course, is only approximate because Welty's trademark was clear prose, and whether speaking in her own voice or that of a character, the conversation continued to reflect the real world and seldom entered the realm of studied literary language.

Once characters start talking and an author puts them in action, said Welty, humor is automatic, "Because anything that's done in action and talk is a comedy."[7] Welty usually selected for public reading stories with lots of conversation, which are generally also her more humorous fictional works. When asked about her tendency to read comic pieces, she noted, "I think that's because I usually use the form of dialogue when I want to write a comic story. So it works out that way. Also, it's nice to hear the laughter of people. I must say, that goes to my head and makes me feel very fine."[8] The Southern tendency to talk, then, inevitably leads to social interaction and entertainment, and for Welty talk conjured up the comic muse.

Southern literature is noted for its use of the grotesque, from the bizarre and insane characters of Edgar Allan Poe and the backwoods hell-raisers and con-men of the frontier humorists, to the Christ-haunted figures of Flannery O'Connor and the demon-possessed tragic heroes of Faulkner. Welty, too, made a home in her fictional world for such vagrant figures as deaf-mutes, circus freaks, pygmies, murderers, misfits, social outcasts, maladjusted loners, and the outright deranged. Perhaps it is the exaggeration and incongruity inherent in the grotesque that appeals to the Southern sensibility, which loves to embroider and expand upon the truth until it reaches the level of fantasy, as it often does in Welty's fiction.

---

[6] Ibid., 17.

[7] Prenshaw, *Conversations*, 46.

[8] Ibid., 268.

She, however, humanizes even the most outrageous character, sometimes with a touch of irony, as in the case of "The Petrified Man," who turns out to be a sex maniac, and sometimes with a touch of gently whimsy, as in the case of the crippled Little Lee Roy, who turns out to have had a startling career as "Keela, the Outcast Indian Maiden," a side-show geek who bites the heads off live chickens. Little Lee Roy's experience is one his children would not believe, even if they took the time to listen, which they do not. Indeed, reality often seems more incredible than fiction in Welty's world, a paradox that world shares with ours. Finally, however, all these stories are themselves prime examples of the tall tale, except through her narrative skill, Welty induces readers to accept her collection of human oddities as if they were kinfolk. The yarn-spinners and ring-tailed roarers of the Old Southwest had nothing on Welty when it comes to making the incredible seem normal and the insane sound sensible.

Of course, in Welty's fiction, the grotesques are always contained within a larger sense of community. Like the frontier humorists, she largely focused on the lives of the ordinary common folk. Her characters are the salt of the earth—farmers, laborers, store clerks, beauticians, housewives, widows, orphans, salesmen, rednecks, moonshiners, and the unemployed; many are respectable enough, but most have achieved little in life. If the meek shall inherit the earth, then the future belongs to the characters of Welty's fiction. Such people also populate the work of Faulkner, O'Connor, and Erskine Caldwell, but those authors seldom invested their characters with the grace and dignity provided by Welty's compassion.

As noted in her response to O'Connor's statement about the seriousness of comedy, Welty believed that the humorous and serious are inextricably interwoven: "It's in the fabric of life—and I try to show what I see or find there, sometimes comedy, sometimes tragedy, and sometimes both,"[9] or as she said on another occasion about humor, "It intrudes, as it does in life, in

[9] Ibid., 189.

even the most tragic situations."[10] This principle is amply demonstrated in the stories of *A Curtain of Green*.

The grimace of tragedy and the smile of comedy coexist in an uneasy relationship in the story "The Hitch-Hikers," where the sweet poignancy of an unfulfilled love affair is brought into rude conjunction with the sudden and brutal murder of a drifter by his traveling companion. The murder of a wife by her frustrated husband in "A Flower for Marjorie" is recounted not as a tale of terror but as viewed through the soft romantic lens of a surrealistic narrative in which fact and fiction become indistinguishable for narrator and reader alike, both of whom are surprised to discover that the murder really happened. In anger over the unjust death of her husband, Mrs. Larkin in "A Curtain of Green" almost allows her outrage to break out in the slaying of an innocent black boy until a storm of gentle rain brings her to her senses. The affirmative force in the scheme of things as often as not prevails in these stories, as it should in classical comedy.

Despite several tales of terror and murder, Welty does not allow *A Curtain of Green* to move towards the melodrama of the gothic novel or the easy emotions of pulp fiction. In fact, she seems to be satirizing such popular genres in "Old Mr. Marblehall," whose main character has a steady reading diet of tales of horror and science fiction from pulp magazines:

> He reads Terror Tales and Astonishing Stories.... These stories are about horrible and fantastic things happening to nude women and scientists. In one of them, when the characters open bureau drawers, they find a woman's leg with a stocking and garter on.... "The glutinous shadows," these stories say, "the red-eyed muttering old crone," "[t]he moonlight on her thigh," "an ancient cult of sun worshipers," "an altar suspiciously stained...." ...It is richness without taste, like some holiday food.[11]

---

[10] Ibid., 303.
[11] Welty, *Collected Stories*, 95.

Mr. Marblehall's bigamous double life seems a domestic parody of *Dr. Jekyll and Mr. Hyde*, and when he moves from his mundane house in the suburbs as Mr. Bird (a reference to "The Raven" perhaps), the mansion he approaches reminds one of the House of Usher in Poe's tale (and, as with Usher, Marblehall's name suggests the building in which he resides). The humor becomes evident when that story is viewed as a satire, and the characters are seen as grim caricatures in the vein of Edward Gorey or a Charles Addams cartoon.

The jazz musician in "Powerhouse" weaves a darkly detailed story about receiving a telegram that reported his wife's death and that contained a gory account of her suicide, but this turns out to be a tall tale he spins for the simple satisfaction of improvisation as he does in his free-style jazz piano music. Behind the beat of his music resides the unexpressed outrage of the black experience in America, which Welty suggested only through indirection.

"A Visit of Charity" might have been a story to be treated with sympathy or pathos about two old women in a nursing home, yet Welty turns the story into a black comedy as the two old crones argue and spar with each other mercilessly. Before the startled eyes of the visiting girl scout, whose interest is not to provide charity but to gain points for a merit badge, the women bicker like witches around the cauldron in *Macbeth* and turn the story into a comic tribute to the tenacity and nastiness of human beings, including little old Southern ladies.

Welty's 1954 novella, *The Ponder Heart*, is an exemplum of how the traditional elements of Southern frontier humor can be carried to a higher level of literary artistry, as did Twain and Faulkner before her. Like the vernacular narrators of the tales recorded by the frontier humorists in the columns of the nineteenth-century newspapers, Edna Earle Ponder was turned loose by Welty in columns within *The New Yorker*, before book publication, to share her fantastic tall tale about her Uncle Daniel. So engaging is her disarming personality, the easy flow of her colloquial language, and the appeal of her country common sense, that the audience soon finds itself irresistibly engrossed in the comic doings of the residents of Clay,

Mississippi. The voice is so understated and gently humorous in its style that the reader is led to accept the most outrageous propositions as ordinary events.

Welty easily adapted many of the technical devices perfected by the earlier humorists to serve her own purposes. There is, for example, the use of the comic catalog, as when Edna Earle recites a list of those things the mindlessly generous Uncle Daniel has given away:

> Things I could think of without being asked that he's given away would be—a string of hams, a fine suit of clothes, a white-heifer calf, two trips to Memphis, pair of fantail pigeons, fine Shetland pony (loves children), brooder and incubator, good nanny goat, bad billy, cypress cistern, field of white Dutch clover, two iron wheels and some laying pullets (they were together), cow pasture during drought (he has everlasting springs), innumerable fresh eggs, a pick-up truck—even his cemetery lot, but they wouldn't accept it.[12]

Very cleverly, the author brings us up short with the final item, pointing the way to the ultimate conclusion of all things in this world of infinite variety.

There are also the memorable and eccentric characters who populate the writer's imagination and cause us to reflect on the extreme examples of human behavior they represent: the intrepid Elsie Fleming who rode a motorcycle around the Wall of Death at the State Fair; the low-class, appropriately named Peacock family who are the kind of people who "keep the mirror outside on the front porch, and go out and pick railroad lilies to bring inside the house, and wave at trains till the day they die";[13] or the vividly described lawyer Dorris R. Gladney with his "Long, black, buzzardy coat, black suspenders, beaky nose and on his little finger a diamond,"[14] almost stepping out of a cartoon or an animated film. Of course, the cen-

---

[12] Eudora Welty, *The Ponder Heart* (New York: Harcourt, Brace and Company, 1954) 8.

[13] Ibid., 29.

[14] Ibid., 88.

tral members of the Ponder family—Grandpa Sam, Uncle Daniel, and Edna Earle—are comic enough on their own, without the supporting chorus of funny paper characters.

One noteworthy feature of the frontier humorists, and their descendants Twain and Faulkner, was their tendency to litter the pages of their stories with corpses—people are stomped by stampeding bulls and horses, frightened to death by apparent ghosts and shocking events, poisoned by disappointed lovers, or shot by cuckolded husbands or avenging agents of various kinds, usually as a result of an overriding system of justice in the scheme of things. Edna Earle Ponder's story, despite her cheerful disposition, is bracketed by corpses—first the sudden death of her grandfather, who popped a blood vessel on learning that Uncle Daniel had unexpectedly taken Bonnie Dee Peacock for a wife, and then Bonnie Dee's mysterious death, which instigates the raucous murder mistrial that forms the final part of the novel. Edna Earle's poker face and unperturbed demeanor allow us to see these events not as tragedies but as typical incongruities of an already absurd and irrational universe. Since a rough type of justice is enacted in the end, however, Welty finally supports a belief in moral order.

Like many comic figures before him in English and American literature, from Falstaff to Sut Lovingood, Uncle Daniel is a wise fool—a man who speaks more honestly than he should and is given license to do so by society because of his antic disposition and questionable sanity. Too smart to be institutionalized but too abnormal to be left alone, Uncle Daniel goes his way in pursuit of ideal love while giving away all his earthly possessions. Had his quest been a spiritual one, he would have deserved canonization as a saint. Instead, he finds himself accused of murdering the one woman who seemed to fulfill every romantic ideal he had in his muddled mind.

Uncle Daniel's main problem is the Ponder family heart—physically given to running out early, but also possessed by a special kind of love. Edna Earle says:

> I don't know if you can measure love at all. But Lord knows there's a lot of it, and it seems to me from all the studying I've

> done over Uncle Daniel—and he loves more people than you and I put together ever will—that if the main one you've set your heart on isn't speaking for your love, or is out of your reach some way, married or dead, or plain nitwitted, you've still got that love banked up somewhere. What Uncle Daniel did was just bestow his all around quick—men, women, and children. Love! There's always somebody wants it. Uncle Daniel knew that. He's smart in a way you aren't child.[15]

He is, then, a fool for love, and we cannot help but admire the singular way he acts out literally the things he believes: "whatever Uncle Daniel might take it into his head to tell you, rest assured it was the Lord's truth to start with, and exactly the way he'd see it. He never told a lie in his life."[16]

Such touchstones of truth in literature, and many of them populate the plays of Shakespeare and his contemporaries, usually cause great discord in their literary worlds, which are otherwise characterized by hypocrisy, flattery, and social lies. Touchstones of truth are clever comic devices for making readers laugh at their own duplicity and thus encourage readers to mend their behavior. The outcome of the novel demonstrates that love may see Uncle Daniel through, but Edna Earle is required to commit a sin of omission by preventing him from telling a story that will unfairly implicate him in his wife's death.

The unvarnished truth is not always the best response to life's difficulties, and the special value of comedy may lie in the kind of exaggeration and fact-stretching that makes life funny. As Edna Earle makes clear at the trial, it is often necessary to say "I'm going to kill you" or "I'll break your neck"[17] and not intend such statements literally and, in fact, as in the case of a parent and child, make such statements out of love and concern. Truth is found

---

[15] Ibid., 69–70.
[16] Ibid., 17.
[17] Ibid., 111.

in what is intended and not in what is said. The view of the human condition that informs *The Ponder Heart* suggests that by not taking life too seriously, not demanding too much of ourselves, and laughing at our failures, we may come closer to the truths which make life and survival possible.

As John Donald Wade noted in his essay on "Southern Humor," "Life is volatile—the grave running into the comic, the comic into the grave, each perhaps dependent upon the other for its being."[18] Beneath the surface of Welty's sympathetic narrative voice and sensitively crafted sentences is a deep undercurrent of terror, tragedy, and death, yet it is the comic sensibility that reaches more deeply and keeps the characters afloat on the sea of hope and circumstance.

Eudora Welty once said that comedy was the thing "I love to write best of all"[19] and she has acknowledged the creative risks involved: "Yes, I like writing comedy. It's very difficult and it's much harder, because one false step—and I've made many of them.... That's why I have to work very hard on the comic theme, because it's so much more difficult to do. One false step and the whole thing comes down in a wreck around you."[20] There is little evidence of false steps on Welty's part in her short stories and novels. She handled her comic skills like a master and amply demonstrated the necessity of humor as a healthy corrective in depicting the human tragedy. Through laughter, man and woman survive.

Welty not only employed traditional forms of American and Southern humor, but she also demonstrated an implicit faith in people and their potential for survival. Her characters tended to affirm their faith in the scheme of things and found ways to adjust to the inevitable disillusionments of existence. She had, in other words, a comic vision that posited the possibility of salvation and regeneration.[21]

[18] John Donald Wade, "Southern Humor," in *The Frontier Humorists*, ed. M. Thomas Inge (Hamden CT: Archon Books, 1975) 38.

[19] Prenshaw, *Conversations*, 77.

[20] Ibid., 303.

[21] Parts of this essay appeared in my book *Faulkner, Sut, and Other Southerners* (West Cornwall CT: Locust Hill Press, 1992) 163–69. They have been revised and expanded here.

Erskine Caldwell, Hillbilly Celebrity: Retailing Rurality in the Modernist Marketplace

BY JOANNA GRANT

There is a small yet impressively stocked used and rare bookstore near my house in Rochester, New York. Gutenberg's Books, by virtue of its name, reflects some of the aura of its namesake, that precious literary artifact, the Gutenberg Bible. One of the few copies of that book in existence today reposes in a specially designed display module on the ground floor of the Harry Ransom Humanities Research Center in Austin, Texas. In February 2004, that particular Gutenberg Bible stood at the entrance to the brilliant exhibition of modernist treasures gathered together to accompany the State and Fate of Modernism, a symposium held there then.[1] We attendees approached the cases with a mixture of awe and excitement—here was a first edition of *Ulysses*, there some of Faulkner's manuscripts. How much do you think they're *worth*? I wondered to myself, and I heard quite a few others ask the same question.

At Gutenberg's Books in Rochester, Richard Aldington's *Death of a Hero* (the first edition) is worth $47, while a collection of Gertrude Stein short stories costs approximately $90. Those were too much for my slender purse, but I could afford and did buy an autographed paperback copy of

---

[1] The exhibition essay, "Exhibiting Modernism: A View from the Air," was written by Daniel Albright of Harvard University. The essay appears along with other contributions from noted contemporary authors and critics in the collection entitled *Make It New: The Rise of Modernism* (Kurt Heinzelman, ed. [Austin: University of Texas Press, 2003]).

Erskine Caldwell's *God's Little Acre*—for $15. Why so cheap? I wondered. As it turns out, autographed mass market Caldwell paperbacks are fairly easy to find, as he wasn't averse to publicity appearances and book signings, especially later in life.[2] Also, the stock of his signature, and of his *oeuvre*, has fallen since his auspicious debut in 1932 with *Tobacco Road*. The accepted story of Caldwell's life depicts a meteoric rise to heights of critical acclaim and popular appeal, followed by a catastrophic fall into "literary pandering" to a low- and middlebrow audience (like the ones named by Adorno and Horkheimer as consumers of the products of the "culture industry" in *The Dialectic of Enlightenment*[3]).

Accusations of having degenerated into a pulp peddler and a "smut" dealer dealt Caldwell an unfortunate ending to a career that began with publication in *transition*, one of the most esteemed highbrow little magazines of the modernist era. During those early heady years, he was often compared to Mark Twain, H. L. Mencken, and Ernest Hemingway. Caldwell was then viewed (and, more importantly, marketed) as a rough-hewn genius, a satirist with a left-leaning social conscience who had some truths to tell the bourgeoisie. So what happened?

It cannot be denied that Caldwell's literary output declined in quality as it increased in quantity in his later years, as his desire for profit and his refusal to listen to any kind of editorial criticism brought on a marked decline in the caliber of his work. This process led to "critical evisceration" as Caldwell became more committed to his "vision of literature as a commodity and not a form of art."[4] However, individual psychology may not have been the only factor contributing to the fall of Caldwell's star and to his metamorphosis from "one of the most important novelists now writing in the United States" and "something of a celebrity" to "virtual...dismiss[al] from the canon of American literature."[5]

---

[2] Dan B. Miller, *Erskine Caldwell: The Journey from Tobacco Road* (New York: Alfred A. Knopf, 1995) 370–71.

[3] Critic V. P. Hass, review of Erskine Caldwell's *Episode in Palmetto, The Saturday Review of Literature*, 1950, quoted in Miller, *Journey*, 348.

[4] Miller, *Journey*, 347, 346.

[5] From *The Nation*, 1941, the citation is from Miller, *Journey*, 308, 349.

Other, subtler, more interesting forces played their roles in the demotion of this awkward and truculent son of the South from what seemed his assured berth in the literary pantheon. Those of us who grew up in a South where "Tobacco Road" remained a shorthand for a kind of existence we hoped to avoid or escape may follow Caldwell's effort to represent Southern culture—and the repercussions of that representation—with both scholarly and personal interest. This essay will examine how the figure of the Southern poor white (like that of the American Negro and other "species" of so-called "savages") was constructed as a modernist Other, representing a form of fashionable primitivism. Such a critical perspective has been enabled by pioneering work in the new field of "hillbilly studies" by scholars such as Anthony Harkins. The Southern poor white has long been seen as a fascinating if repulsive figure due to its paradoxical construction as a primitive, laughable foil to the more sophisticated, cosmopolitan, Northern consumer of its representations as well as a kind of Anglo-Saxon "Noble Savage" figure. It appears that the critical and cultural fortunes of Caldwell and his Southern poor white subjects are intertwined.

Caldwell constructed his celebrity, his literary stardom, on the backs of his depictions of poor white characters in such widely-read novels as *Tobacco Road* and *God's Little Acre*. While his characters remained susceptible to being interpreted as examples of fashionable primitivism or deeply-felt, left-leaning testimony as to the need for the uplift of poor whites, Caldwell was able to maintain the precarious balancing act between mass market appeal and critical acclaim. As representations of the hillbilly moved from high art to mass-produced Hollywood kitsch (as in the case of *The Beverly Hillbillies*), Caldwell's own career began to falter. His stature was also diminished by his own desire to maximize his earning potential by throwing himself into paperback publishing at a time when the doyens of highbrow culture, particularly the Agrarians and the New Critics (who had always frowned on Caldwell anyway), considered such activities as beyond the pale. While remaining a bestselling author of what might be called Southern-fried soft-porn pulp, he forfeited the cachet of intellectual and artistic integrity.

During the early years of his career, Caldwell was seen as a hillbilly celebrity, a rough-hewn genius, and a poor white darling of the Northeastern intelligentsia. The paradoxical, ambivalent nature of such acclaim is gestured at in the lengthy blurb (with photograph) featured on the back of my copy of Caldwell's *succés de scandale, God's Little Acre* (1933).

Caldwell remained at his zenith through the 1940s. Upon the 1940 publication of his collection of short stories entitled *Jackpot*, Caldwell indeed hit the jackpot when he received "enthusiastic testimonials" from H. L. Mencken, John Steinbeck, Carl Van Doren, and Sinclair Lewis.[6] Caldwell was included in anthologies celebrating and popularizing the best of the "little magazines." During that era, many lists of the best contemporary American writers included his name in their rolls.[7] The accolades kept rolling in: "William Faulkner declared Caldwell one of the five best contemporary American writers, along with himself [naturally], Hemingway, Fitzgerald, and Dos Passos."[8]

How did Caldwell rise to such heights? In the early years of his career, he (and his editors, especially Maxwell Perkins of Scribner's) marketed his product shrewdly and successfully, making sure that he was seen in the right company and presenting the right credentials. Modernist writers such as Malcolm Cowley praised his "violent poetry, simple, romantic, arbitrary and effective." Critic T. K. Whipple, speaking as a representative of the literary left of the 1930s, admired Caldwell's speaking for "the picturesque, proletarian, peasant American"; he *really* admired Caldwell's "proletarian 'credentials' as presented on the book jacket."[9] That carefully calibrated self-presentation, one blurring the lines between producer and product, was similar to the aforementioned blurb from the back cover of *God's Little Acre.* Well-groomed yet virile, serious yet with a twinkle of iconoclastic humor in his eyes, Caldwell is boomed as "the son of a Presbyterian minister…[b]orn

---

[6] Miller, *Journey*, 307.

[7] Miller, *Journey*, 308.

[8] Louis Nordan, foreword, in Erskine Caldwell, *God's Little Acre* (Athens: University of Georgia Press, 1995) vi. This is the edition that I use as my source for quotations in the body of this paper. My signed edition (the back cover of which I refer to, and is reproduced in this article) was far too delicate to withstand the making of notes in the margins and the other abuses perpetrated on primary source texts during the writing process).

[9] The citation is from Miller, *Journey*, 117, 118; ibid., 118.

in 1903 in Coweta County, Georgia, in a spot too remote to have a name.... He worked his way through the Universities of Virginia and Pennsylvania, graduating from neither... [He has been] a mill laborer, cotton-picker, hack-driver, stage-hand, reporter, cook and waiter...in 1938 [he] gave a series of lectures on 'Southern Tenant Farmers' at the New School for Social Research.[10] The blurb offered a careful deployment of a constructed authorial image, one tough yet romantic, much like the vision of Southern culture that Caldwell espoused.

Traditionally, modernist writers were supposed to be above such things, disdaining the vulgar embrace of the herd, a position espoused in the slogan for Margaret Anderson's periodical *Little Review*: "Making no compromise with the public taste." Recently, critics such as Catherine Turner and Joe Moran have revised and complicated this notion, demonstrating that modernist authors "did not like mass culture.... [H]owever, [they] never turned their backs on it...if they really wanted to 'make it new'—in the broad sense of changing human perception and experience in the world—they would have to reach an audience."[11] And, as Moran illustrates in his book *Star Authors*, in the age of proliferating mass media one needs to sell oneself to make it big. Moran uses Mark Twain—to whose persona and output both Caldwell himself and his works were compared—as one of many examples. Twain "sold himself" successfully, however reluctantly, as did Dickens and Wilde, two other "transatlantic stars."[12] In modern publishing, the authors, publishers, and consumers of literary products comprise what Pierre Bourdieu theorizes as a "field" in which persons and institutions grapple with each other for precedence; the production of culture and the artifacts (like books) that make it up is an "anti-economy," one in which "symbolic capital"—i.e., credibility and

[10] Please see the accompanying illustration.

[11] Catherine Turner, *Marketing Modernism Between the Two World Wars* (Amherst & Boston: University of Massachusetts Press, 2003) 4.

[12] Joe Moran, *Star Authors: Literary Celebrity in America* (London & Sterling VA: Pluto Press, 2000) 16.

About the Author

ERSKINE CALDWELL

He has lived all over the place, particularly through the length and breadth of the South. Born in 1903 in Coweta County, Georgia, in a spot too remote to have a name, Caldwell was the son of a Presbyterian minister. He worked his way through the Universities of Virginia and Pennsylvania, graduating from neither. For a time he held a variety of jobs, working as a mill laborer, cotton-picker, hack-driver, stage-hand, reporter, cook and waiter. Exactly six feet tall, he has the physique of a football pro (another job he has held), and a round, candid, innocent face. He is deeply interested in the problems of the submerged Southerners he writes about (although some of the less perceptive members of his audience have seen them simply as grotesque butts for his Rabelaisian humor), and in 1938 gave a series of lectures on "Southern Tenant Farmers" at the New School for Social Research. He now lives in Arizona.

Caldwell's other best-known books are *Trouble in July,* published as #567 in this series and *Tobacco Road* (#627)—the dramatization of which ran for seven years on Broadway—*Journeyman* (#646) and *Tragic Ground* (#661).

Published by the New American Library

BACK-COVER BLURB OF ERSKINE CALDWELL'S NOVEL *GOD'S LITTLE ACRE* (New American Library edition).

prestige as measured by the correct proportion of good reviews to healthy sales—is converted into economic success. Oddly enough, or perhaps not, "the most 'anti-economic' and most visibly 'disinterested' behaviors…contain a form of economic rationality."[13] So—one can grub for dollars using all kinds of advertising and publicity stunts as long as one can maintain the pretense that that isn't what one is actually doing.

In his early years, Caldwell achieves this feat through a combination of good sense and good timing. While he was in the process of flunking out of the University of Virginia (note the masterful touch: he has the drive and acumen to get into a good university, and the bohemian credibility that comes from abandoning it), he was thrilled by the library's collection of little magazines, "intoxicated by the violence, sexuality, and uncompromising realism he discovered."[14] Caldwell's own writings chronicle the violent and darkly comic doings of Southern grotesques, dwelling lovingly on the ugly and the obscene. In doing so, he affiliates himself with such other American modernist writers as Sherwood Anderson and Ernest Hemingway, with whom he was often compared; those authors had blazed the trail Caldwell was to follow.

As Turner demonstrates, Anderson, Hemingway, and their publishers had effected a change in the public taste, creating a market for modernist works by appealing to what Stuart Sherman in an article in *The New York Herald Tribune Books* called "the craving to be formed." Drawing on the work of Joan Rubin, Turner demonstrates that advertisements for modernist literature "presented culture as a commodity that offered a solution to people's personal insecurities."[15] Anderson and Hemingway—and Caldwell—participated in the seemingly disinterested marketing of their products by adhering to and circulating protestations that their books told the truth about American life. By doing so, those authors aligned themselves with influential critics such as Van Wyck Brooks, who believed that

[13] Pierre Bourdieu, *The Field of Cultural Production: Essays on Art and Literature* (New York: Columbia University Press, 1993) 62.

[14] Miller, *Journey*, 83.

[15] The citation is from Turner, *Marketing*, 17.

the sense of crisis in American culture and letters could be blamed on the repressive Puritan past and on the current work of sell-out authors bent only on "material success." These sentimental hacks and scribbling women, according to Brooks, had "thrown veils over the barrenness and emptiness of our life."[16] What was called for, Vernon Louis Partington opined, was a new "brutal realism" that would enable "the animal called man [to] stand...before us naked and unashamed."[17] The appeal to a masculinist brand of sensationalism is obvious, and constitutes a central component of these critics' and authors' hopes to escape the feminine, the sentimental—or, in Caldwell's case, the "genteel," romantic school of Southern literature, the mode predominating Southern letters at the beginning of the twentieth century.

Accordingly, Caldwell produced *Tobacco Road* and *God's Little Acre*, creating characters that echoed archetypal images of the South. Such characters include his tragicomic poor white patriarchs Jeeter Lester and Ty Ty Walden and their oversexed womenfolk. Of course, Caldwell's representations of poor whites don't emerge out of thin air; Caldwell utilizes hillbilly stereotypes, as Harkins demonstrates in *Hillbilly: A Cultural History of an American Icon.*

In this study, Harkins enumerates the "standard tropes that defined hillbillies throughout popular culture: social isolation, physical torpor and laziness, unrefined sexuality, filth and animality, comical violence, and utter ignorance of modernity."[18] Some historians of American rurality and its literary representations may criticize Harkins's book for its "homogenizing" of the different regions of rural America.[19] Rural Minnesota and rural Mississippi differ in many ways, of course, and some scholars would offer

---

[16] Van Wyck Brooks, *America's Coming-of-Age* (Garden City NY: Doubleday Anchor Books, 1958) 124.

[17] Vernon Louis Partington, "The Development of Realism," in *The Reinterpretation of American Literature*, ed. Norman Foerster (New York: Harcourt Brace, 1928) 158–59.

[18] Anthony Harkins, *Hillbilly: A Cultural History of an American Icon* (New York/Oxford: Oxford University Press, 2004) 105.

[19] Historian and literary critic Janet Galligani Casey made such a point during a seminar on "Modernism and Rurality" that was the occasion for the writing of the original version of this paper. This seminar took place in Vancouver, British Columbia, at the sixth annual Modernist Studies Association conference. I would like to take this opportunity to thank Professor Casey for her seminar leadership and for her contributions to this project. I would also like to thank my fellow seminar participants for their enthusiasm regarding this piece; my especial thanks go out to Aaron Shaheen, who provided me with thoughtful and detailed suggestions for revision.

objections to the eliding of the various "species" of poor white, rural American into the overdetermined figure of the hillbilly. However, this shortcoming also constitutes one of the book's strengths. Harkins deals with an image of the sexualized, primitive hillbilly/poor white that has to a certain extent become divorced from its referent while insisting upon its truth, a classic modernist maneuver. To a considerable extent, modernist authors and their audiences cared little for empirical evidence if it endangered the beauty and utility of an idea or vision. The long half-life of stereotyped images of the rural South has great implications for aficionados of Southern literature and culture, especially as the power of those stereotypes persists in the face of rapid demographic change.

The descriptions of poor whites/hillbillies recovered by Harkins could easily serve as descriptions of characters in any of Caldwell's novels. In an infamous scene in *Tobacco Road*—the one that probably put more bottoms on seats than any other when the novel was adapted to the stage—Ellie May, the girl with the harelip, "scrape[s] her bottom on the sand" in a masturbatory fashion as she drags herself across the yard like a dog in heat towards her brother-in-law Lov. Later, she copulates with him in full view of her family.[20] In *God's Little Acre*, Ty Ty Walden frequently praises his son's wife's "rising beauties [her breasts]," which make him want to "get…right down on [his] hands and knees like these old hound dogs you see chasing after a flowing bitch."[21] Caldwell's hillbillies fight and make love like animals. Indeed, as Griselda observes in *God's Little Acre*, "There was a mean trick played on us somewhere…God put us in the bodies of animals and tried to make us act like people."[22] Caldwell's poor whites don't always measure up to that evolutionary challenge.

As Harkins demonstrates, there is an unsettling and thrilling similarity in the representation of poor whites and blacks in the primitivist discourse of the early twentieth century. Of course, tensions between "white trash" and blacks and the fear of miscegenation are some of the hallmarks—and

---

[20] Erskine Caldwell, *Tobacco Road* (New York: The Modern Library, 1947) 24.

[21] Erskine Caldwell, *God's Little Acre*, foreword by Louis Nordan (Athens Georgia: University of Georgia Press, 1995) 88.

[22] Caldwell, *Acre*, 208.

favorite bugbears—of Southern literature. For instance, in the "Becky" section of Jean Toomer's 1923 novel *Cane*, the townsfolk exhibit horror toward her mixed offspring. Harkins deepens our understanding of how images of the poor white and of Southern rurality were shaped and packaged in the early twentieth-century marketplace. According to Harkins, a kind of creative miscegenation was practiced in the early days of the film industry:

> mountaineer [and other poor white] characters' viciousness, ignorance, and primitiveness mirrored the portrayal of nonwhite characters in numerous other silent films. Race and notions of proper racial hierarchy were central to both the narratives and ideological underpinnings of many silent film producers and directors, most notably Kentucky native D. W. Griffith. In the same way, Griffith consistently used characters of African, Chinese, Latino, and Indian descent to show the latent violence in all people of color, the dangers of interracial sexual desire, and the superiority of whites. Through narratives of nonwhite servitude, he incorporated mountaineers, coded as "nonwhite," to highlight the superiority of "normative" white society.[23]

It seems rather astounding from our contemporary standpoint that brandishing images of hillbillies, crackers, and clay-eaters could ever have been considered an expression of modernity and sophistication, or that Southern poor whites could have occupied a space in the modernist imagery analogous to that of such Others as the American Negro or dark-skinned peoples from other locales. That reaction seems to lurk just beneath the surface of Harkins's bemused description of the hillbilly cartoons that ran in "such a self-consciously sophisticated publication as *Esquire*," which "blend[ed] a woman's magazine format (mixing fiction, illustrations, and lifestyle features) with a male-oriented (and, in many cases, outrightly

---

[23] Harkins, *Hillbilly*, 61.

misogynist) outlook, and 'high brow' culture with 'low brow' sex-driven cartoons and 'pin ups.'"[24] Caldwell, who published in *Esquire*, gained great fame and wealth by exploiting the same kinds of stereotypes while asserting an interest in vigorous, regenerative truth-telling.

Caldwell's exploitation of the primitivist poor white was further complicated by his identification with the left and with fashionable Communism. In the 1920s and 1930s, the rise of what historian George Tindall called the myth of the "Benighted South" blended uneasily with the subsequent Depression era's "general celebration of 'the folk'...[that grew out of a desire for] escape into a romanticized rural past." In his chapter on the origin of the country/"hillbilly" music industry, Harkins examines how the fashionable image of the white primitive was packaged and consumed by radio listeners and buyers of early recordings and sheet music.[25] In a typical piece of modernist juxtaposition, this "authentic" music of the rural poor was packaged and retailed as commercial recordings, and was broadcast to living rooms across America by means of radio waves.

Caldwell's work mirrors this tension in its unsettling and shifting mixture of reverence for and ridicule of its subjects. For all of his righteous indignation against wealthy landowners and mill owners in *Tobacco Road* and *God's Little Acre*, Caldwell is not above poking rather cruel fun at his characters, particularly his female ones. This may be seen in *Tobacco Road* when the car salesmen fleece Sister Bessie of her savings, "wink[ing] at each other" as they mock her country ways and her facial deformities.[26] Bessie has no nose, possibly the results of a venereal disease such as syphilis.

Be that as it may, Caldwell in the 1930s successfully marketed himself as a warrior of the proletariat. He was aided in this respect by the censors' repeated attempts to ban his work. Attempted censorship, and even outright banning, as we know, can be great publicity, and it certainly worked for Caldwell. He and his supporters were able to claim persecution by the philistine, repressive forces of organizations such as the New York Society

[24] Ibid., 105.

[25] George Brown Tindall, *America: A Narrative History*, Brief 3rd ed. (New York: W. W. Norton, 1993) 284; Harkins, *Hillbilly*, 89.

[26] Caldwell, *Road*, 119.

for the Suppression of Vice. According to Miller, the dramatic version of *Tobacco Road* was taken to court thirty-six times. Caldwell "logged thousands of miles defending *Tobacco Road* and became recognized as one of the nation's leading advocates of artistic freedom. And with the rise of fascism in Europe, he began to liken his trials to the struggles for liberation going on around the globe."[27] The author was no longer just an author; he had become a fashionable cause.

Caldwell's identification with the fashionable left benefited immensely from his cementing of, first, a professional and, then, a romantic partnership with the photographer Margaret Bourke-White, the star of *Life* magazine's staff. They capitalized on the growing interest of American Communists and other left-leaning intellectuals in Southern working-class culture, inventing and popularizing the fashionable photo-essay genre of the 1930s, one whose occasional distortions of the truth in the guise of documentary realism has been commented on at length. Caldwell had already rendered the character of Will in *God's Little Acre* into a proletarian Christlike figure who dies for the cause of the workingman, like Joe Hill. In their bestselling *You Have Seen Their Faces*, Bourke-White's portraits of poor whites and blacks, whose thoughts are "voiced" by Caldwell's captions, went "a long way toward establishing the image of the South in Northern liberal circles as a land of wasted yeomanry reduced to hapless peonage by corrupt landowners; a place where honorable, virtuous Negroes were lynched at the slightest provocation with the smirking complicity of a pot-bellied white sheriff."[28] The North might have loved Caldwell; the Soviets might have lionized him; even the French might have praised him; but we can see how people in the South might have been less than thrilled at being represented in this way. However, Caldwell's mantle of truth-telling protected him through World War II. Harkins quotes a defender of Caldwell's, whose letter to *Esquire* concludes that "the poor whites seem happy enough in all their squalor, so we may as well leave matters as they are."[29] As long

[27] Miller, *Journey*, 202.

[28] Ibid., 157.

[29] The citation is from Harkins, *Hillbilly*, 112.

as the image of the poor white kept its primitivist charge and held the attention of the intelligentsia, Caldwell could do no wrong. We today who preoccupy ourselves with trying to know the South, hoping to chart its changes and its passages, can profit, no doubt, from looking at how past authors have created images of the South that responded well to contemporary shibboleths and preoccupations.

The problem of identifying oneself with a popular cause, however, is that one runs the risk of becoming the victim of changing times. American Communists and other left-leaning intellectuals were stunned by Stalin's non-aggression pact with Hitler. Later, the outbreak of the Cold War made the fashionable Communism of the Depression years seem dated if not dangerous. At the same time, representations of the hillbilly began to lose their association with cutting-edge primitivism as they became transformed into pop culture kitsch in the Ma and Pa Kettle films, *The Real McCoys*, *The Andy Griffith Show*, and, of course, *The Beverly Hillbillies* (see Harkins, chapters 5–6). Perhaps not surprisingly, by the World War II years—which mended the national economy and forced the closing of the play *Tobacco Road* due to saturation of the drama market—reviews of Caldwell's books exhibited signs of waning enthusiasm. In a review of Caldwell's *Journeyman*, for instance, Horace Gregory of *The New York Herald Tribune* deprecated Caldwell's "present tendency to repeat himself."[30]

Caldwell also suffered from the perennial curse of the Bright Young Thing, the ease with which a familiar media darling becomes yesterday's news when a new star comes to town. But why did Caldwell's reputation fade so fast when, for example, John Steinbeck's went from strength to strength after the 1939 publication of *The Grapes of Wrath*? Perhaps the answer emerges from a comparison of Caldwell's and Steinbeck's uses of sentiment, the sacred, and the supposedly documentary, and from a consideration of the roles these narratives and styles play in the kinds of stories Americans like to tell about their collective nature and character. On the

[30] The citation is from Miller, *Journey*, 205.

one hand, Americans crave the truth, ever seeking to investigate and to understand the world. But on the other hand, Americans want to identify themselves with the common man, one with God and right on his side. The brutality of Caldwell's grotesque, objectifying vision simply could not withstand the emotional rush of Henry Fonda's film delivery of Tom Joad's parting lines from *The Grapes of Wrath*: "I'll be ever'where—wherever you look. Wherever they's a fight so hungry people can eat, I'll be there."[31] Steinbeck even acknowledges the sacrality of American womanhood in his—admittedly controversial—depiction of the character Rose of Sharon nursing the starving man at the novel's end, casting the pair as a Depression-era Madonna and child.

Perhaps the recent renewal of "highbrow" critical interest in Caldwell may be attributed to the rise of a postmodernism that has created an academic audience more prepared to accept flat, cartoonish, and brutish characters, ones suspicious of the kind of grand narratives of psychology and biblical allusion and typology deployed by a Steinbeck. For example, when comparing the end of *The Grapes of Wrath*—Casey's death, Tom's apotheosis, Rose of Sharon's selfless gesture—with a roughly comparable sequence in Caldwell's *God's Little Acre*, obvious differences emerge. In Caldwell's telling, the Christ figure, Will, can't keep his hands off his sister-in-law, and his death accomplishes nothing.

Critics became less enamored of Caldwell's characters and their predilections, however, once their novelty grew stale. A fusion of sentiment and manly vigor, as in Steinbeck's fiction, exposed the undercurrent of voyeurism and sadism ever present in Caldwell's *oeuvre* to a public not entirely willing to accept it. No wonder that Caldwell found success in pulp fiction, where such excesses were not only tolerated but encouraged.

The bad reviews increased dramatically as Caldwell began to write more and more quickly in order to capitalize on what remained of his literary reputation. Increasingly, Caldwell's publishers relied on lurid covers and cheap

---

[31] John Steinbeck, *The Grapes of Wrath*. (New York: Penguin Books, 1992) 572; the movie version of the novel was released in 1940.

paperback prices to move his books. Caldwell began to gain notoriety as a writer of supposedly "dirty" books, and indeed he published some stories in pornographic magazines. This was enough to put him beyond the pale as far as Allen Tate and his associates were concerned. The Agrarians had always viewed Caldwell as a traitor to their homeland, and now they were able to write him off as both a whore and a hack. As Miller observed:

> Caldwell's pioneering status as an author and promoter of mass-market paperbacks was the most potent ingredient in his critical decline.... Caldwell first encountered this snobbery in 1948 when he attended a discussion on contemporary American literature at the University of Kansas. On the way to the conference, Caldwell had...host[ed] a publicity event for NAL [his publisher] in a local drugstore. When he reached the university, he noted an unmistakable aloofness and coolness among the participants, who included such eminent critics as Allen Tate.[32]

On the face of it, a drugstore hardly seems like a disreputable public space. Yet, considering Tate's conceptions of literature and the author, that venue does partake more of the bawdy house than of the ivory tower.

Caldwell's vision of the South—as a region peopled with violent, deformed, sex-crazed grotesques—had always run counter to the vision of the Agrarians, who wished to enact their own "platform for a genteel 'squirearchy' of cultural domination."[33] Donald Davidson, right-leaning mentor to the Vanderbilt Fugitive/Agrarian movement, denigrated mass culture in terms of which the left-leaning Adorno and Horkheimer would have approved, stating that the "industrialists in art...will naturally make their appeal to the lowest common denominator."[34] According to this logic, then, Caldwell, who had heavily invested in the now terminally lame image of the hillbilly and the teachings of inartistic propagandists, had to forfeit

---

[32] Miller, *Journey*, 370.

[33] Walter Kalaidjian, "Marketing Modern Poetry and the Southern Public Sphere," in *Marketing Modernisms: Self-Promotion, Canonization, Rereading*, 300.

[34] Donald Davidson, "A Mirror for Artists," in *I'll Take My Stand: The South and The Agrarian Tradition, by 12 Southerners* (New York: Harper Torchbooks, 1962) 35.

his unearned place in the American literary canon. The Agrarians' marketing strategies secured them control over the competitive field of American letters, until their claims to prestige and value were discredited in their turn.

Now, with the rise of "hillbilly studies" (an outgrowth of cultural and gender studies), Caldwell appears to be making a comeback. His depictions of coarse, brutish men and rapacious women, characters whose desires seem to override evolution, render his work particularly interesting to contemporary scholars of Southern literature and culture. As Barbara Ladd observes, "[r]ace is one of the most salient problematics in southern literary studies; the other is gender."[35] One can't help but wonder how long this revival will persist, and how much my autographed copy of *God's Little Acre* may appreciate or depreciate in value over the next few years.

This battle over the hillbilly image is far from over, as the media's focus on the desirable votes from NASCAR dads of the Bible Belt indicate. In fact, these NASCAR dads live in an increasingly polyglot South, one whose cacophony of voices in different languages might silence Caldwell for good. According to many people today, that would be a good thing. But if such Caldwell characters as Jeeter Lester and Ty Ty Walden could speak today, perhaps they would counter that, however disrespected they might become, however short and brutal their lives might remain, they will survive. And some might say that *that* would be a good thing.

[35] Barbara Ladd, "The Changing Profession: Literary Studies: The Southern United States, 2005," *PMLA* 120/5 (October 2005): 1630. Ladd goes on to cite Michael Kreyling's assertion of the importance of the "mid-twentieth-century conservative intellectual historians Richard Weaver and Eugene Genovese['s identification of the] erasure of 'sexual predation' and female subjugation from southern intellectual history." Sexual predation constitutes a favorite leitmotif of Caldwell's work, though it should be noted that women can be just as guilty of these offenses as men in his fictional world.

Ignatius Reilly's Polish Compatriot: Finding *Ferdydurke* in *A Confederacy of Dunces*

BY JOE SAMUEL STARNES

The multiple similarities in John Kennedy Toole's *A Confederacy of Dunces* and Witold Gombrowicz's *Ferdydurke* are striking considering that the two novels were written twenty-five years apart in cultures as divergent as Poland in the late 1930s and Louisiana in the early 1960s. Both novels feature thirty-year-old protagonists, anti-hero characters created by authors of approximately the same age as their main character at the time of writing. Both books took many years after their original writing to be published in English: *Ferdydurke*, begun in 1935 and published in Polish in 1937, was translated from Polish to Spanish in 1947 and then to German and French in the late 1950s and early 1960s. The first English translation was published in 1961, derived from the French, German, and possibly the Spanish translations[1]; *A Confederacy of Dunces*, written in the early 1960s, finally found publication in 1980 solely because of the persistence of Toole's mother, who sought readers for the book after Toole's suicide in 1969.

Both authors were outcasts of a sort. Toole, unable to get his novel published, died by his own hand at the age of thirty-one. Gombrowicz was on a cruise off South America in 1939 when the Germans occupied his homeland. Stranded in Buenos Aires, he remained in exile in Argentina and did

---

[1] Danuta Borchardt, "Translator's Note," in Witold Gombrowicz, *Ferdydurke*, trans. Danuta Borchardt (New Haven: Yale Nota Bene, 2000) xvii.

not return to Europe for twenty-three years; he never returned to Poland.[2] Gombrowicz died, at the age of sixty-four, in 1969, the same year as Toole.

Both novels have been vilified by many readers and revered by others: *Ferdydurke*[3] was banned and burned for decades by Nazis and then by Communists in Poland; *Confederacy* suffered years of rejection from New York printing houses before being published by Louisiana State University Press. Even after winning the Pulitzer Prize and selling successfully, topping *The New York Times* paperback bestseller list for a month, Toole's novel still is frowned upon by many genteel New Orleans residents for its unflattering portrait of eccentric, immoral, and corrupt characters, as well as its occasional bathroom humor and sexual content, complaints also lodged against *Ferdydurke*.

Joey Kowalski, Gombrowicz's narrator, and Ignatius Reilly, Toole's protagonist, are adults that refuse to grow up, jaded by a fear, even a hatred, of the cultural institutions of school and work. Perplexed by the opposite sex, both characters live in societies deep in turmoil from racial and religious strife, governed by dangerous demagogues. The two novels are irreverent and often outrageously comic—with Toole's work being one of the funniest American novels ever written—but both authors also project a dark "worldview," to use one of Ignatius' favorite terms, of anger and bitterness at the conformity required and the normalcy expected in the world beyond their childhoods, beyond the doors of their cozy private rooms. Joey and Ignatius, each the age of Jesus when he began his ministry, share a paralysis in the face of cultures they find inane and ridiculous. They both prefer to stay indoors, writing in their notebooks rather than trying to coexist in societies ruled by a gauntlet of dictatorial authority figures: "cultural aunts" and school teachers in Poland; and Ignatius's mother, college professors, factory owners, and policemen in New Orleans. The revolt of both protagonists is one of not confronting the world outside; instead, they seek to hide away

[2] Czeslaw Milosz, *The History of Polish Literature* (Berkeley: University of California Press, 1983) 432–37.

[3] The meaning of the title is unclear. "The title itself, *Ferdydurke*, has no meaning in Polish, although there is some conjecture that the word was a contraction and alteration of the name Freddy Durkee, the chief character in Sinclair Lewis's *Babbitt*, which was widely read in Poland in the early 1930s. Gombrowicz himself never explained the title" (Borchardt, "Translator's Note," xx).

from the systematic demands that compromise their philosophical beliefs and their art. Gombrowicz was ahead of postmodern culture in his stylistic challenge to society and culture; Toole took bitter and ironic swings, not only at traditional societal leaders of industry, military, and war, but at postmodern figures themselves: beatniks, sexual and social revolutionaries, and liberals of the early 1960s—and he did it at a time when it certainly was not fashionable to take such a position. Both authors were politically incorrect before the term was coined. It is fitting that the symbolism in the two books flaunts the adult world by sticking their rear-ends out: Gombrowicz, with his frequently cited "pupa," and Toole, through the obese Ignatius's flatulence caused by trouble with his pyloric valve. In effect, both Gombrowicz and Toole commit the literary equivalent of the teenage prank of "mooning" proper society, an "*ass*ignation," if you will, of the derriere as a symbol of revolt against mainstream social mores.

How did these two novels—written in different cultures, languages, and times—come to echo one another in so many ways? It is certainly possible that Toole read the 1961 English language edition of *Ferdydurke,* which in the US was published by Harcourt. Toole was well-read and educated with a master's in English from Columbia University and some doctoral studies at Tulane University. According to a recent biography, Toole began writing *Confederacy* in 1962 and completed the novel in early 1964. This timing would have allowed *Ferdydurke* to be an influence for Toole during the writing of his novel.[4]

Regardless of the question of Toole's possible exposure to *Ferdydurke,* Poland in the mid-1930s and Louisiana in the early 1960s have much in common. Both were places with racial uneasiness and were subject to demagogic leaders. Also, both cultures were overshadowed by other nearby countries or states, and both areas were often looked down upon by their

[4] Rene Pol Nevils and Deborah George Hardy, *Ignatius Rising: The Life of John Kennedy Toole* (Baton Rouge: Louisiana State University Press, 2001) 79–133.

JOHN KENNEDY TOOLE, (1937-1969)
Photo courtesy of Louisiana State University Press.

neighbors. Of Toole's novel, Andrei Codrescu wrote, "The South, at the beginning of the Civil Rights Movement, was America's designated hell. Southern writers were a suspect species, with a few rare exceptions."[5] Gombrowicz faced a similar situation in Poland, where proximity to Western Europe created what Susan Sontag calls "the Polish sense of being marginal to European culture."[6]

In Poland, Jozef Pilsudski—a revolutionary Socialist from Krakow—led that nation after World War I, defeating Soviet forces in 1920 near Warsaw. In 1921, a peace treaty established a border between the Soviet Union and Poland, cutting through the middle of ethnically mixed areas, with large Byelorussian and Ukrainian-speaking populations on both sides. After five years of political turmoil, Pilsudski took over the government as dictator. "He revealed himself to be a man of whims and resentments, acting more by instinct than by any clearly formulated principles," wrote Csezlaw Milosz in *The History of Polish Literature*. Pilsudski founded a concentration camp and sent several members of opposing parties there. He died in 1935, but the political situation only worsened as Adolf Hitler's power grew. Poland was fraught with political tension, including Nazi influenced anti-Semitic regulations imposed at universities. According to Milosz, "The tone of Polish literature changed in 1930 with an economic crisis, the violation of the constitution by the military junta, the emergence of Fascist groupings on the Right, propagating anti-Semitism. In intellectual circles a feeling of impotence and presentiments of an imminent European catastrophe prevailed."[7]

Toole's Louisiana is unique for its insularity and cultural distinctiveness (manifested in Mardi Gras, jazz, voodoo), yet even the fiercely independent Deep South was not nearly as close to outright war as Gombrowicz's Poland. Nevertheless, Louisiana was gripped by racial tensions as the Civil

[5] Andrei Codrescu, "*A Confederacy of Dunces*, Making the Natives Wince," *Chronicle of Higher Education* 46/32 (April 14, 2000): B7.

[6] Susan Sontag, "Foreword," in Witold Gombrowicz, *Ferdydurke*, trans. Danuta Borchardt (New Haven: Yale Nota Bene, 2000) xiv.

[7] Milosz, *The History of Polish Literature*, 380–84.

WITOLD GOMBROWICZ, (1904-1969). Photo Courtesy of Yale University Press.

Rights Movement took hold and broke down the barriers of segregation. Nearby Mississippi and Alabama experienced numerous protests that resulted in violent clashes, as well as bombings, lynchings, and other attacks on blacks by whites. In New Orleans during 1960, integration of four all-white schools resulted in rioting that resulted in considerable bloodshed—shootings, stabbings, and beatings of blacks.

Like Poland after World War I, New Orleans's population consisted of a mix of races. The city was comprised primarily of blacks and whites, though, unlike much of the rest of the South, New Orleans claimed a diversity of religions, with large numbers of Catholics and Protestants. New Orleans also boasted a complex blended culture fused from the presence of Cajuns, Creoles, and Southern whites. Louisiana's version of Pilsudski emerged in the form of demagogue Huey Long, the former populist governor and US Senator assassinated in 1935, and his younger brother, Earl Long, a three-term governor sometimes known as "Crazy Earl."

While neither *Ferdydurke* nor *Confederacy* directly addresses the dangerous political landscape of racist causes alive in Poland or Louisiana, the plots of both novels are rife with characters of Fascist tendencies—mini-dictators and low-level tyrants. Both Joey and Ignatius fear being held against their will. As Ignatius writes in his journal, "Like a bitch in heat, I seem to attract a coterie of policemen and sanitation officials. The world will someday get me on some ludicrous pretext; I simply await the day that they drag me to some air-conditioned dungeon and leave me there beneath the florescent lights and sound-proofed ceiling to pay the price for scorning all that they hold dear within their little latex hearts."[8] Joey is in fact abducted, while Ignatius evades his mother's attempt to put him into a mental institution. Although the abductions are handled by the authors with a comic touch, much more sinister, factual associations existed during the times in which these novels were written. Joey's abduction by the schoolteacher Pimko at the beginning of *Ferdydurke* is prescient, foreshadowing the mil-

[8] John Kennedy Toole, *A Confederacy of Dunces* (New York: Wing Books/Random House, 1996) 269.

lions of European Jews who would be seized and confined in concentration camps. While certainly not as numerous as the atrocities committed by the Nazis, abductions did occur in the South, both of blacks and of white Civil Rights protesters. The two novels, while focusing on the individual imprisonment of the protagonists, offer metaphors that demonstrate the diabolic danger of nationalized racism.

Although the novels are told from different points of view (Gombrowicz uses a very direct first person voice, prone to digressions on art, culture, and societal institutions; Toole employs an omniscient third-person narration that follows the thoughts of multiple characters), the monologue of Joey and the flamboyant dialogue and lengthy journal entries of Ignatius often mirror one another in thought and form and positions. Although Toole follows an almost cinematic style of storytelling, the narrative parts that are told in Ignatius's voice function as first-person segments of journal entries and lengthy dialogue within the larger, omniscient work. Ignatius is a keeper of "unorganized" notebooks that "one day he would assume the task of editing these fragments of his mentality into a jigsaw puzzle of a very grand design; the completed puzzle would show literate men the disaster course that history had been taking for the past four centuries."[9]

The beginning of each novel features images of adults as adolescents, since both lead characters refuse to exist as grown-ups in the world. Ignatius is described as being at a department store waiting for his mother, where he behaves like a spoiled ten-year-old child when questioned by a policeman who finds him, a large thirty-year-old man in a hunting cap, suspicious. "Let me see your driver's license," the policeman asks him. "I don't drive." Ignatius responds, then continues, "Will you kindly go away? I am waiting for my mother."[10] Before his mother rescues him (He is an adult wholly dependent on his mother.), Ignatius is drawn into a ridiculous scene where he whips the officer with a lute string. In *Ferdydurke*, Joey is alone in his

---

[9] Ibid., 34.

[10] Ibid., 3.

home when he is visited by the schoolteacher Pimko, who Joey fears. The teacher reads part of Joey's writings, summons him to return to high school, telling him his education is not complete; Joey is unable to protest, so he returns to school and enrolls, unable to fight against the juvenile form in which he has been cast. Near the end of the second chapter, Joey says, "I felt sure that, had reality asserted itself for one moment, the incredibly grotesque situation in which I found myself would have become so glaringly obvious that everyone would have exclaimed: 'What is this grown man doing here?' But against the background of general freakishness, the case of my particular freakishness was lost."[11]

Both Joey (in his diatribes that take up much of the narrative) and Ignatius (in his dialogue and journals) decry the power and authority of what Gombrowicz described as "cultural aunts"—that is, women who appoint themselves judges of culture and art, not because they possess a deep belief in culture or art, but because the women believe in upholding social appearances. Joey says, "world culture has been beset by a flock of superfluous hens patched-on, pinned-on, to literature, who have become finely tuned to spiritual values and well versed in aesthetics, frequently entertaining views and opinions of their own.... Oh, they are on to the fact that they must be independent, profound, unobtrusively assertive, filled with auntie kindliness."[12] It is these cultural aunts that Joey rails against, the sweet saccharine coating of art, not for art's sake, but for the sake of manners and upkeep of dignified Polish culture. In his diatribes, Joey attacks the cultural aunts, embracing his own immaturity while undercutting their societal order.

Reading *Ferdydurke* helps illuminate for the reader what Ignatius tries to do in *Confederacy* when he visits a showing of paintings by the ladies art guild in the French Quarter. He is out to offend and rebuke the cultural aunts. Ignatius, a very heavy man, is wearing a costume with a pirate's earring and scarf, and he is carrying a cutlass and is pushing a hot-dog vendor's

---

[11] Gombrowicz, *Ferdydurke*, 37.
[12] Ibid., 6.

cart for Paradise Vendors on which he has scrawled a blatantly suggestive handwritten sign that advertises "TWELVE (12) INCHES OF PARADISE." After offering the women hot dogs, he turns to their artwork, which he insults heartily. Ignatius says, "You women had better stop giving teas and brunches and settle down to the business of learning how to draw. First, you must learn how to handle a brush. I would suggest that you all get together and paint someone's house for a start." When the leader of the women's group asks Ignatius to leave and tells him they don't want him there, he accuses them of being out of touch with reality. "Apparently you are afraid of someone who has some contact with reality, who can truthfully describe to you the offenses which you have committed to canvas.... You women should all be on your knees begging forgiveness for what I have seen here on this fence."[13]

The failure for people to make "contact with reality" is a cornerstone of both novels, and Joey's and Ignatius's wicked criticism is certainly not limited to women. Both characters abhor the pretentiousness they encounter, particularly of the shallowness of art as they see it. Ignatius, in his journal, attacks American art by criticizing work that declares the greatness of the Mississippi River. He seeks to destroy such cultural myths, and even goes as far to condemn Mark Twain:

> This river is famed in atrocious song and verse; the most prevalent motif is one which attempts to make of the river an ersatz father figure. Actually, the Mississippi River is a treacherous and sinister body of water whose eddies and currents yearly claim many lives. I have never known anyone who would even venture to stick his toe in its polluted brown waters, which seethe with sewage, industrial waste, and deadly insecticides. Even the fish are dying. Therefore, the Mississippi as Father-God-Moses-Daddy-Phallus-Pops is an altogether false motif begun, I would imagine, by that dreary fraud, Mark Twain. This failure to make

[13] Toole, *A Confederacy of Dunces*, 287.

> contact with reality, is, however, characteristic of almost all of America's "art." Any connection between American art and American nature is purely coincidental, but this only because the nation as a whole has no contact with reality. That is only one of the reasons why I have always been forced to exist on the fringes of its society, consigned to the Limbo reserved for those who do know reality when they see it.[14]

This quote from Toole's novel echoes Gombrowicz's attack on his generation of writers, who the latter author believed fail to address topics inwardly but who instead write superficially on topics of history and nature. According to Gombrowicz, those writers—by ignoring their inner emotions as they pass from childhood into adulthood—avoid reality by writing on "remote and indifferent matters," such as beekeeping or royal families. "What a cheap and simplistic way of avoiding reality, what a shoddy escape into specious loftiness?" [15] Joey, like Ignatius, pursues this issue of reality throughout the novel, often pleading with the reader to look at things his way. "And once you open your minds to Reality this alone may bring you great relief—at the same time stop worrying that it will impoverish and shrivel your spirit—because Reality is always richer than naïve illusions and idle notions."[16]

Both Joey and Ignatius rail against these "naïve illusions and idle notions"—tendencies they fear will lead already marred societies into total ruin. But neither character is in any position to influence anyone except through the possibility that what they write down may be taken seriously.

Both Joey and Ignatius have been harshly described by some reviewers and academics. According to Robert Boyers, "Gombrowicz' fiction is nourished by his understanding of art as insurrection, and is characterized by a strenuous effort to indict what passes for sanity in the twentieth century. His insurrection, then, is largely defensive in nature—he mocks and imaginatively destroys what he cannot tolerate, what threatens to enlist him in

---

[14] Ibid., 141.

[15] Gombrowicz, *Ferdydurke*, 5–6.

[16] Ibid., 79.

procedures that seem to him insane, but his responses to experience are basically bizarre and compulsive—he is a very sick man."[17]

Ignatius receives no better reception. Walker Percy, the Southern novelist who championed the book, describes Ignatius as a "slob extraordinary, a mad Oliver Hardy, a fat Don Quixote, a perverse Thomas Aquinas," and Percy also characterizes Ignatius as an "intellectual, ideologue, deadbeat, goof-off, glutton, who should repel the reader with his gargantuan bloats, his thunderous contempt and one-man war against everybody—Freud, homosexuals, heterosexuals, Protestants, and the assorted excesses of modern times."[18] Reviewer Charles Larson described Ignatius as a "misfit, an iconoclast, a liar, a virgin, a raconteur, and, above all, a grossly overweight mamma's boy."[19]

As both novelists make clear, it is not Joey and Ignatius who are insane but the societies in which the characters live—societies consumed by racial politics and nationalistic demagogues. Joey and Ignatius are two characters who will not succumb, at any cost, to the groundswell of conformity. In a reading that could go for Joey as well, Andrei Codrescu accurately describes Ignatius as "a merciless camera lens trained on the eternal stupidity that, far from dated, flourishes unchecked in our day."[20]

As might be expected of thirty-year-old agoraphobic men, Joey's and Ignatius's mental trauma is tormented by internal desires and anger toward the opposite sex. Joey is tortured by the very presence of a sixteen-year-old girl, obsessed with her "calves," by her willingness to succumb to men both young and old, by her being "modern." Again, he is decrying the tendency of people around him to conform to trends and societal norms. "Oh this cult, this obedience, the girl's slavery just because she is a schoolgirl and because she's modern!" Joey says.[21] Ignatius is confounded by Myrna Minkoff, a folk-singing, freethinking, liberal from New York who counsels him to turn to sex to relieve his mental stress, something the celibate mas-

---

[17] Robert Boyers, "Gombrowicz and *Ferdydurke:* The Tyranny of Form," *The Centennial* Review, Vol. 14/1 (Winter 1970): 288.

[18] Walker Percy, "Foreword," in Toole, *A Confederacy of Dunces,* vii–viii.

[19] Charles J. Larson, *Detroit News,* June 17, 1980, in Gale Authors Online.

[20] Codrescu, "Making the Natives Wince," B7.

[21] Gombrowicz, *Ferdydurke,* 165.

turbator Ignatius claims he finds repugnant. He refers to Myrna as the "minx."

However upset they are by the presence of these women in their lives—both women actually exist on the periphery (the sixteen-year-old of Joey's affection stays in her room, while Myrna and Ignatius communicate via letters from New York and New Orleans)—Joey and Ignatius are paralyzed, unable to do anything in response. And though they claim to be repulsed by their untouchable female counterparts (most women in general, for that matter), both Joey and Ignatius are "rescued" by a woman. Joey runs off with Zosia, a young woman who is his cousin, and later convinces her that he "kidnapped" her. Myrna arrives to take Ignatius to New York, whisking him away from the ambulance his mother has sent for to take him to the mental hospital. For both Joey and Ignatius to move beyond their isolation, they need help of a conspiratorial kind from a woman.

The two novels possess several other similarities in plot and symbolism. Not only are Joey and Ignatius reluctant to leave their rooms, the two abhor the idea of leaving Warsaw or New Orleans, their respective cities. When about to leave the city limits with his traveling partner, Kneadus, Joey in *Ferdydurke* fears the world beyond what he knows. He says, "I stopped at the city limits, and I felt that I couldn't continue without the herd and its works, without the human among humans. I caught Kneadus by the hand. 'Don't go there, Kneadus, let's turn back, don't leave the city, Kneadus.'" [22] In *Confederacy of Dunces*, Ignatius says, "Personally, I have been out of the city only once… Outside the city limits there are many horrors."[23] His one venture outside of New Orleans, a bus ride to Baton Rouge for a job interview, was a terrible experience for him in which he got sick on a two-level bus, the much-hated Greyhound Scenicruiser. He took a taxi home and did not leave New Orleans again. These characters' fear of the world beyond what they already know might reflect Gombrowicz's and Toole's attitudes

[22] Gombrowicz, *Ferdydurke*, 207.

[23] Toole, *A Confederacy of Dunces*, 247.

toward their respective eras—the 1930s in Poland (with war looming in Germany) or the 1960s in the US (with the Civil Rights struggle, the Cold War, and Vietnam).

Another similarity between the two books is the image of what Czeslaw Milosz calls the "wriggling heap." He writes of *Ferdydurke*, "A recurring motif in the novel is the pandemonium of a wriggling 'heap' (kupa) of bodies as the characters throw each other to the floor in a kind of frenzy." In *Ferdydurke*, two such struggles occur on the floor, both involving the families with whom Joey has been staying. In *Confederacy*, most of the novel's characters end up in a melee that is reported in the newspaper with the headline "WILD INCIDENT ON BOURBON STREET." This struggle in the street is a key turning point for most of the characters in Toole's novel, just as the struggles are an essential point for Joey's escapes. In their novels' denouements, Gombrowicz and Toole each turn to these wild scrums of various characters because in a world of total irrationality issues cannot be resolved logically and peacefully, but instead are destined for "wriggling heaps" of madness.

The most obvious and frequently used metaphor in both novels is the human rear-end. Joey frequently refers to his beloved "pupa," a Polish word with many meanings, including "buttocks, behind, bum, tush, rump." However, Gombrowicz uses "pupa" in a broader sense, as a metaphor for "for the gentle, infantilizing and humiliation that we inflict on one another," according to translator Danuta Borchardt in explaining why the Polish word "pupa," as found in the original text, was not translated into English.[24] Similar to Gombrowicz's "pupa," Toole employs Ignatius's belches and flatulence as a metaphor for his disgust. In Percy's words, Ignatius's "pyloric valve periodically closes in response to the lack of a 'proper geometry and theology' in the modern world."[25] In the manner of Ignatius's famous closed valve, both novels' protagonists shut themselves off from the world, preventing passage into adulthood. Like children obsessed

---

[24] Borchardt, "Translator's Note," xviii–xix.

[25] Percy, "Foreword," ix.

with bathroom humor, both authors return to these images again and again, even in their closing words. The moon, in Gombrowicz's final chapter, hangs like a huge buttocks in the sky. "From the pupa, however, there is absolutely no escape," he writes, closing with two rhyming lines of verse. "It's the end, what a gas / And who's read it is an ass!"[26] At the conclusion of Toole's novel, Ignatius—who, for only the second time in his life is leaving New Orleans (this time, he claims, for good)—finds relief from his pyloric valve and its tendency to slam shut. "As if the air were a purgative, his valve opened."[27] For Ignatius, a new life in New York means an end to the gastrointestinal disturbances caused by the insanity of life in Louisiana. Having found the societies they live in unstable and on the brink of sliding into madness, Joey and Ignatius cling to their immaturity and figuratively pull down their pants and moon the world. The much deeper message behind these metaphors is a damning condemnation of their cultures, a warning to the reader that society has run amok and a darker future awaits.

[26] Gombrowicz, *Ferdydurke*, 281.

[27] Toole, *A Confederacy of Dunces*, 462.

Southern Shadows: Mammoth Cave Meets Plato's Cave in Davis McCombs' *Ultima Thule*

BY JERALDINE R. KRAVER

It should not surprise readers that so many of the poems in Davis McCombs's *Ultima Thule* include descriptions of darkness and light. After all, the sonnet sequences framing that collection of poetry guide the reader into the labyrinth that is Mammoth Cave, the world's longest cave system. Mammoth Cave's more than 360 miles of connected tunnels snake intricately beneath 20 square miles of wooded hills in south-central Kentucky, the cave and its environs providing McCombs with the setting for the three sections of his collection. In the first section, "Ultima Thule," the poet speaks through the voice of cave guide and slave, Stephen Bishop (1820–1856), the first man to map the extensive cave system. The second section, "The River and Under the River," explores the history of the cave and depicts the physical and spiritual world of the region. In the final sequence, "The Dark County," the collection comes full circle: having retraced Bishop's steps and having illuminated the cultural and natural history of the cave, McCombs shifts to his own experiences as a ranger in Mammoth Cave National Park.

As poet W. S. Merwin notes in his preface to *Ultima Thule*, one cannot think about caves without harkening to Plato. Indeed, Plato's "allegory of the cave" remains the most familiar passage from that philosopher's seminal text *The Republic.* Plato envisions a world divided into the visible realm of objects grasped with the senses and the intelligible realm of eternal Forms grasped by the mind. In Plato's allegory, knowledge of Forms is available to the prisoner who, escaping from the darkness of the cave, ascends to where the sun "[makes] our eyes see perfectly and [makes] objects perfectly visible." Through the illuminating power of the sun, Plato continues, "the soul gains understanding and knowledge and is manifestly in possession of intelligence." [1] Without the sun to irradiate objects with truth and reality, the prisoner remains trapped in the darkness of objects or illusions. Freed from the realm of imagination—that is, by exiting the cave—the individual achieves knowledge and the attendant happiness that comes with fulfilling the rational desire for wisdom.

Throughout *The Republic*, Plato differentiates the visible and the intelligible worlds by juxtaposing appearance and imagination against reality and knowledge. Through the metaphor of the divided line, he traces the progression from the visible to the intelligible. At the lowest, most primitive level of reality is the realm of physical objects, shadows, and images apprehended through imagination, conjecture, or belief. At the highest level are Forms, directly apprehended by intuition—that is, the capacity of human reason to comprehend the true nature of reality. It would be error, Plato admonishes, to mistake shadows and images for reality. We are seduced by our particular and immediate experiences into believing that we know the immutable, eternal, unchanging Forms. However, knowledge and wisdom are based not on particular experience of objects or on belief (metaphorically speaking, the shadows and projections of the cave) but on transcendent Forms that exist independent both of our experience of them and of their appearance. To perceive Forms is to achieve knowledge and wisdom—to know objects only is merely to have belief.

---

[1] Francis McDonald Cornford, *The Republic of Plato* (Oxford University Press, 1977) 219. Chief among the Forms Plato discusses is the Form of the Good, described through the metaphor of the sun. Plato explains that as the sun radiates light in the visible realm, thus enabling us to see objects, so does the Form of the Good emmanate truth in the intelligible realm. In effect, the Form of the Good is the cause of all other Forms; it is the source of all Goodness, Justice, and Beauty in the world.

In McCombs's collection, Stephen Bishop speaks in the opening sonnet sequence. This tack allows McCombs to confront Platonic notions of objects and Forms. Bishop's position as a slave compels speculation about how one is to distinguish mere objects from eternal Forms when denied access to the site of knowledge; should we be surprised, McCombs poses, that the slave seeks wisdom and the knowledge in the only place where he is free? Through his encounters with the objects that compose the world below ground and by dint of his imagination, Bishop indeed comes to know Forms like Beauty, Goodness, and Truth. Thus, Bishop's explorations effectively contest Plato's rejection of experience as the way to achieve wisdom. Bishop's engagement with the tunnels and crevasses of Mammoth Cave suggest that, despite Plato's assertions otherwise, one can encounter universal Forms through particular experiences.

In *The Republic*, the philosopher-king is able to distinguish the one true Form from its multiple manifestations. He can "discern that essence as well as the things that partake of its character, without ever confusing one for the other."[2] Plato explains that the philosopher-king—as one who knows rather than simply believes—acts as a "guide," leading those who dwell in the darkness of the cave into the sunlit world above ground and to a similar state of knowledge. Conversely, Bishop's path to the essence of things is not up and out from the cave but, rather, farther down and into it. Through Bishop's experience, McCombs dramatizes that the path to wisdom might in fact be by means of the imagination, and he asserts that the philosopher-king who guides us might very well be a slave.

I.

> I was drawn to wonder, the margins of the map.
> Breath and a heartbeat. A fading lamp.
> I was coffled to the light.
>
> —from "Ultima Thule"

---

[2] *The Republic*, 183–84.

Critics have praised McCombs for not taking the bait, so to speak, about issues of race. Craig Arnold, for instance, notes that "It is to McCombs' credit that he does not turn these poems into post-modern meditations on slavery."[3] Nonetheless, Bishop's status as a slave undergirds all aspects of the opening sonnet sequence—as it must. In "Fame," Bishop notes that "The Doctor boasts I was the merest germ / of a man when he bought me," or, in the final poem of the sequence, "Ultima Thule," Bishop describes himself, in language that clearly references his status as a slave as "coffled." Despite the services he rendered as a guide and despite his popularity with tourists, Bishop was, until the final year of his life, the property of other men.

Among the visitors who recorded their memories of Bishop was Nathaniel P. Willis who, in 1852, purchased a private tour. Describing Bishop as "picturesque," Willis explained, "[he is] part mulatto and part Indian. With more of the physiognomy of a Spaniard, with masses of black hair, curling slightly and gracefully, and his long mustache, giving quite an appearance. He is of middle size, but built for an athlete. With broad chest and shoulders, narrow hips and legs slightly bowed. Mammoth Cave is a wonder in which draws good society and Stephen shows that he is used to it." Willis also described Bishop's ability to create a mood for more traditional tourist parties. Recalling his party's arrival at a "not a very attractive-looking place," where a mummy had once been located, Willis writes, "Stephen set down his lamp, after showing us the hollow niche in the rock against which the fair one was found sitting, as if, with his sixteen years' experience as guide, he had found this to be a spot where the traveler usually takes time for reverie. It cost me no coaxing to have mine. With the silence of the spot, and all the world shut out, it is impossible that the imagination should not do pretty fair justice to the single idea presented."[4] For tourists such as Willis—who embrace the shadows and the darkness as part of the cave's very nature—contemplation and imagination reveal its mystery

---

[3] Craig Arnold, "*Ultima Thule*," *The Austin Chronicle*, August 4, 2002, http://www.austinchronicle.com/issues/dispatch/2000-08-04/books_vsbr.html (accessed November 5, 2005).

[4] Julian Dibble, "A Marketable Wonder: Spelunking the American Imagination," *Topic Magazine* 2 (Autumn 2002), http://www.webdelsol.com/Topic/articles/02/dibbell.html (accessed November 5, 2005).

and its beauty. During their private tour, Willis asked Bishop for his views on slavery, and Bishop confided his plan to purchase his freedom and that of his wife and child and to relocate to Liberia. Dr. Croghan, who purchased both the cave and Bishop from the previous owner, stipulated in his will that his slaves, Bishop among them, be freed—but not until seven years after his death. Bishop was freed in accordance with Croghan's will. However, Bishop would die one year later, at age thirty-six, never having been able to gather sufficient money to purchase his family's freedom.

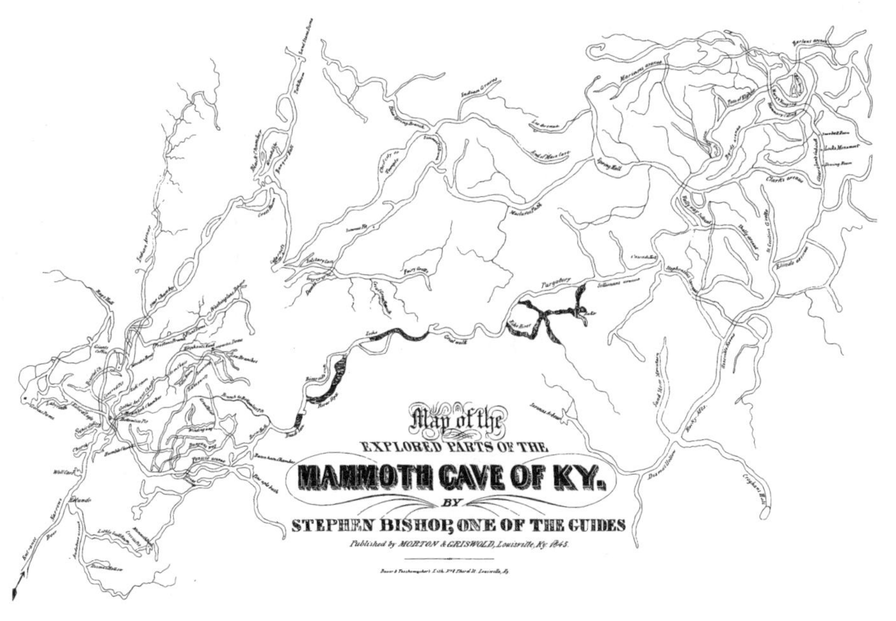

Freedom for the man who had mapped and mastered Mammoth Cave was available only underground. If the slave in Plato's allegory breaks his shackles and acquires freedom and wisdom by ascending to the world above the cave, Bishop breaks his only by descending farther down into the darkness. In the poem "Star Chamber," Dr. Croghan, fascinated by the heavens, tells Bishop about gravity and tides and the pull of the moon:

when we observe the waxing of the Moon,
everything cognate to her nature—marrow
in bones and in trees, flesh of the river
mussel—increases also.

Bishop concedes that perhaps above ground all living things are affected by the moon; however, in the cave, he describes how a lantern hung in a certain way will reproduce a night sky, and, wobbled slightly, "a comet, / smoky pestilent, streaks across the Ether." In the Star Chamber, Bishop asserts, "I control the spheres." Beneath the surface of the Earth, he acquires a measure of control over the shadows and over his own life.

Through the persona and the experience of a slave, McCombs contests Plato's application of Forms. In *The Republic*, Plato affirms "the existence of a single essential nature or Form for each set of things which we call by the same name."[5] There is a single *a priori* truth that stands above each individual's experience. Yet, for Bishop, on the surface of the Earth, above the corridors of Mammoth Cave, Forms like Beauty, Goodness, and, perhaps most important for the slave, Justice, are more shadow than Form. Plato would contend that the slave's experience of Justice, especially the absence of it, is merely an encounter with a particular manifestation of Justice, not the Form. However, despite Plato's warning that one should not mistake the particular manifestation for the eternal Form, to a slave, separated from his family and having to live as the property of another man, all justice seems arbitrary and the Form of Justice inaccessible. Thus, in the poems, Bishop travels more deeply into the cave, to the "margins of the map," to locate among the corridors and caverns what free men find on the surface. His explorations reveal that knowledge of Forms can be located in the shadows of the caves, a place Bishop describes in "Shadow Land" as "a region nearer / to the source of things." Through this inversion, McCombs frames a curious estimation of Plato's divided line.

---

[5] *The Republic*, 325.

Mapping the cave system and guiding white visitors empower Bishop in a world where others like him are powerless. However, whatever agency he possesses is underground only. In terms of Plato's model, Bishop, though mobile, remains like those coffled in the cave whom Plato depicts as being trapped in a world of impermanence, in the realm of sensible objects. In his explorations of the particular and immediate experiences that visible objects provide, Bishop is, Plato would contend, effectively fooled. He remains unenlightened. Yet, from the perspective of the slave, chained from without and free to explore only within, the particular and immediate experiences of the visible world are the only source for the wisdom and knowledge afforded to those who dwell in the sunlight.

II.

he
of all people, would prefer the company of rain
to my own

—from "Stephen Bishop's Grave"

Bishop first entered Mammoth Cave in 1838 at seventeen years old. His owner, Franklin Gorin, purchased the cave tract as a potential tourist attraction, hoping to capitalize on the discovery inside the cave of prehistoric human remains, including a number of mummified corpses of indigenous people, some still dressed in elaborate ceremonial costume.[6] Gorin described Bishop as "a self-educated man…[with] a fine genius, a great fund of wit and humor, some little knowledge of Latin and Greek, and much knowledge of geology, but his great talent was a knowledge of man."[7] Bishop's tours were part topography lesson and part entertainment, and his knowledge of the cave was unmatched. He became an attraction nearly as famous as the cave itself. In McCombs's poetic interpretation of that situa-

---

[6] Gorin was not the first to try. From its discovery by white men in the late 1700s through the end of the War of 1812, Mammoth Cave was exploited primarily for its reserves of calcium nitrate, or niter, a byproduct of bat guano used to make gunpowder. During the war, the caves became a subterranean factory for niter, manned by as many as seventy slaves at a time. After the war, when prices collapsed, the caves were opened for tourists.

[7] United States Department of the Interior, National Park Service, Mammoth Cave National Park. *Steven Bishop, Cave Guide*. http://www.nps.gov/maca/stephen.pdf (accessed November 5, 2005).

tion, “Visitations,” the poet captures the strange relationship between the slave-guide and the visitors to the cave:

> It is the women
> on the tours that give me pause, delicate,
> ghost-white, how, that night, I'm told,
> they wake to find themselves in unfamiliar
> beds, and lost, bewildered, call my name.

The tourists find the caves disturbing long after they depart, and, disoriented in the unfamiliar darkness of night, they call for a guide. Unlike the visitors, Bishop feels most comfortable in the darkness; only the whiteness of the visitors gives him “pause.” The “monstrous shadows” cast by the glow of the oil lamp disturb the tourists, but, Bishop explains, “These I do not fear.” Having studied and mapped the passageways and tunnels, Bishop knows the reality beyond the shadows. Others may speculate about what they see in the caves, but, as Bishop asserts in “Cave Formation,” “Who better to conjecture / on these matters than I?” Although it is a darkened world, Bishop has knowledge enough to distinguish between the illusions cast by shadows and the cave formations that create them. For Bishop, it is the above-ground world of Forms privileged by Plato that appears “a mapless country” (“Candlewriting”), whose turning seasons he hardly notices. And it is these Forms, illuminated by the sun, that are illusory to Bishop; those Forms are more like shadows than are the dark recesses of the caves that neither disturb nor disorient him.

By assuming the voice of Stephen Bishop, McCombs upends the Platonic imperative and makes the cave a place of understanding, knowledge, and, for the slave, authority. Like those shackled before the shadows and images of the cave wall, Bishop is a prisoner. However, neither personhood nor power, knowledge nor wisdom await him above ground. Only in the cave does Bishop begin contemplate the nature of his identity. In “Candlewriting,” the first poem of the opening sonnet sequence, Bishop ponders the seven letters of his name, which he had learned to write “with a taper on a stick" using the smoke from a tallow candle against the limestone walls. During his "mapless" years, his name was merely sounds on the wind that "meant me, Stephen." More than 100 years later, McCombs, reflecting in an interview on his art and his own experiences as a cave guide, describes a six-hour tour he calls "Wild Cave," which involves crawling, squeezing, and climbing: "There are places on that tour where you crawl into these little passageways and you're on your stomach, you're writhing around in the dirt and the mud and you look up on the ceiling and there is Stephen Bishop's signature."[8] Although others may claim deeds and titles to the twisting passageways and bottomless crevasses, it is Bishop who truly owned Mammoth Cave.

III.

> The services of a guide cannot, as a rule
> be dispensed with; we alone can disentangle
> the winding passageways.
>
> —from "Tours"

Bishop's explorations revealed the size and the scope of the cave system. By surveying the cave's narrow crevices and traversing its innumerable chasms and corridors, he discovered 100-feet-high vertical shafts, underground lakes and rivers inhabited by eyeless albino fish, and chambers encrusted with delicate white gypsum. In his first year of exploration, Bishop doubled the size of the known cave. After Gorin sold his property, including Bishop, to Dr. John Croghan in 1839, Croghan had Bishop chart his geographical discoveries, a process described in "Cartography":

> At Locust Grove, Great House, I pass days
> in the garden—a stone bench, ornamental
> cherries, August's dappled light. Once, a hawk's

---

[8] "Park Ranger Poet Inspired by Cavernous Depths of Mammoth Cave," *Book News* (August 30, 2000) http://archives.cnn.com/2000/books/news/08/30/cave.poet.ap/ (accessed November 5, 2005).

shadow crossed my paper, startling me
from the dark rooms and corridors of my map

Bishop named the many places he had discovered, names that define the cave's features to this day. The influence of his self-study of Western literature is apparent in his choices: alongside the more prosaic (though colorful) names like "Fairy Grotto," "Dismal Chamber," "Snowball Room," "Little Bat Avenue," or "Giant Room," are the "River Styx," "Lake Lethe," and "Purgatory." Identifying the rivers and lakes of the cave system by names that reflect, for example, the river of hate and separation ("Styx"), the lake of oblivion and forgetfulness ("Lethe"), and the place of purification ("Purgatory") intimates that Bishop's travails as a slave afford him a Platonic appreciation of what appears, at first glance, mere darkness and shadow. Plato maintains that the intelligible world is knowable through reason—a disciplined application of understanding. In his study of the caves, McCombs suggests, Bishop sought to make the shadowy recesses tangible and real. What Bishop's explorations (and McCombs's poems) propose is that insight and discovery may be gleaned as easily from investigating the shadows of the visible as from emerging into the light.

At the same time that Bishop, simply using the power of recall, is composing "an eye-draught of the known Cave passages," Dr. Croghan himself is plotting the movement of the moon "by aide of lenses and tubes." The doctor relies on all manner of mathematical equations and scientific instruments to map what he sees above ground. This is the kind of systematic knowledge that characterizes Plato's intelligible realm. Conversely, Bishop plots from memory and intuition, explaining, "The mind moves and the hand follows." Bishop's map remained unsurpassed for sixty years. Perhaps even more important than Bishop's achievement in cartography, according to McCombs, is the fact that Bishop saw beyond the cave's visible topological marvels. The poem "Tours" depicts how visitors come to the caves, "From drawing rooms and formal gardens / …from sunlit lives they enter / the chill, grand and instantaneous night." That such visitors are unable to perceive the beauty of the caves is apparent in both "Tours" and

"Tuberculosis Sanitarium," where Bishop notes how they imagine all manner of modifications. In fact, Dr. Croghan would fail in an attempt to establish in Mammoth Cave a sanitarium for the tubercular; others would propose that carriage lanes or "capacious ballrooms" be built in the cave. These notions emerge from an inherent "rough-hewn" fear of the cave. An awkwardness in the tangled passageways compels tourists to "fill / with talk the natural silence." In descending from the light into the shadows, they fail to perceive the grand beauty of the caves themselves. Yet, this beauty attracts Bishop and draws him to wonder and to wander where "No one has ever come" ("Ultima Thule"). The cave lures him deeper into its recesses, where, through his explorations and in "the half-light on the dark side," the darkness yields its own knowledge ("Shadow World"). "Cave Formation" describes what one sees "Safe from the withering glare of daylight," including eyeless fish and coral-like rock formations. There is much to be learned from the world below ground, perhaps more than above in the sunlight that "withers" more than it illuminates.

IV.

> Behold how the shades in the Cave
> gather and deepen, extend in darker zones
> from the center of the flame where I stand.
>
> —from "Shadow World"

In Plato's cave, firelight casts the shadows of objects that the cave dwellers mistake for the real. Only the prisoner who is exposed to the natural light of the sun encounters the real or the true. Above ground, he turns his sights to the sun and recognizes the ultimate Form, the Form of the Good. Throughout *The Republic*, the sun serves as a key metaphor, for it is this "precious light" that enables one to see. Describing the power of the sun, Plato writes, "When [the soul's] gaze is fixed upon an object irradiated by truth and reality, the soul gains understanding and knowledge and is manifestly in possession of intelligence."[9] Those who dwell in the dim

[9] *The Republic*, 220.

realm of shadows, in "the twilight world of things," however, are duped by a world of opinions and beliefs only.

In his underground explorations, Bishop relies on all manner of manufactured light in order to illuminate the sensible world around him and to discover the truth behind the shadows. Recall his assertion in "Ultima Thule": "I was drawn to wonder, the margins of the map. / Breath and a heartbeat. A fading lamp. / I was coffled to the light." In the same way that those above ground rely on the natural light of the sun to illuminate, Bishop, in his quest for knowledge, depends on the light he carries into the recesses of the cave to reveal. "Dripstone," for example, tells of what he sees in the blue flare of a "Bengal Light."[10] On the walls of a cave grotto, the light reveals glistening globules and nodules that grow on the walls in the darkness beneath the Earth. When they are struck, they make "melodious tones, liquid and wavering." The doctor has sent Bishop into the caves to extract one of the nodules for his research. However, exposed to the natural light their essence changes for the worse, and Bishop laments,

How sad I grew
to see the changes wrought in them by sunlight.
How lustreless they appeared under glass,
their sparks extinguished, their music fled.

The Bengal Light that Bishop uses in his explorations at once "driv[es] darkness from the corners" and reveals the beauty that resides among the shadows, a beauty that, antithetical to Platonic notions, withers in the light of the sun.

In "Bottomless Pit," Bishop explores farther into the darkness, to places where visitors do not travel. Across precipices and by the light of burning oiled paper, Bishop discovers "rivers beyond," including those that featured "fish with no eyes," "strange inhabitants / that emerged into the circle of my

---

[10] A blue-colored light usually used for signaling.

light." Despite Plato's proviso, there is much to learn from the shadows and the darkness of the caves. In "Cave Formations," Bishop talks of "Theories I have learned / to keep from other, educated men." Such men, Bishop indicates, cannot imagine that the conclusions of an uneducated slave—albeit one intimate with the cave—would have merit. Thus, he chooses not to share what he learns with these men, "lest they, like bats, fly shrieking at the torch-bearer." In Plato's allegory, the cave dwellers reject what they are told by the prisoner who has returned from the world above with news of eternal Forms. In *Ultima Thule*, it is those above ground who reject what the cave dweller comes to tell them about the objects and the shadows. No credence is given to those chained to the objects and manifestations of the visible world, for knowledge resides above ground, in the intelligible realm. Forms cannot be discovered in shadows; the philosopher-king is not a slave, or so think the people who dwell above the Earth. And, yet, Bishop envisions himself as such a "philosopher king," one with the knowledge to enlighten.

The concept of seeking the intelligible in the world of the visible challenges Plato's epistemological methodology. It is a reversal of the philosopher's journey. For Plato, the freed prisoner recognizes that all his prior experiences in the cave have been delusions. Only by leaving the cave does he have access to reality rather than perceptions. And, Plato continues, it is the responsibility of the educated and the wise, having "climb[ed] the ascent to the vision of Goodness," to return to the cave and enlighten the ignorant. In contrast, Bishop emerges from the cave, map in hand, to teach the lessons of the shadows to those in the light. But to accept the lessons of the cave, to accept that one can in fact locate knowledge and reality in the darkness of the cave, challenges the notion that what one encounters above ground, in the world illuminated by the sun, is real and not perception. What has been perceived as the Form of the Good may be nothing more than shadows, and what we have mistaken for knowledge may be nothing more than belief.

More than a century later, McCombs, too, will learn what the cave can teach. He concludes his collection with a sonnet sequence in his own voice.

Like Bishop, it is the voice of a cave guide. In his closing lines, McCombs writes,

> I've wondered, stare out
> into the dark, and ask what brought us here,
> all of us, what artifact will tell the future
> of a longing wild and inarticulate,
> of a dark place loved and gotten in the blood?

Ultimately, the allegory of the cave depicts the journey from ignorance to enlightenment, the individual achieving knowledge and, hence, happiness. In *The Republic*, Plato's captive replaces shadows with sunlight, opinions with knowledge, material particulars with ideal Forms by ascending out of the cave. Bishop, and McCombs after him, and readers of *Ultima Thule*, through the poems collected in that significant poetry collection, likewise achieve wisdom by descending into it.

What Floyd Said*

BY DAVIS MCCOMBS

A late wind scuffs the water of the pond
and you will look for me there,
for what, if anything, survives
the glass-topped coffin or the looted grave.

It's not that I might still endure, mud-
plastered in the glow of a single bulb
that scares you; it's the possibility
that I don't. No, that *you* won't.

That night you saw the figure of a man
carved in shadow by the taillight,
the tip of a cigarette quickly
extinguished, and gasped my name.

Do you think I shuffle, mumbling,
down a gravel road at dusk,
or that I linger in the grip
of some damp rat-hole still? Do you?

The wagon lurched into the dark
and the moment vanished. Even
the cave in its nest of undergrowth
cries with an open beak to be fed.

You know this. Think of the Entrance
as it is tonight, how the bats at twilight
will ascend black ropes of water
unraveling toward the mossy slabs.

Look for me there at your peril,
for a year played into a shallow grave
by the crickets' tuneless fiddling:
a sound like a season wasting its breath.

* *Floyd Collins was trapped and died*
in Sand Cave, Kentucky, in February 1925.

The Reality of William Christenberry's South[1]

BY ROBERT L. MCDONALD

> The South, what we mean when we talk about the South, is not a geographical place and is only related to geographical place by pure arbitrary contingency. The South is instead nothing in the world but an idea in narrative form, a discourse or rhetoric of narrative tropes, a story made out of sub-stories, a lie, a fiction to which we have lent reality by believing in it.
>
> —Jefferson Humphries[2]

This quotation by Jefferson Humphries has haunted me since I first came across it several years ago in his and John Lowe's intriguingly titled collection *The Future of Southern Letters*. The word "lie" in particular catches my attention every time I read it: the proposition that the subject I have spent the better part of my professional career—indeed, most of my life—trying to understand is, after all, just a postmodern "story," an "idea," a "contingency." My problem is not that I disagree with Humphries. It's that the truth he tells appears so logically inescapable.

---

[1] All images reproduced courtesy of William Christenberry and Hemphill Fine Arts (www.hemphillfinearts.com). The author thanks Mary Early and Lisa Bertnick at Hemphill for their assistance with the illustrations.

[2] Jefferson Humphries, "The Discourse of Southernness," in *The Future of Southern Letters*, ed. Jefferson Humphries and John Lowe (New York: Oxford University Press, 1996) 120.

Where logic fails, however, art often provides answers. In many respects, the photographs, paintings, sculptures, and mixed-media assemblages of Alabama native William Christenberry may be viewed as a direct refutation of the notion that the South itself is more conception than reality. Christenberry not only "believes in" the South; for the past forty years he has devoted himself to capturing and revealing its materiality, its spirit, and, through these, its condition. He is, to borrow his word, "obsessed" with what he calls "a totality of expression about this place"—the Alabama Black Belt that has been home to his family since before the Civil War.[3] To be sure, Christenberry is interested in the idea of the South, but that idea is grounded in a real place whose dimensions he has explored and expressed in various media utilizing his unique aesthetic—an alchemic marriage of documentary effort and artistic imagination.

The importance of Christenberry's biography in comprehending his artistic vision has been noted by critics since he began showing his work professionally in the early 1960s. He has often told the story of how he was born in Tuscaloosa in 1936 and how he continues to be nourished by vivid memories of a childhood and young adulthood spent roaming the woods, fields, and farms near his grandparents' homes in rural Hale County, Alabama.[4] He earned both a bachelor's and master's degree in art at the University of Alabama in Tuscaloosa, but it was not until 1960, while teaching as an instructor at that institution, that he found the proverbial thread he would subsequently weave into a massive and varied tapestry depicting his vision of the American South—a vision that would win him international acclaim and that would also involve considerable controversy.

Browsing in a Birmingham bookstore one day, Christenberry discovered a reprint edition of James Agee and Walker Evans's classic photo-text documentary, *Let Us Now Praise Famous Men*, which reflected the human toll of tenancy and poverty in Depression-era Alabama. Recognizing familiar landmarks in the photographs, Christenberry purchased the book and

[3] Zoe Ingalls, "Sweet Home Alabama: An Artist Looks Back in Wonder." *Chronicle of Higher Education*, May 19, 2000, B10.

[4] For example, see Thomas W. Southall, *Of Time and Place: Walker Evans and William Christenberry* (San Francisco: Friends of Photography, in conjunction with the Amon Carter Museum [Fort Worth, TX] and the University of New Mexico Press [Albuquerque], 1990) 25. Throughout my essay, references to Christenberry's comments on his work that are not cited come from various personal conversations I have had with him.

took it home to show his grandmother, who identified the families Evans depicted in his photographs as local tenants that she had known well. As fate would have it, Agee and Evans had visited Hale County to gather material and take photographs for the book during the very summer in which Christenberry was born. This coincidence amplifying his admiration for *Let Us Now Praise Famous Men*, Christenberry seems to have perceived his discovery of Agee and Evans's collaboration as a kind of artistic summons.

In telling the story of his discovery of *Let Us Now Praise Famous Men*—one of the many biographical vignettes he has apparently internalized so deeply that he repeats lines verbatim from interview to interview—Christenberry emphasizes, interestingly, that "it was Agee's prose more than Walker's photographs that affected me."[5] "I had never run into a writer who described so clearly, so beautifully, the things I had experienced as a child," Christenberry has said. "The smell of that landscape. Of course, the appearance of it. And, just the minute detail."[6] He can recite from memory Agee's famous ironic and acerbic passage about the very inadequacy of his medium, for the artist as well as for the public in whose hands the work will eventually wind up: "If I could do it, I'd do no writing at all here. It would be photographs; the rest would be fragments of cloth, bits of cotton, lumps of earth, records of speech, pieces of wood and iron, phials of odors, plates of food and excrement. Booksellers would consider it quite a novelty; critics would murmur, yes, but is it art; and I could trust a majority of you to use it as you would a parlor game... A piece of the body torn out by the roots might be more to the point."[7] Agee's words "overwhelmed" Christenberry, he says, because he later recognized immediately that "what [Agee] was doing in the written word was exactly what I was trying to do" in art.[8]

Christenberry's work from this time, particularly the 1960 series of abstract expressionist paintings that includes *Tenant House I* (figure 1), reveals the artist's attempts to achieve Agee's ideal of rendering memory

[5] Christenberry, quoted in R. H. Cravens, introduction, in William Christenberry, *Southern Photographs* (Millerton NY: Aperture, 1983) 12.

[6] J. Richard Gruber, *William Christenberry: The Early Years, 1954–1968* (Augusta GA: Morris Museum of Art, 1996) 35.

[7] James Agee and Walker Evans, *Let Us Now Praise Famous Men* (1941; reprint, New York: Houghton Mifflin, 1988) 13.

[8] Peter J. Brownlee, "Interview with William Christenberry," *Southern Quarterly* 32/3 (Spring 1994): 93.

materially through broad, vivid, passionate brushstrokes. It was during this period that Christenberry first took photographs of the Alabama landscape, which he brought into the studio to prompt his memory of color, texture, and mood for paintings and drawings. He soon realized, however, that canvas, paint, and brushes alone were insufficient materials to achieve his vision. Even a year living in New York—where he went on the advice of a mentor at Alabama, "seeking the spirit" of the avant-garde—left him dissatisfied with his work.[9] Although painting and drawing almost feverishly, Christenberry describes his move North as the only true creative "dry spell" that he has experienced in his career.[10] That move North might have been disastrous but for the distance it took him from Alabama, which gave him an opportunity to reflect on the relationship between his artistic goals and his Southern home. One particularly extraordinary positive experience turned that year into one of the most "formative" years in Christenberry's life: he was able to meet and establish what would be come a lifelong friendship with Walker Evans.[11]

In the course of one of their early conversations, after showing Evans some of his paintings, Christenberry mentioned that he had taken photographs of many of the same landmarks and places that Evans had recorded for *Let Us Now Praise Famous Men*. When Evans asked to see them, Christenberry obliged, showing him a few of the small, square-format images. The combination of saturated color and soft focus—evidence of their having been taken with a simple point-and-shoot Brownie camera and developed at a local drugstore—gave the photographs, in the words of one recent critic, the appearance of a "winsome bruising..., the look of the irrecoverable."[12] Evans was impressed, admiring their unpretentiousness, their snapshot-like quality which derived from the photographer's

---

[9] Gruber, *William Christenberry*, 50.

[10] Ibid., 43.

[11] Brownlee, "Interview with William Christenberry," 92.

[12] Roger Cardinal, review of *Of Time and Place: Walker Evans and William Christenberry* by Thomas Southall, *History of Photography* 16/1 (Spring 1992): 83.

FIGURE 1. TENANT HOUSE I (1960), *PAINTING*.

unaffected point of view. He told Christenberry, "Young man, there is something about how you use that little camera, it has become a perfect extension of your eye. You know exactly where to stand. And I encourage you to take it seriously."[13]

Christenberry was "surprised" by Evans's enthusiasm, since he had taken the photographs primarily to inform his painting and "had never thought of [them] as anything other than something I enjoyed making."[14] Almost immediately, Christenberry followed Evans's advice and began to view the medium of photography itself as a native art—"an intuitive, natural response to what I saw"[15]—and not simply a means for inspiring his work in other genres. Even though in 1977 he moved from the Brownie to the much more complex Deardorff 8x10 view camera, at the urging of artist-friends like Lee Friedlander and William Eggleston, Christenberry has never lost the calculated framing of the image that excited Evans: the direct, almost clinical study of facades and landscapes that, captured on film, both documents and amplifies their significance.

Christenberry left Alabama in 1961, and has never returned there to live—following the year in New York, he moved to Memphis, taking a teaching position at Memphis State, and in 1968, he moved to his current home, in Washington DC, joining the faculty of the Corcoran School of Art. Like many artists, Christenberry has found the distance from the South not only conducive to, but perhaps necessary for, his continued artistic exploration of the region. He continues to return to Alabama each summer to make photographs, a seasonal pilgrimage he began in 1961 after that conversation with Evans about his collection of Brownie snapshots. As curator Trudy Wilner Stack has observed, Christenberry's biography continues to provide "inexhaustible fodder" for "the unfolding disclosure" of his artistic vision.[16]

If Christenberry's artistic vision begins in the personal, however, it expands to encompass regional iconography and, beyond that, transcendent

---

[13] Gruber, *William Christenberry*, 48.

[14] Southall, *Of Time and Place*, 19.

[15] Craven, introduction, 20.

[16] Trudy Wilner Stack, "Material Remains," in *Reconstruction: The Art of William Christenberry*, ed. Trudy Wilner Stack (Jackson: University Press of Mississippi and the Center for Creative Photography [Tucson], 1996) 31.

ideas of the relationship between reality and memory, form and meaning, and surfaces and unimagined depths. Indeed, there is a constructive element to that vision. This is important because a recurring theme in writing about his work in general, and especially about his photography, is the notion that Christenberry is compelled by "the urge to record change" and "an equally strong need to preserve, to hold something of the landscape intact."[17] Christenberry himself has fed this notion by acknowledging his massive collection—though he says he dislikes the verb "collect"[18]—of old advertising tins, hand-painted signs, and scraps of aged wood and metal, and by commenting that at least part of his impulse for making art derives from his need to "possess" something of the physical material from which his memories are made. But his art's origins in his motivation to record and to preserve only partly explains its impact. An examination of Christenberry's treatment of certain topics across various media suggests that he holds as strong an interest in *composition* as in documenting—in making something new from what *is* but soon will be *was* (to paraphrase Faulkner).

Here are two illustrations. Christenberry's photographic catalog contains a number of unintentional series—images of the same structure or landscape, typically shot from precisely the same point of view, spanning years (and, in some instances, decades). These series are unintentional, because the artist himself admits that he found himself developing chronicles of certain places, particular viewpoints on spaces in the landscape, before he realized it: "I was not really conscious of what I was doing, in terms of the passage of time, for a long, long time," he said in an interview. Then, one year, "all of a sudden it became very clear to me: I'm going back to the same places every year. I look at the place maybe the same way, maybe take a slightly different stance or view of it, and yet I'm really recording something of the life of this place. You can see it change like we can see ourselves change."[19]

[17] Craven, introduction, 20.

[18] Brownlee, "Interview with William Christenberry," 91.

[19] Ibid., 94.

Series of this kind include *Coleman's Café* (1967–1980), *The Green Warehouse* (1973–2001), *The Bar-B-Q Inn* (1971–1991), and what has become one of his most famous single bodies of work, *The Palmist Building* (1961–1996) (figures 2, 3, 4).[20] Certainly, the photographs in these series are documentary, and they serve to illustrate the time passing. But in this respect, they are also foundational, demonstrating Christenberry's virtuosity in crossing media to achieve his vision. Because the café, the warehouse, the church, the Palmist building, as physical structures, are each always in flux, subject to the alterations and deteriorations that accompany the passage of time, the photographs of those structures, taken in composite, in a sense become more real than the structures themselves.[21] And even as they are objects of art, for Christenberry the photographs also serve a practical and utilitarian function, orienting the artist in his relationship to his subjects and providing a point of departure and reference for his desire to render those subjects concretely.

As Agee had attempted in words to fabricate lived experience, in the mid-70s Christenberry began experimenting with ways to literally build directly upon experience by constructing sculptures of certain subjects he had first captured on film. After selecting the subject, framing it in the camera, and taking the photograph, Christenberry, feeling short of his desire to "[make] feeling visible,"[22] used wood, nails, and paint to build what he calls *constructions* that reference both the moment and the product of the photographic encounter with the subject, as the structure's form is reconstituted in three dimensions. These were in no way intended to be scale-models, Christenberry insists—they are fabrications, made from memory and the record of his photography. He has made only twenty or so of these constructions, each of them completed primarily because he could not feel

[20] All of these series are fully reproduced in Christenberry's recent book *Disappearing Places* (Düsseldorf: Richter Verlag, 2002).

[21] I am thinking here of Edward Weston's observation that the art of photography "provides the photographer with a means of looking deeply into the nature of things, and presenting his subjects in terms of their basic reality. It enables him to reveal the essence of what lies before his lens with such clear insight that the beholder may find the recreated image more real and comprehensible than the actual object" (Edward Weston, "Seeing Photographically," *Classic Essays on Photography*, ed. Alan Trachtenberg [1943; reprint, New Haven: Leete's Island, 1980] 174).

[22] Brownlee, "Interview with William Christenberry," 90.

FIGURE 2. PSALMIST BUILDING, HAVANA JUNCTION, ALABAMA (1971), *PHOTOGRAPH.*

FIGURE 3. PSALMIST BUILDING (SUMMER), HAVANA JUNCTION, ALABAMA (1980), *PHOTOGRAPH.*

FIGURE 4. PSALMIST BUILDING (WINTER), HAVANA JUNCTION, ALABAMA (1981), *PHOTOGRAPH.*

satisfied with what he was trying to express about the place utilizing the photographic medium alone. In each case, as Trudy Wilner Stack has observed, "the structure is removed from its setting, displacing trees, fields, roads, littered yards and utility poles"—it is abstracted yet specifically located nonetheless as the artist has mounted each structure on a base that is covered with actual red Alabama soil, "common ground" for viewing and contemplating that construction.[23] Christenberry thus processes the subject from his personal encounter with it, making two- and then three-dimensional representations so that in composite the subject exists virtually as a new entity, as symbolic as it is representational, as subjective as it appears objective. Some of the more recent of these pieces, such as 1994's white-washed *Ghost Form* (figure 5), are less literal and more self-consciously metaphorical. Derived from such photographs as *Abandoned House in Field* (1971) (figure 6), this sculpture is intended, according to Christenberry, to permit viewers simply to "respond to [the] almost primal feel" of the traditional dogtrot house's purity of form. In this piece, and in comparable works using other media—such as his 1996 ink drawing of the subject (figure 7)—the artist takes an image typically associated with poverty and imbues it with both gravity and a kind of hollow beauty.[24]

A less linear relationship, and perhaps the supreme example of Christenberry's multi-media genius, can be seen in his most controversial work, a constellation of drawings, photographs, paintings, and sculptures that refer, sometimes explicitly and other times obliquely, to the Ku Klux Klan. Much has been written about Christenberry's famous *Klan Room* (1962–present), the massive installation of various "found" Klan paraphernalia and ephemera, paintings, sketches, constructions, and most disturbing of all, dolls dressed in homemade satin robes illustrating the various aspects of life inside the KKK (figure 8). Less noticed, however, is the pervasiveness of Klan allusions throughout his work, including in his photography.

---

[23] Stack, "Material Remains," 37.

[24] Critic Allen Tullos quoted in Stack, "Material Remains," 26.

FIGURE 5. PSALMIST BUILDING (1996), *SCULPTURE.*

FIGURE 6. GHOST FORM (1994), *SCULPTURE.*

FIGURE 7. ABANDONED HOUSE IN FIELD, NEAR MONTGOMERY, ALABAMA (1971), *PHOTOGRAPH.*

FIGURE 8. UNTITLED [GHOST HOUSE] (1996), *INK ON PAPER.*

FIGURE 9. THE KLAN ROOM, INSTALLATION VIEW (1982).

The presence of such allusions is understandable, of course. As a young white man in the South, entering adulthood during the Civil Rights era, Christenberry witnessed firsthand the Klan's ability to fascinate and to terrorize. Whether subconsciously or intentionally, he seems to gravitate toward images that allude to the Klan. One of these is the photograph *The Klub* (1964) (figure 9). Christenberry says that in taking the photograph he sensed something eerie about the building's façade and about the men he had seen when he went inside to get something to drink, but he could not identify what had unsettled him until he received the print: the ghost-white building trimmed in aqua, two lights like eyes staring out from the middle of a hood-like awning, punctuated by the purposeful spelling: Klub. The slightly off-balance framing of the image suggests the photographer's subconscious discomfort with what he was seeing through the Brownie's viewfinder. Another image like this, less specific in its ominousness but more precise in its composition, is the 1980 photograph *Barn with White Object* (figure 10) The "white object," hanging in the shadow of what looks to be a dilapidated tobacco barn, bears an obvious resemblance to a Klan hood. At first glance, the photograph may appear as another example of the artist's fascination with aging structures. However, it is distinctive in Christenberry's catalog mainly because of its unusually imprecise title. For an artist normally so specific in naming his images, his attraction to this subject, even though he did not know what it was, suggests a beckoning. This possibility becomes even clearer after recognizing that the image was shot with the Deardorff view camera, which requires great effort to set up and take each exposure. It is not a snapshot, but rather an image that he must have contemplated and carefully framed before recording.

Another set of Christenberry's photographs bears on his contemplation of the Ku Klux Klan, though the popular imagination would not associate their ostensible subject, the wooden country church, with the organization. It is hard to look at a grouping of these photographs, however, and not begin to identify subliminal connections. *Church between Greensboro and Marion, Alabama* (1973) (figure 11) and *Church across Early Cotton* (1964), for example, both radiate a mesmerizing whiteness, a crisp austerity that is pronounced by the hood-like pointed roof of one and the soaring spire of the other. *China Grove Church* (1979) (figure 12) depicts a white wooden church nestled—or is it lurking?—around a curve in a dirt road lined with lush greenery. The photograph is taken in broad daylight, but the viewer might wonder how the scene would appear at night, an automobile's headlights finding the flat-white structure in the darkness. The link between fundamentalist religion of the type often practiced in country churches like these and the passion that inspires Klan activity is not terribly difficult to establish. A visit to the Klan's website even today invites guests to click on a link to discover "Christian Books and Things—Your Source for Christian, Confederate, and Ku Klux Klan Souvenirs" and repeatedly urges guests to visit the website for Thomas Robb Ministries, "A Christian ministry that still teaches the Old Time Religion … the faith of our ancestors!"[25]

The essential shape of these churches, especially the hood-like pitched roofs and steeples, becomes a central if not defining element in Christenberry's *Dream Building* sculpture series. Unlike the realist or formalist sculptures mentioned earlier, these pieces are overtly symbolist in conception and execution. The series began, Christenberry says, literally with a dream: "One night…I dreamed I was on a winding, back country Alabama road and I came around a curve and there before me was a building with no windows and doors. The building had an unbelievably pitched roof. The walls were covered with these outdoor advertising signs that I love. I got up the next morning and the dream was clear as a bell. I said, 'If Jasper Johns—an artist that I admire very much—can dream that he made an American flag and do it, I'm going to make my dream building.'" And so Christenberry made *Dream Building I* (1981) (figure 13), a form that he has repeated, in increasingly exaggerated constructions (figure 14), more than three dozen times, including a large-scale version some 13 feet tall and 6 feet square for the 1980 International Sculpture Conference. The allusion dawns readily on viewers, particularly in context with Christenberry's other

---

[25] www.kkk.com.

FIGURE 10. THE KLUB, UNIONTOWN, ALABAMA (1964), *PHOTOGRAPH.*

FIGURE 11. BARN WITH WHITE OBJECT, NEAR STEWART, ALABAMA (1980), *PHOTOGRAPH.*

FIGURE 12. CHURCH BETWEEN GREENSBORO AND MARION, ALABAMA (1973), *PHOTOGRAPH.*

work, but the artist himself came to understand it only gradually, as if it were a truth finding him: "I was not conscious until several weeks into making that first [building] that what I was doing was replicating the hooded Klansman's head," he has confessed. The pitch of the roof has gotten so steep on some of the constructions that one reviewer has observed that they look like the Washington Monument, to which Christenberry replied, "Isn't that 'the ultimate Klansman.'"[26]

Notably, the dream that inspired the creation of this series occurred just weeks after some person or group—Christenberry is still haunted by not knowing who or why—broke into his Washington studio and stole most elements of his Klan Room tableau, including a Klansman's robe he had acquired and many of his drawings and original Klan dolls. Christenberry had begun the installation two years after his first face-to-face encounter with a fully robed, hooded Klansman, who was monitoring the dim hallway while the group met inside the Tuscaloosa courthouse. Christenberry says he was frozen with fear: "He didn't turn his body to look at me. He didn't even turn his head. He just turned his eyes to the right and looked at me through those eyehole slits." That moment, Christenberry says, "stimulated this need on my part, as I've said many times, to come to grips with that aspect of evil we call the Ku Klux Klan." Christenberry began the reconstruction of the Klan Room following the 1979 robbery and has rebuilt it to a size more than double the original, comprising nearly 600 objects, including drawings, sculptures, paintings, actual Klan ephemera, and the element that many viewers find most disturbing of all: dolls—Barbies and G-I Joes for which he sews robes and dresses as Klansmen and -women of various ranks and roles, and, most recently, soft-sculpture dolls that are similarly dressed but that do not pretend to simulate humanity. "A doll can get under people's skin," Christenberry has said, associating his use of them in the tableau with his long fascination with Dadaism and Surrealism.[27] The effect is chilling, as viewers glimpse the plastic flesh, the static eyes peeking through the gently draped, gorgeously colored satin robes (figure 15).

---

[26]Allen Tullos, "Into the Territory: William Christenberry's Klan Room," *William Christenberry: Disappearing Places* (Düsseldorf: Richter Verlag, 2002) 93.

[27] Ibid., 85–86.

FIGURE 13. CHINA GROVE CHURCH, HALE COUNTY, ALABAMA (1979), *PHOTOGRAPH.*

FIGURE 14. DREAM BUILDING I (1979), *SCULPTURE*.

FIGURE 15. DREAM BUILDING XV (1992–1994), *SCULPTURE*.

The sheer volume of material in the Klan Room—coupled with the fact that the art has been crafted as a space the viewer must inhabit in order to experience—gives this work its breathtaking power. The experiential nature of the room is perhaps the ultimate expression of Christenberry's desire to follow the charge he adapted from Agee's wish that art might be less polite for its abstraction and more challenging in being palpable. In the Klan Room, art becomes not a thing to observe at arm's length, but an entity that encompasses, seduces, challenges, and leaves you unsettled. It is a powerful idea precisely because it is made into an absorptive reality—a place. Arguably the most interesting thing about the Klan Room project, however, is not the controversy it has inspired—and there has been plenty of that—but the way in which the project has been represented in catalogues of Christenberry's work. Obviously, the Klan Room is static, an installation, so to communicate its mood and meaning, Christenberry returns to the medium of evocative precision with which nearly all of his art begins: the photograph. Many people who have seen the space comment that some of Christenberry's images used in the Klan Room—in which he isolates this or that element and only suggests the horrific context through select details—are more arresting than the installation itself (figures 16, 17).[28]

Thinking about William Christenberry makes me think of a wonderfully titled essay, "What We Talk about When We Talk about the South," in which historian Edward Ayres observes that "There is a tendency for Southerners to see time as the enemy, erasing the inscriptions on the land, destroying whatever certain identity the South has ever had."[29] For Christenberry, time is not so much an enemy as it is an ally, a partner in an unfolding vision of an American region—a region whose identity his art reveals not in abstractions or theoretical constructions, but in living-color particulars.

---

[28] For illustrations of many items found in the Klan Room installation, see *Reconstruction: The Art of William Christenberry*, ed. Trudy Wilner Stack (Jackson: University Press of Mississippi; and Tucson: Center for Creative Photography, 1996) 149–63.

[29] Edward L. Ayres, "What We Talk about When We Talk about the South." *All Over the Map: Rethinking American Regions*, ed. Edward L. Ayres, Patricia Nelson Limerick, Stephen Nissenbaum, and Peter S. Onuf (Baltimore: Johns Hopkins University Press, 1996) 81.

FIGURE 16. THE KLAN ROOM: DOLL IN CASE, *SCULPTURE AND PHOTOGRAPH.*

FIGURE 17. THE KLAN ROOM: DOLL WITH CONFEDERATE FLAG, *SCULPTURE AND PHOTOGRAPH.*

The Sunken Mill

BY JESSE GRAVES

A nest of trees across the lake,
taller in their crowns than the treeline,
too far from our shore to make out
a leafshape or trace a pattern over the bark.

Just below them trees about twenty feet,
he said, showing with two extended fingers
angled in their joints as a hammer claw,
was your people's grist mill.

The old feller was blind, and that's what they
called him, Blind Graves. I never knowed
any other name for him, and I never knowed
how he figured that there was a running spring

in the back of that sinkhole cave.
He had water grinding his cornfeed
day and night when the other millers
waited till after light every morning

for the river to fill up the reservoirs
before they could start to work.
Tell me what use had them oldtimers
for lectric lights— they slept when it was dark.

Now there was evening wind and LaFollette
darkening beyond the trees and the underwater
county line. Powell River moves as a basin ghost
beneath the crush of Senator Norris's lake and dam.

That goddamn socialist Roosevelt
flooded all the bottomlands,
for what? So the women could waste
their days with the television stories

and menfolk could plug up one machine
to saw wood, another to strip it
and another to drive the nails.
I wouldn't trade all the power lights

and tools and machinery they ever was
for another night on a chestnut raft,
seining these channels for trout
and listening to the shoals

of the blind man's millwheel.

The Chicken House

BY BERNADETTE RULE

The small town in which I grew up took awhile to make the transformation from rural to urban. In its formative days as a wilderness settlement in the early nineteenth century, my home town was no more than a few buildings along a creek in what had been Chickasaw territory. Surrounded by woods, canebrakes, and grasslands from which fields were being wrested, the town existed to serve the farmers who decided to stop there on their way west; one day more and they'd have come to the Mississippi. Since everyone kept horses back then, no laws prohibited animal habitation inside the growing town's borders. Most people kept a milk cow, a few chickens, and, of course, cats and dogs.

A hundred years later, various of my grandparents, aunts, and uncles moved into Mayfield from their tobacco farms in order to work at the clothing mills. Well into the twentieth century, these people still kept chickens in their backyards—not for the eggs so much as because they simply couldn't imagine life without them. They couldn't imagine going to the outhouse, say, without passing through a drift of colorful, truculent chickens.

Granny Rule made pets of her chickens, and taught them tricks. Her rooster, for example, would crow at her command, no matter what the hour. My Great Aunt Ruth was among the last people in town to keep a large animal—a cow in the shed at the end of her garden, to remind her of the farm.

I suppose it was the automobile (that destroyer of all the old ways) that brought about the change in the end—the law forbidding animals within "city" limits. When horses were no longer essential to transportation, all the stables and sheds in the backyards fell into disrepair. Animals literally breathe life into barns and stables. After a year or two of no cattle-warmth in the wintertime, the foundations of those structures begin to rot. And that was when the garage was born, a cold answer to a cold problem. The garage smelled of machine oil—gone were the rich scents of hay and horsedung, leather and life.

By the time I came along in 1951, our garage was a small white clapboard structure at the end of the maple-lined driveway; it had a peaked roof, but no doors. We rarely kept the car inside the garage, so it stood empty, failing to generate much interest. The interesting feature—indeed the dark, central mystery of our backyard—was the lean-to attached to the back of the garage: the chicken house. No doubt originally built as a garden shed, that structure was my father's domain. On summer nights, Daddy's light cast a mysterious gleam across the backyard, as my sister Bridget and I lay in bed and wondered what he could possibly be doing out there. Perhaps because I associated it with Daddy, the chicken house held a sort of totemic relationship for us as a family.

Part of its allure was its dirt floor, which contrasted with the empty garage's floor of concrete. The chicken house was a veritable cave of smells: a faint whiff of mouse, metal, and oil from Daddy's tools, the slow roasting of unpainted wood in the summer sun. That structure seemed to trap all that wafted in through its two large windows: rotting apples, wild onion, cut grass.

Scraping the table scraps into the garbage can in a corner of the chicken house was my first, and only, official task in the venerable building when I was a child—a task I hated beyond all telling. The lid could be raised automatically by foot pedal, thank God, so I didn't have to touch the thing. Still, when that lid sprang up to reveal a putrid mound of eggshells and peelings, an almost visible cushion of stench nearly smothered me. It may as well

THE RULE FAMILY (FRONT) AND THE CHICKEN HOUSE (RIGHT).

have been a newish grave yawning open before me. My sister Bridget and I so detested this chore that we plea-bargained our way out of it, insisting that since the boys didn't have to wash dishes as we did, they should have to take out garbage. To our relief and amazement, our parents agreed. We were absolved of the task and never had to do it again.

Garbage notwithstanding, the chicken house held me in thrall. Daddy had a long shelf under the windows that, for many years, seemed one tantalizing inch too high for me to see what was on it. I knew that he fixed things there, whistling often. My biggest clue to his chicken house operations resided in an old Peter Pan peanut butter jar full of nails and springs and hooks. By the jaunty way Daddy reached for it, it seemed that jar held the answer to most any problem.

Another reason for my fascination with the chicken house was that things rejected from the house always found their way out there. An iridescent, pearl-lacquered crucifix gleamed incongruously from a rusty nail against the unpainted boards. An old mantel clock came to pieces little by little in the chicken house, face, hands and cabinet appearing on various nails at various times. Years later, even our trusty Hoosier cabinet found its way out there. Daddy always put its drawers to good use, filling them with screwdrivers, files, doorknobs, and string.

At one point, he replaced the door of the chicken house with a door sporting a knob of faceted crystal. It was like an urchin wearing the Hope diamond. How I loved that doorknob, there. It was like the physical incarnation of a magic phrase with the power to open a cave of treasures.

For me, the meaning of the chicken house changed at different points in my childhood. One year our beloved apple tree blew over in a storm, and we woke up that morning to find it canted neatly against the chicken house roof. Before we understood that this meant the end of the tree, we were elated to be able to walk straight up the trunk and onto the chicken house and then onto the garage roof. It was as if we were in a flood, being swept down the Mississippi on the roof of our house. Later, when the tree was gone, the backyard seemed naked and bare…until Daddy planted a garden under the windows of the shed.

For awhile, Bridget appropriated one end of Daddy's work-shelf as her office. That was the year she was a detective. I wasn't allowed near the place for awhile, but luckily she went out of business fairly quickly. During our teen years, Bridget and I used a ladder to climb to the flat roof of the chicken house in order to sunbathe. I read *Portrait of a Lady* up there. The last time we used the roof as a sundeck, I put my foot right through the roof. Daddy also "went through the roof," but I finally understood why he had warned us not to go up there.

During one of those teen summers, after Daddy had repaired the roof, I helped him paint the garage and chicken house. At last I got to watch Daddy work, participating in one of the outdoor tasks that gave him such pleasure. Crouched on a beam of the chicken house roof, he taught me how to scrape and prime a clapboard wall. When he dipped the brush and drew it steadily across the board, Daddy seemed utterly happy, and so was I.

Why did we call it "the chicken house?" Because, for a very short time, we kept chickens. Such an enterprise hadn't yet been outlawed then. And though the chicken house phase was one of the shortest incarnations of the old lean-to shed, it was, without a doubt, the most colorful and dramatic phase, and so the name stuck.

I was very young at the time, still a pre-schooler, but my memories are vivid. One day, Daddy brought home a large pasteboard box full of noise and fluff—dozens of yellow chicks peeping and moving. We each were allowed to hold a chick briefly, but then we had to put them down and leave them alone or, Daddy said, they would die. He set the box in a corner of our house's hall and trained a big silver lamp on the chicks. With light flowing as warm as sunshine from the lamp, they continued their sharp peeping all night long.

They couldn't have stayed in the house more than a night or two. The next thing I remember, the chicken house had been emptied out completely and was lined with stacked, silver cages. I walked amazed among the rows of now-white chickens. They looked wildly around and sometimes right at me, with a bit of a glare, I thought. Daddy said they were not pets. To me, their smell was not as repulsive as the garbage, but it was easily as powerful—it smelled like Aunt Rose's farmyard crammed into a small shed. It was difficult for me to believe that the little yellow fluff-balls were the same creatures as those opinionated hens.

I don't remember gathering eggs, or feeding the chickens, but I do recall one or two dead chickens, floating in a tub of water to be plucked. I didn't like the tearing sound of the plucking, nor the holes where the feathers came out. I didn't like the smell of uncooked, soaking chicken, of wet feathers. Luckily, I was usually encouraged to go off and play.

I cannot imagine what made me go out one Saturday afternoon to watch Daddy kill a chicken for our Sunday dinner. It may have been on a dare. I know I went consciously, understanding what would take place. Daddy and I were the only ones in the backyard, and I stayed back beside the elm. He came out of the chicken house with a squawking hen.

Then, with no more ceremony than you would adopt to screw the lid off a jar, he wrung the chicken's head completely off. I don't know what happened to the head, because I was too absorbed in watching the headless body, darting and flopping around the yard. If it had run up to me I don't know what I would have done, but it went the other direction, thank God. Once the headless body of the chicken slumped to the ground, Daddy took it and hung it up on the clothesline by its feet, with clothes pins. He went into the house to wash the blood off his hands, and I stood by the elm and stared at the chicken on the clothesline. Surely now I had seen it all, I thought. The next day at the table I said I didn't care for any fried chicken. Daddy immediately placed a drumstick on my plate. "Not having any of that nonsense," he said in a matter-of-fact tone. "You like fried chicken, don't you?" I nodded, my chin trembling. "Well, then, eat it." He spoke with the same degree of dispassion he had worn when killing the chicken. I did as I was told—and it tasted as good as ever.

I didn't know what to think of Daddy's attitude. He showed no emotion whatsoever about killing that chicken. He had wrung off its head and then gone about his business, exactly the way he always walked back to his chair and newspaper after spanking one of us. It was a job that had to be done—no more, no less. Whether disciplining his children or providing for his family, he did what had to be done, without apology or analysis.

⁂

Last year, the time came to tear down the chicken house. The maples along the driveway had to be removed, after one of them suddenly fell in a windstorm, narrowly missing the house. No tears, everybody said. It has to be done. The elm was removed years ago, of course. There hasn't been a garden for a long time, not since Daddy died twenty years ago. Mama, who is past ninety now, has lived in the house since 1940. The chicken house is deteriorating. The last time I was home, the corner where the garbage can used to be was open to the wind. The Hoosier cabinet was whiskered with its own paint. The padlock is the only thing holding the door up now. It hardly matters, though—there's nothing to steal there anyway. What was magical and valuable about the chicken house was taken from us twenty years ago.

Where I Live

BY DANA WILDSMITH

"My land has a voice; I'm a singer who sings."
"Road Song," Muriel Miller Dressler

"I think we're neighbors. Tell me again where you live." Kathy's on the phone with me about some Little Theater business and I've tried twice already to explain where I live, but she's just not getting it. I run down the directions one more time: follow Harry McCarty all the way to the end, even after it turns dirt, to where it dead-ends into Briscoe Mill. "Is Briscoe Mill the name of a subdivision?" No, it's a road. "But what's the name of the subdivision?"

I live on a hundred-and-something-year-old family farm, which makes it one of Barrow County's original subdivisions, I suppose; that's what I should tell Kathy. My parents bought these forty acres from the last generation of Edwards to live on the last remnant of what had been hundreds of acres of Barrow County farmland. Death after death, the Edwards family subdivided their land among their children and their children's children until they had deed-whittled it down to an ell-shaped plot of Southern woods, a pointy-roofed farmhouse, Lona Bell's flower beds, and Lona Bell. A year or more after this last Edwards daughter had signed the papers and moved to a singlewide just down the road, I'd see out my kitchen window Lona Bell's cotton-bonneted head bent over the dahlia bed nearest the road, digging bulbs to transplant to her yard. She considered this earth still hers to dig in every sense but the legal one, and I wasn't about to argue against her claim being the more abiding.

The Edwards family had farmed my land in cotton and tobacco through all this last century and a chunk of the one before. Clarence Edwards's plow furrowed ditches and ridges, which still, seventy-five years after his final plowing, cause my steps to rise and dip when I walk there under thirty-foot sweet gums and pines. I've seen no photos of those farming years, so it's easy for me to forget that once the hill behind my house bumped up as bare as a knuckle ringed with barbed wire pasture fence. Every ten yards or so Clarence set posts he'd rough-axed from trees he'd cleared from his fields. When I sink to my knee in another leaf-hidden fence post hole, I remember his farm as I've never seen it. It's as if the former Mr. Edwards has reached up and snagged me from the earth he worked to remind me his life was hard, hard, and always only one misstep from something broken or somebody dead.

Max and Fred are the farm boys who run the hill and swim the lower creek these days, two orphan pups tossed out like beer cans on the side of a road and recycled by us into a couple of Good Old Boy dogs. They love trucks and chasing deer and fishing, but when we head out to work the land, it really puts a grin on their faces. And don't tell me dogs can't smile—when I tuck the limb saw under my arm and shove my leather gloves (not the cotton gardening gloves, signal for boring, stay-in-one-place work) in my jacket pocket, those guys start grinning all over themselves. *We're working now,* say Max and Fred. *This is how days should be lived, yessir.*

They don't know that I'm using them. Or maybe they do, but don't care. They have their agenda; I have mine. Mine is to trim dead branches, cut back cat brier, keep privet from making any more alien inroads into the woods. That's my public purpose, at any rate, should anyone ask. My private and truest reason for going into the woods is to escape everything indoors, everything "seared with trade...that wears man's smudge and shares man's smell," as Gerard Manley Hopkins, that most sensual of priests, put it. When I'm wild to get away from heat pumps and leaf blowers and windows that serve no purpose because they are never opened, I go to the woods. My daughter calls me a Luddite, and she's probably right. I do tend to resent and avoid the technologies of our times because these work to persuade us to not think of nature as a member of the family. Not a member of the family? Not ours to love, and therefore not our responsibility.

Lately I've been having dreams, nightmares, really, about invasions onto my land. In one dream, I have come home from work to find Barrow County road trucks and Bobcats filling in my creeks with dirt because "we can't allow open creeks; they're a hazard." In another, I step out of the woods by the garden shed and have to snatch Max away from dozens of snakes' heads popping out of the ground like March's first asparagus while people I don't know mill about wondering aloud why I'm so upset. In last night's dream, as I was walking the road picking up fast-food bags and lottery tickets and beer cans that drivers had chucked from their car windows, I began to find bag after elephant-sized bag of garbage filling and spilling over our ditches.

A week or two ago as I rounded the curve where our dirt part of the road begins, I had to brake for a lottery ticket booth smack in the middle of the road. This wasn't a dream, mind you. This was a real wooden pink and white Georgia Lottery booth, the kind you see in gas station minimarts, standing at attention on the dirt, ready for business. Suddenly I wasn't sure if I was dreaming or not. But, nope, there it was, as four-square as an outhouse. What can this possibly say about my life when a metaphor takes solid form and blocks my drive home from Quality Foods? And who but a Luddite poet would see this stolen and dumped booth's appearance as a metaphor for our society? It's not as if illicit goods have never ended their sorry journey on our road before. I find more than my share of crack pipes and stashed appliances swiped from construction sites and even condoms soggy from stolen love. But the lottery booth was plunder on a Powerball scale, and it stopped me cold.

Now, I have to tell you the first thing I did when I saw that lottery booth was laugh. Then I drove quickly around it so I could tell anyone who was home what I'd found. This was a good story, and a good story to a writer is better than a winning lottery ticket, or it's right up there, anyhow. But the thing is, now I can't unwrap my mind from the idea of someone stealing a five-foot-high wooden booth and carefully positioning it in the middle of my road, its cheery pink-and-green logo greeting oncoming drivers as squarely as some new highway sign. What could have possessed this ambitious thief to invest so much time and trouble? Was Lottery Booth Thief simply an extremely tidy person, someone like me who won't have a litterbag in the car because a passenger might put litter into it?

Trash has been on my mind this month because of a cedar tree making headlines here, a tree gaining fame through its demise. Local property owners ordered this fifty-year-old, sixty-foot cedar cut down in order to clear the way for a new building, the placement of which was, according to the owners, decreed by building and zoning regulations. I have no doubt the owners are speaking truth. I'm certain the neighbors know the owner is speaking truth, but truth doesn't get at the heart of the neighbors' anger. What the property owners aren't getting is how much the locals needed that tree. City dwellers spend their days learning to not notice trash in the gutters, trash on the edges of yards, trash wind-blown to concrete gutters and the feet of concrete buildings. It's ugly. But a sixty-foot cedar can't be made ugly, even should trash pile around its roots like the trash bags of my dreams. Before the cedar fell, its neighbors had only to look up to see something undefiled. Their lives needed that luxury of beauty, even though they have not said as much, stating their anger rather in terms of the size and age of the tree, as if a tree's right to life might be substantiated through statistics.

I needed the luxury of the beauty of my woods during all my years of roaming as a Navy wife before I came home to my forty acres. And it *is* a luxury. More and more these days when someone asks how much land I have and I tell them, "forty acres," they respond that I own a subdivision. I suppose I do. My land is subdivided into the wet-weather creek right behind my house, the flat stretch of small hardwoods leading to the footbridge across the wetlands and Fred's fishing creek, then the hill rising thick in pines and cedars to the clearing where the apples trees my sister planted make a half-circle around the wooden bench I rest on in sight of the dogwood thicket, watching while Max and Fred explore. Trying to choose which area pleases me more would be like trying to name one's favorite child.

Not that all is lovely here. I constantly grieve and fret over piles of deadfall rotting among the pines. Cat brier I haven't cut back wends its ugly way up sassafras trunks, choking the life from trees and weaving a low connective path for fire, should fire come. Dry blackberry canes snag like old brown claws from the sides of deer paths. Heavy widow-maker pine snags dangle above my head wherever I stand. And both creeks always need cleaning out. After the most recent ice storm, my friend Terry Kay, knowing how driven I am, admonished me, "Don't over-do the clean-up. God meant nature to have its own design." He's right, Terry is. And that is the luxury I would fight for—the luxury of contrast. In the natural subdivision that is my land, nothing is predictable. How ever many times each day the dogs and I tramp these acres, some little something is always changed from the time before. Those changes require of me attention, consideration, and the kind of figuring out that leads to poems.

Hopkins the poet used the ritual of form, sonnet form, to figure out where to go with his unease in an industrialized world and with his guilt, as Hopkins the priest, over-loving the lush world. He went to where "morning at the brown brink eastward springs…with warm breast and with ah! bright wings" He went to whatever nature thrived in monastery gardens as I go to my woods, in order to find again "the dearest freshness deep down things." It was not by accident that Hopkins wrote of the world being "charged" with God's grandeur. He well knew how every charge exacts its price. The price he paid was a guilt-tingled duality; mine is the same.

I, who have so much compared to subdivision dwellers, want more. More land to let run to woods, more time in the woods. Out there in the trees, my dogs become more dogly, I become less a woman of 2005 America. I let go and let go until I teeter right on the last edge of my socially acceptable self. And this is when I like myself best. "Why does one not like things if there are other people about?" asked Lawrence of Arabia. It isn't quite that I don't like things when people are about; it's more that I like them better when people are absent. When people and things leave me, or when I leave them, I do the fullest job of seeing them, and loving them for what I see.

In a subdivision such as the one Kathy's brain keeps trying to picture me in, I wouldn't be able to step back far enough to see well. I know because I've been there; I've tried. Those years when I had no choice, I tried to learn to not need escape, but it never quite worked. Years ago when Lona Bell came for her bulbs, I knew she couldn't leave them behind because for her and her mother and her mother's mother, those flowers had been their escape, their way of stepping back and recovering gentleness in a subsistence life, their poetry.

My mother now lives where Lona Bell's parents lived out their married life. I can step from my porch to Mama's in thirty seconds to let her read these pages. "Aw, honey," she'll say, "don't take yourself so seriously."

Family Jewels

BY KRISTIN BERKEY-ABBOTT

Some women hoard the family jewelry.
As each child comes of age, reaches
an important milestone, the matron doles
out an appropriate piece.

I hide the last bags of pecans
in my vault of a freezer. I will receive
no more nuts when these are gone.
My grandmother has sold the land,
the trees bulldozed for a subdivision.

As children, we were sent to scout
the nuts from under the leaves. Some children get
Easter egg hunts, but we had the real autumnal treasure.
Whoever brought in the most got to dictate
dessert for the evening: buttery cookies or a pie
crunchy with nuts in the crust and the topping.

For punishment, we had to shell the nuts,
pick the prize pieces away from the bitter bits.
I enjoyed the enforced time out
even as my hands stained brown,
the cool air calming me, the crack
of the shell draining my aggression.

Now my children don't even realize
that nuts grow on trees. They approve
of grocery store nuts, even though they're stale
and oddly chewy. So unlike the ones I hoard
in the freezer, ration out for special occasions.
I portion out these prizes, savor
every last nugget, mourn the loss
of family and homeplace and majestic trees.

Tennessee Song

BY BILL BROWN

How can I give up little night fires
on the Mississippi's cracked sand,
the roll and pitch of the old man,
wood duck's squeal, a flash
of teal in the deep river bends;

how can I give up the mystery of hymns
born from the dark labor of hands,
shotgun shacks, feed troughs, and
floods that hang a back break
of hay in cotton wood limbs;

drought corn roots clutch July soil,
husks touched brown, cobs missing
kernels like toothless grins,
road stench of flattened black snakes,
truck windows flapping the ears of hounds;

how can I not love burned-out trailers
stacked with feed, their use diminished
but not undone, an engine lynched in an oak,
a jake-leg mechanic lowering it down,
a winding of buzzards in the sun;

a clutch of fox bones bleached by moon,
old women spitting snuff in a can,
a sentinel of herons on cypress knees,
a dead tractor honored on a hilltop crown,
bee boxes swollen with the labor of bees;

night fires on the river's cracked sand,
hymns born from the labor of hands,
windows flapping the ears of hounds,
a winding of buzzards in the sky,
a sentinel of herons on cypress knees,
honey in a jar stuffed with cone,
how can I not love all of these?

CONTRIBUTOR'S NOTES

Thomas Aiello is a doctoral candidate in the department of History at the University of Arkansas, specializing in twentieth-century US intellectual and cultural history. His work has appeared in *Americana: The Journal of American Popular Culture*, *The Southwestern Review*, *The McNeese Review*, *The Neoamericanist*, and *North Louisiana History*, among others. Aiello received his MA in twentieth-century American and European history from the University of Louisiana at Lafayette in 2004.

Kristin Berkey-Abbott earned a Ph.D. in British Literature from the University of South Carolina. Currently, she teaches English and Creative Writing at the Art Institute of Ft. Lauderdale. She has published in many literary journals, including *The Beloit Poetry Journal*, *North American Review*, and *Poetry East*. In 2004 Pudding House Publications published her chapbook, *Whistling Past the Graveyard.*

Bill Brown has composed four collections of poetry, most recently *The Gods of Little Pleasures* (Sow's Ear). He is the co-author of the writing textbook *Important Words, for Poets and Writers* (Heinemann). His recent work has appeared in *Appalachian Journal, Atlanta Review, Smartish Pace, Tar River Poetry, Southern Poetry Review,* and *The North American Review.* He teaches part time at Peabody College of Vanderbilt University. In 1999, he received the Tennessee Arts Commission's Poetry Fellowship.

James E. Cherry, a native west Tennessean, is a poet, fiction writer, educator, and social critic. He is the author of *Bending the Blues* (H & H Press). His previous work has appeared in *Signifyin' Harlem*, *Langston Hughes Review*, and *DrumVoices Revue.*

Jim Clark was born in Byrdstown, Tennessee. His two books of poems are *Dancing on Canaan's Ruins* and *Handiwork*, and he also edited *Fable in the Blood: The Selected Poems of Byron Herbert Reece*. Clark lives in Wilson, North Carolina, where he is professor of English and writer in residence at Barton College, director of the Barton College Creative Writing Symposium, and an editor of the literary journal *Crucible.*

Luminita M. Dragulescu is a doctoral student at West Virginia University; she specializes in twentieth-century American literature. Her focus is on issues of collective and individual memory, traumatic memory in particular, in texts produced by whites and African Americans and which revolve around racial, economic, and political tensions.

David Gold lives in Los Angeles, where he teaches at California State University. He is currently working on a history of rhetorical education at public women's colleges in the South.

Joanna Grant is a Ph.D. candidate in English at the University of Rochester in upstate New York. As an expatriate Southerner who has lived out of the South for many years, she has had considerable opportunity to witness and to contemplate how Southerners think of themselves and others, and how others think of them.

Jesse Graves was born and raised in Sharps Chapel, Tennessee, a farming community north of Knoxville that has been the subject of much of his work and study. He is currently a Ph.D. candidate in the department of English at the University of Tennessee, where he won the 2004 John C. Hodges Graduate Poetry Award and the 2005 James Agee Conference Award in Poetry. He holds an MFA in creative writing from Cornell University.

Randall Horton is from Birmingham, Alabama. He is a candidate for an MFA in Creative Writing in Poetry at Chicago State University. Currently he is the editor for the *Warpland Journal* and has served as assistant editor for Tia Chucha Press's *Dream of a Word Anthology*.

David Huddle, a native of the Virginia Blue Ridge, is a poet, novelist, and teacher of writing. His recent works include the novel *La Tour Dreams of the Wolf Girl* and *Summer Lake: New and Collected Poems*. He teaches at the University of Vermont and the Bread Loaf School of English.

M. Thomas Inge is the Blackwell Professor of Humanities at Randolph-Macon College in Ashland, Virginia. His recent publications include *Conversations with William Faulkner,* the four-volume *Greenwood Guide to American Popular Culture,* and *William Faulkner: Overlook Illustrated Lives.* His works in progress include studies of the influence of William Faulkner, Walt Disney and the art of adaptation, and connections between comics and American literature. He is editor of the journal *Studies in American Humor*.

Anna Sunshine Ison grew up surrounded by yard art, mannequins, gourds, and hand-made quilts on her family farm in Rowan County, Kentucky. A graduate of Queens University of Charlotte and the University of North Carolina at Greensboro, her work has appeared in *The Greensboro Review, The GSU Review, Urban Latino*, and *I to I: Life Writing by Kentucky Feminists*. She is a Junior Foreign Service Officer currently serving at the United States Consulate General in Monterrey, Mexico.

Mark Allan Jackson is visiting assistant professor at Depauw University in Greencastle, Indiana.

Edwin C. (Ed) King was born in Dixie, Brooks County, Georgia, in 1929. He served twenty-eight years as a Marine, retiring as a colonel. Now fully retired, he lives in Ormond Beach, Florida. He is fascinated by colonial, early American, and Southern history.

Jeraldine R. Kraver is associate professor of English and director of English education at the University of Northern Colorado. She has published works on Henry James, Benjamin Disraeli, and Katherine Anne Porter. A graduate of the University of Kentucky, she has studied the work of two Kentucky-based poets, Davis McCombs and Affrilachian poet Nikky Finney.

Davis McCombs was a park ranger for the National Park Service, based at Mammoth Cave National Park, near Bowling Green, Kentucky, from 1991 to 2001. He currently serves as director of the Creative Writing program at the University of Arkansas. His poetry collection *Ultima Thule* was awarded the Yale Series of Younger Poets prize in 1999.

Robert L. McDonald has authored numerous publications on Southern literature and culture, including the book *Reading Erskine Caldwell: New Essays*. A professor of English and associate dean for academic affairs at Virginia Military Institute, he edits the journal *Studies in American Culture*. He is also a photographer who exhibits his work nationally; a portfolio of photographs from his Southern Places series appeared in *CrossRoads: A Southern Culture Annual 2005*.

Born and reared in the Southeast Alabama town of Abbeville, Alabama, **Nancy Gregory McLendon** attended Samford University in Birmingham and the University of South Alabama in Mobile. She teaches English at Wallace Community College in Dothan, Alabama, and is pursuing a Ph.D. at Auburn University. She is grateful to her mother Marian Glover Leonard for the encouragement and inspiration which made the writing of "Sylvia's Story" possible and appreciates proofreading and suggestions by Dr. Edward Matthews, Missouri State University.

Robert Morgan is the author of eleven books of poetry, most recently *The Strange Attractor: New and Selected Poems* (2004), and eight volumes of fiction, including *Gap Creek* and *Brave Enemies.* A native of western North Carolina, he has taught at Cornell University since 1971. At present he is working on a biography of Daniel Boone to be published by Algonquin Books of Chapel Hill in 2007.

Michael Newton was awarded a Ph.D. in Celtic Studies from the University of Edinburgh in 1998. He has written several books and numerous articles on Scottish Highland tradition and history, and has given lectures and taught workshops at venues such as the Smithsonian, the Library of Congress, Slighe nan Gaidheal in Seattle, and the Toronto Scottish Gaelic Learners' Association. He is the Humanities Liaison of the Renaissance Computing Institute of North Carolina.

Ted Olson teaches at East Tennessee State University in Johnson City, Tennessee. In addition to editing *CrossRoads: A Southern Culture Annual* for Mercer University Press, he is the author of a recently published book of poetry, *Breathing in Darkness* (Wind Publications), and a study of traditional Appalachian culture, *Blue Ridge Folklife* (University Press of Mississippi), and the co-author (with Charles K. Wolfe) of *The Bristol Sessions: Writings About the Big Bang of Country Music* (McFarland & Co., Publishers).

Ron Rash is a past winner of an NEA Poetry Fellowship. His third book of poems, *Raising the Dead,* was published by Iris Press. He has published recently in *Poetry, Southern Review, Sewanee Review, Yale Review,* and *Kenyon Review* and has a story in the *2005 O. Henry Prize Stories.* His first novel, *One Foot in Eden,* was published in paperback by Picador. Henry Holt has issued two later novels, *Saints at the River* and *The World Made Straight.*

Bernadette Rule is the editor of a book by Fred Turnbull, *Remember Me to Everybody: Letters from India, 1944 to 1949.* She has composed five collections of poetry, with *New and Selected Poems* forthcoming from Larkspur Press. She teaches in the writing program at McMaster University in Ontario, Canada.

Carly Sachs teaches Creative Writing at George Washington University. Her work has appeared in *Best American Poetry 2004, goodfoot, PMS, Another Chicago Magazine, Runes Review, Alimentum,* and *No Tell Motel,* and her poetry has been featured on the buses of Cleveland, Ohio. Her anthology, *the why and later*, is forthcoming from deep cleveland press. Her first collection of poems, *the steam sequence,* won the 2006 Washington Writers' Publishing House Book.

Roger Sharpe is the author of *Ceremony of Innocence: A Memoir* (2005). In Fall 2006, he ran for a seat in the US House of Representatives (fifth district, North Carolina).

John Sparks is a minister, historian, and writer living in eastern Kentucky. His published works include *The Roots of Appalachian Christianity: The Life and Legacy of Elder Shubal Stearns* (University Press of Kentucky), for which he received Morehead State University's Chaffin Award for Appalachian Literature in 2004, and *Raccoon John Smith: Frontier Kentucky's Most Famous Preacher* (University Press of Kentucky). The piece in *CrossRoads 2006* was the winner of the Appalachian Writers' Association's Wilma Dykeman Essay Prize for 2005.

Joe Samuel Starnes is the author of the novel *Calling*. Born in Anniston, Alabama, he grew up in Cedartown, Georgia, and has lived in New Jersey for several years. He holds a BA from the University of Georgia's Grady College of Journalism and Mass Communication and an MA in English from Rutgers University. He has worked in newspapers and media relations in Georgia, Florida, Texas, New Jersey, and New York.

Kyes Stevens lives in Waverly, Alabama. Having earned her MA and MFA degrees from Sarah Lawrence College in New York, she is the director of the Alabama Prison Arts and Education Project at the Center for the Arts and Humanities at Auburn University.

Hugh M. (Max) Thomason is retired from Western Kentucky University's Department of Government, having served as head of the department and professor of Government. He received his AB degree in History from North Georgia College (from which he received the Distinguished Alumnus Award) and his MA and Ph.D. degrees in Political Science from Emory University.

Maureen E. Torpey is a master's student at Buffalo State College in New York. With a BA in English and Irish Studies from Boston College, she delights in studying the comparisons between Irish literature and other world literatures. Her essay is an outgrowth of a paper presented at the 2005 Methodist College Southern Writers Symposium.

Andrew J. Walters graduated from East Tennessee State University in 2005 with a BA in History and a minor in Appalachian Studies. His academic interests include the social and cultural history of Appalachia and the South during the Civil War and into the twentieth century. A native of southwest Virginia, he is currently pursuing an MA in History at Virginia Tech.

Dana Wildsmith grew up in South Georgia, and she now lives in North Georgia. Her books of poetry include *Our Bodies Remember* and *One Good Hand.*

Tammy Wilson has lived more than half her life in western North Carolina, where she was a 2002 Blumenthal Writer. She has published more than thirty stories in such journals as the *North Carolina Literary Review, The MacGuffin*, *The Kennesaw Review,* and *Epiphany*. Her story, "Paradise Found," was a finalist for the 2004 Iowa Award in Short Fiction.